WORSHIP WORKBOOK FOR THE GOSPELS

Cycle B

ROBERT D. INGRAM

MUSIC SECTIONS BY
ROBERT A. HOBBY
AND
BERKLEY J. GUSE

ART BY
GAIL THROCKMORTON WARNER
ANGIE LATTA
AND
ROBERT D. INGRAM

CSS Publishing Company, Inc.
Lima, Ohio

Dedicated to

Barbara,

my best friend and wife of many years
who gives me time and support to write.

WORSHIP WORKBOOK FOR THE GOSPELS

Copyright © 1996 by
CSS Publishing Company, Inc.
Lima, Ohio

Scripture quotations are from the *New Revised Standard Version of the Bible*, copyright 1989, by the Division of Christian Education of the National Council of the Churches of Christ in the USA. Used by permission.

Library of Congress Cataloging-in-Publication Data

Ingram, Robert D., 1946-
  Worship workbook for the gospels. Series II. Cycle B / Robert D. Ingram : music sections compiled by Robert Hobby and Berkley Guse.
     p.   cm.
  Includes bibliographical references and index.
  ISBN 0-7880-0809-9
  1. Worship programs. 2. Public worship—Handbooks, manuals, etc. 3. Common lectionary (1992)—Handbooks, manuals, etc. I. Hobby, Robert A. II. Guse, Berkley J., 1965-   .   III. Title.
BV198.I54   1995
264—dc20   95-13960
                                                                                                              CIP

This book is available in the following formats, listed by ISBN:
0-7880-0809-9 Book
0-7880-0810-2 IBM 3 1/2 computer disk
0-7880-0811-0 Macintosh computer disk
0-7880-0812-9 Sermon Prep

PRINTED IN U.S.A.

Table of Contents

Editor's Note Regarding The Lectionary

During the past two decades there has been an attempt to move in the direction of a uniform lectionary among various Protestant denominations.

Preaching on the same scripture lessons every Sunday is a step in the right direction of uniting Christians of many faiths. If we are reading the same scriptures together we may also begin to accomplish other achievements. Our efforts will be strengthened through our unity.

Beginning with Advent 1995 The Evangelical Lutheran Church in America will drop its own lectionary schedule and adopt the Revised Common Lectionary.

We at CSS Publishing Company heartily embrace this change. We recognize, however, that there will be a transitional period during which some churches may continue for a time to use the traditional Lutheran lectionary. In order to accommodate these clergy and churches who may still be referring to the Lutheran lectionary we will for a period of time continue to list the Lutheran lections along with the Revised Common and Episcopal texts.

How To Use This Book

The resources and ideas in this book are meant to inspire worship planners, not enslave them with demands for exact reproduction of these materials. The reader is encouraged to adapt and modify the contents to fit the culture of the congregation being served.

With one exception, these resources and ideas were designed to aid worship planners in proclaiming, interpreting, applying and celebrating the lessons found in the four gospels of the New Testament. This book is not intended as a preaching resource. There are more preaching resources on the market than any one pastor will ever need. Instead of focusing on the sermon, the materials in this book focus on the rest of the worship service. They help worshipers hear God's Word and provide a medium for the worshipers to respond to the God whose voice they have heard.

Because the TV generations tend to take in more with their eyes than with their ears, many of these resources are visually oriented. Even many of the printed resources are salted with visual imagery.

The author tried to stay with the scripture text, even when working with passages that are traditionally used at certain times in the Christian year. Because of this, worship planners will need to blend seasonal emphases into these resources. On the other hand, non-lectionary preachers will find this feature beneficial when they use these texts at other times throughout the year.

Worship planners will also need to be selective in using the resources focused on a passage of scripture. Several angles of interpretation and application are used with each passage. If planners are not careful in choosing which ideas and resources to use together in one worship service, the end result could make worshipers feel schizophrenic.

Note: At the beginning of each chapter is a brief note printed in italics. These are provided for those churches that print a quote in the worship bulletins for worshipers to use during their quiet time before the service begins. Worshipers may use these to meditate upon, or just to get a hint as to what direction the worship service will be going. These could also be printed in newsletters along with the scripture texts and sermon titles for the coming Sundays.

Printed Resources

The resources meant to be printed in worship bulletins include two characteristics that should be highlighted for the sake of worship planners. First, they encourage dialogue between God and God's people. For example, greetings are written in such a manner that although a worship leader initiates the dialogue, the worshipers respond to God, not to the worship leader. This puts worship leaders in the position of speaking truths about God, or, even more importantly, serving as God's spokesperson to address the people. This style changes worship away from being a conversation between the people leading worship and the people filling the pews. Instead, the worship service is turned into a conversation between God and all the people in worship.

A second important characteristic of the printed resources is that they encourage the worshipers to participate in what is happening. For example, the prayers are written to be prayed in unison or responsively. There are no prayers included in this material that are intended for the pastor to pray on behalf of the people. This is because ministry is the work of all believers, and the liturgy of the church is one of the believers' areas of ministry.

Finally, the word "benediction" is replaced in these resources by the words "commissioning and blessing." For too many people the Latin word "benediction" has come to mean "the end" rather than a blessing which the worshipers receive before they go back into their daily lives and work. The commissioning and blessings included here are written to bestow blessings, as well as to give a final charge or commission to God's people. Thus comes the title used throughout this book.

Words appearing in bold face type are meant to be spoken by the whole congregation. Words in regular face type are spoken by the pastor or other worship leaders. Abbreviations used for responsive greetings, prayers and litanies are:

All	— All the congregation, pastors and others
Chr	— Choir
Cng	— Congregation
Ldr	— Leader (a pastor, liturgist, or whomever)
Ld1	— Leader 1
Ld2	— Leader 2, etc.
Lft	— All the people on the left-hand side of the sanctuary
Men	— All men and boys
Off	— Officers of the congregation
Pst	— Pastor
Rgt	— All the people on the right-hand side of the sanctuary
Wmn	— All women and girls

Hymns and Service Music

The hymns listed in this section are gleaned from several denominational hymnals in hopes that at least a few appear in the hymnals being used in the reader's church. The choruses are from several books that provide collections of these. Each piece of music is chosen to relate to, echo, or respond to the gospel lesson in some way. Again, several angles in applying the lesson are used in choosing the hymns. Most of the hymns can be found in one of these three hymnals:

Lutheran Book of Worship. Minneapolis: Augsburg Publishing House, 1978.
The Hymnal 1982. New York: The Church Hymnal Corporation, 1985.
The United Methodist Hymnal. Nashville: The United Methodist Publishing House, 1989.

Most of the choruses can be found in:
Songs for Praise and Worship. Waco: Word Music, 1992.

Reading the Scriptures

It is the author's conviction that reading the Word of God and celebrating the sacraments are the most important things that we routinely do in Christian worship. The sacraments easily hold the contemporary worshiper's attention, but not so the reading of scripture. When worship leaders pick up a Bible to read, they can look out over the congregation and watch the minds click off and the eyes glaze over. This is no judgment against the scriptures, but it is certainly a statement about the biblical illiteracy, lack of understanding, cultural biases and spiritual laziness that block the hearts of most people filling church pews today.

Because it is so hard for contemporary worshipers to truly listen to and understand the scriptures, worship planners need to put much more emphasis on helping worshipers with this task. Material in this section should help move the congregation toward a more effective hearing of God's Word.

Worship planners can be of even more assistance to the congregation if they preface the reading of scripture with a brief explanation of the passage about to be read. Telling the worshipers a little about the context of the passage or about what was happening in the time that the passage was written will help open ears to hearing what God is saying.

Unfortunately, none of these practices will overcome the lazy attitudes reflected in so many Christians today. Too many feel they do not have to hear, read or study God's Word. All they have to do is go to church and their pastor will tell them everything they need to know about what God is saying. Such lazy Christians plop themselves into the church pews only for the sake of getting something that will help them get through the week ahead. They do not come with the intention of giving anything, not even their worship. It will take more than careful planning of worship to overcome this tragedy in the Christian church today.

Responses to the Word

How can any human hear God, Creator of the universe, speaking to him or her, and not respond in some way? Worship planners who do not provide some manner for the worshipers to say "Yes" to God are shortchanging the people and the God whom they serve. The old-fashioned altar calls of the frontiers provided the worshipers a means of giving a response to God, and thus changed the nature of the North American continent.

These materials provide a starting place for worship planners to think about what the worshipers will need to be able to respond to God after hearing the message of the gospel lesson. Of course, these responses are just the beginning. The real response is what gets lived out in the daily lives and work of the worshipers the rest of the week. But the rituals experienced in services of worship can point worshipers to ways of faithfully responding to God with their daily lives.

Drama and Movement

Only a few published plays and skits are mentioned in this section. Much of this kind of information that could be printed here would be dated by the time the reader would want to use it. Instead, it is recommended that the reader request the most recent play catalogues from publishers such as:

Anchorage Press
P.O. Box 8067
New Orleans, LA 70182
504-283-8868

Baker's Plays
100 Chauncy St.
Boston, MA 02111
617-482-1280

Contemporary Drama Service
P.O. Box 7710
Colorado Springs, CO 80933
1-800-93-PLAYS

Dramatic Publishing Co.
P.O. Box 129
Woodstock, IL 60098
1-800-448-7469

Dramatists Play Service
440 Park Ave. S.
New York, NY 10016
212-683-8960

Friendship Press
P.O. Box 37844
Cincinnati, OH 45222-0844
1-800-889-5733

Lillenas Publishing Co.
P.O. Box 419527
Kansas City, MO 64141
1-800-877-0700

Pioneer Drama Service
P.O. Box 4267
Englewood, CO 80155
1-800-333-7262

Publishers Group West   Samuel French
4065 Hollis St.   45 W. 25th St.
Emeryville, CA 94608   New York, NY 10010
1-800-788-3123   212-206-8990

Visuals

At the beginning of each chapter is a sketch that can be enlarged and reproduced as the cover for worship bulletins. These sketches can also provide ideas for congregational artists and craftspeople creating banners and other visual helps for enhancing the worship services.

Once again the material listed in this section is only a beginning point. Let the congregation's local artisans use their imaginations to give expression to the content of the gospel lessons. Part of being created in God's image is our ability to be creative ourselves. Artists have been suppressed for too long in many churches. It is time to give them some space for proclaiming, responding to, and celebrating God's Word.

Anthems and Special Music; Organ and Other Keyboard Music

The music suggestions provided are twofold. One area is choral; the other is organ. Since the intent of this resource book is to provide ideas for proclaiming the gospel lessons, it seemed appropriate that the choral selections also be based on the gospels. While some of the readings have a plethora of choral suggestions, others have little or no anthems to be found. In the latter cases, some anthems related to the themes of the gospel are suggested. Appendix I contains a listing of additional choral pieces for each church season that could be utilized in that time frame. Choral/vocal settings with various voicings, including solo and unison settings usable for a soloist, are provided throughout to meet the various needs of churches.

The organ suggestions given are, with a few exceptions, based on the hymns selected by the author. A minimum of two hymns were selected for each day. Since there is great diversity of tunes with hymn texts, it seemed appropriate to include the tune name of the chorale prelude in parentheses after the title. Furthermore, in cases where a tune was selected more than one Sunday, additional suggestions were provided. The reader will want to note that the composer's name is listed prior to the title of a collection when he/she is one of multiple contributors to that collection. If the composer's name appears after the title of the collection, he/she is the sole composer for the collection. This will be valuable information when ordering from the publisher. Like the choral music, additional organ music suggestions are listed in Appendix I for each season of the church year.

Each musical entry also includes an abbreviation which indicates the publisher of the piece. This abbreviation appears in the form of two to four capital letters at the end of the entry. (See example below.) Appendix II contains a complete list of these publishing companies and the capital letter abbreviation used for each one.
(Example: Variations on Nun komm, der Heiden Heiland — R. Lind — CPH. CPH stands for Concordia Publishing House, as listed in the appendix.)

FIRST SUNDAY IN ADVENT

Revised
 Common: Mark 13:24-37
Episcopal: Mark 13:(24-32) 33-37
Lutheran: Mark 13:24-37 or
              Mark 11:1-10*

Gail Throckmorton Warner

Note: Each day that we take up the work commissioned by Christ is a day that we are awake and alert.

* See Passion/Palm Sunday for materials on this text.

Printed Resources

___ Greeting

Ldr: On this first Sunday of Advent,
      we cannot help but notice all the false messiahs
      claiming that all the signs point to them
      as the second advent of Jesus Christ.
Cng: **Lord, forgive these self-deceiving messiahs**
      who lead people to the destruction,
      not the salvation, of their eternal souls.
Ldr: So many waste their energies poring over obscure texts,
      calculating the date and time of Christ's advent,
      twisting numbers and signs to fit their misguided schemes.
Cng: **Lord, forgive these self-proclaimed fools,**
      who cannot keep their minds on the work you assign
      while we await the return of our true Messiah.
Ldr: This is not a time to spend ourselves
      chasing after all those who claim divine inspiration.
      This is a time to be steady at our work,
      trusting, believing, staying awake to Christ's coming.
Cng: **Lord, teach us such faithfulness,**
      in the midst of all the confusions and futility of this age.

___ Prayer for Illumination

In this confusing and chaotic time, O Lord,
   it is hard to discern truth from fiction.
Teach us once again the lesson of the fig tree.
Reassure us one more time
      that, even though heaven and earth pass away,
      your words are eternal and will never fail.
Clear the cobwebs of sleep from our minds,
      and awaken us to hear the gospel. Amen.

___ A Prayer for Pastors

God of truth and faithfulness,
   I am a doorkeeper.
Save me from wasting my energies
      futilely calculating the end of time.
Instead, help me stay awake and alert,
      watching always for the signs of the Messiah.
Clear my eyes to see beyond the visible.
      Tune my ears to sounds never before heard.
Strengthen my voice to sound the alarm,
      and my legs to leap for joy.
I am a doorkeeper, O God,
      keep me faithful to my calling
      and fill my mouth with your truth,
      from now until the end of time. Amen.

___ Commissioning and Blessing

What I say to you, I say to all: Keep awake!
      Beware! Keep alert!
You do not know when the Messiah will return.
So, each one should do his work,
      the task that Christ has assigned you,
      so that all will be ready
      when the time has come.
And the time will come.
      The Messiah will not fail you.
      Promises will be kept,
      and the faithful will be saved.
So, keep awake!
      You do not know when the time will come. **Amen.**

Hymns and Choruses

(The asterisk [*] indicates hymns or choruses that are addressed to God and can be used as prayers.)

___ "Awake, My Soul, and with the Sun"
___ *"Come, Thou Long-Expected Jesus"
___ "Hark! A Thrilling Voice Is Sounding"
___ "Hymn of Promise"
___ "Lo, He Comes with Clouds Descending"
___ *"My Lord, What a Morning"
___ "Oh, that the Lord Would Guide My Ways"
___ "People, Look East"
___ "Rise, My Soul, to Watch and Pray"
___ "Rise Up, O Saints of God"
___ "Sing with All the Saints in Glory"
___ "The Advent of Our God"
___ "Wake, Awake, for Night Is Flying"
___ "When We All Get to Heaven"
___ *"While We Are Waiting, Come"

Reading the Scripture

___ Recruit seven people of different ages to read the gospel text. Have the youngest reader (preferably an elementary child) begin the reading and then let the next oldest person read, and so on, until the oldest person concludes the lesson. Assign the verses of the lesson as follows:

Verses 24-25   First reader (the youngest)
Verses 26-27   Second reader
Verses 28-29   Third reader
Verses 30-31   Fourth reader
Verses 32-33   Fifth reader
Verses 34-36   Sixth reader
Verse 37   Seventh reader (the oldest)

___ This entire lesson can be spoken by a single person, taking the role of Christ talking to the disciples. This person should memorize the text. Costuming the person to look like Christ could be used to add to the drama of the reading, and to help the congregation receive the words as those of Jesus Christ.

Responses to the Word

___ Call the worshipers to take up their assigned tasks that are to be accomplished while waiting for Christ to return. Ask people to stand and state for all the congregation to hear what ministry task they will, or are, undertaking in service to the "master of the house." Another way to accomplish this would be to ask worshipers to write on a piece of paper the

11

area of ministry they will undertake. This paper could be inserted in worship bulletins and handed out prior to the service. The worshipers could put the completed papers in the offering plates as a way of presenting their intended service to God.

___ Challenge the worshipers to pray silently that God reveal a task that needs to be done. When they have had ample time to pray, then challenge them to take on the task they heard God assigning. Tell them to set this task ahead of their usual Christmas preparations, and to make it a priority in their lives. Some may not have heard God assigning a task to them. Challenge these people to keep praying, and to remain alert for a word from God. Call upon all the congregation to work and to pray as if Christ were already at the door.

___ This would be a good time for the worshipers to join in an affirmation of faith that emphasizes the second coming and the end of time.

Drama and Movement

___ Ask a group of adults to prepare and present several vignettes that show faithful servants working and keeping awake to the coming of Christ. The same group should also prepare several vignettes that show a contrasting group of "sleeping" servants that are not going to be prepared for Christ's return. For example, faithful servants can be shown ministering to the poor, healing the sick or broken, caring for the orphans and widows, and so on. The "sleepers" can be shown trying to figure out the exact time of the second coming, or mouthing pious platitudes about "When Christ comes..." but doing nothing to alleviate human suffering in the meantime. A sermon could follow the vignettes to emphasize that each servant of Christ has work to be done while waiting for our Savior to return.

___ Have an interrupter suddenly enter the sanctuary and interrupt the worship service. A loud noise should accompany the interruption, adding to the shock to the congregation. The person interrupting the service could say something like the following:
"Are you awake? You do not know when the master of our house will return. This might have been the time. What were you doing? What were you thinking? Was it something that you would want Christ to discover you doing and thinking when he returns? What I say to you, I say to all: Keep awake."
This could be repeated several times during the same service.

Visuals

___ Many people grow ficus as a houseplant. Ask if you can borrow one or more of these members of the fig family. Use these plants to decorate the sanctuary, or to add to the Christmas decorations that may already be in place on this First Sunday in Advent.

___ Recruit some members of the congregation to make two banners. Put a black sun and falling stars on the first banner, and a black moon and falling stars on the second banner. At the bottom of one banner have a person portrayed sleeping, and the bottom of the other portray a person awake and praying.

___ Have some craftspeople cut out cardboard angels. They should paint and decorate these angels, and then hang them in the sanctuary in such a way that it appears that they are going out to "the four winds, from the ends of the earth to the ends of heaven."

___ Have members design two banners. One should look like a clock with no hour or minute hands. The other should look like a calendar with no year or month marked on it.

Anthems and Special Music

(Mark 13:24-37)
An Advent Carol — J. Lindh — Unison w/keyboard — CG
God Make You Blameless — T. Gieschen — Unison or SATB w/keyboard — AF
All The Days of My Life (cantata in 7 movements) — L. Talma — Tenor Solo w/piano, clarinet, cello, percussion — AMC
Light One Candle to Watch for Messiah — Yiddish folk/W. Wold — Unison w/keyboard — from *With One Voice* — AF
My Lord What a Morning — African-American Spiritual — SATB unaccompanied — from *With One Voice* — AF
O Blessed Lord Our God — H. Schütz — 2-part — ECS
People Look East — French Carol/B. Rose — SATB w/opt. keyboard — from *With One Voice* — AF
Wake, Awake, for Night is Flying — F. Zipp — SAB unaccompanied — from *Sing for Joy* — CPH
Wake, Awake, for Night is Flying — F. Tunder — Unison — CPH
Ye Watchers and Ye Holy Ones — G. W. Cassler — SATB w/organ, opt. trumpet — AF
Zion Hears the Watchmen's Voices — J. S. Bach/J. Rutter — Tenors or Unison voices w/keyboard — from *Carols for Choirs 2* — OUP

(Mark 11:1-10)
See Passion/Palm Sunday

Organ and Other Keyboard Music

Come, Thou Long Expected Jesus (Hyfrydol) — Partita on Hyfrydol — C. Callahan — CPH
People, Look East (Besancon) — found in *Wood Works on International Folk Hymns* — D. Wood — SMP
Wake, Awake, for Night Is Flying (Wachet Auf) — found in *30 Chorale Preludes* — F. Peeters — CFP

SECOND SUNDAY
IN ADVENT

Revised
  Common: Mark 1:1-8
Episcopal: Mark 1:1-8
Lutheran: Mark 1:1-8

Note: John came with a baptism for repentance. Jesus came with the baptism of the Holy Spirit for the transformation of our lives. Shall we be satisfied with just repentance any longer?

Angie Latta

Printed Resources

___ Greeting

Ldr: John the baptizer appeared in the wilderness,
     proclaiming a baptism of repentance
     for the forgiveness of sins.
Cng: **Lord, people came from all over Judea to confess their sins,**
     and to be baptized by John in the river Jordan.
Ldr: And John told the people
     that he baptized with water,
     but one was coming after him
     who would baptize them with the Holy Spirit.
Cng: **Lord, we have come today, confessing our sins**
     and reaffirming our baptisms
     in the name of Jesus Christ,
     who baptizes us with your Holy Spirit.

___ Prayer of Confession and Assurance of Pardon

Let us prepare the way of the Lord in our hearts,
     by silently confessing our sins.
Let us pray for forgiveness for the times
     that we have mistreated our families and close friends.
(Pause for silent prayer.)
Let us pray for forgiveness for the times
     that we have ignored the suffering and needs of others.

(Pause for silent prayer.)
Let us pray for forgiveness for the times
    that we have not loved our enemies.
(Pause for silent prayer.)
Let us pray for forgiveness for the times
    that we have sought selfish pleasure above God's will.
(Pause for silent prayer.)
Let us pray for forgiveness for the times
    that we have failed to stand up for what is just and right.
(Pause for silent prayer.)
Let us pray for forgiveness for the times
    that we have refused to forgive those who have wronged us.
(Pause for silent prayer.)
Let us pray for forgiveness for the times
    that we have put selfish gain ahead of service to God.
(Pause for silent prayer.)
Let us pray for forgiveness for the times
    that we have failed to love as God has loved us.
(Pause for silent prayer.)
Let us pray for forgiveness for all the times
    that we have failed to appreciate God's forgiving our sins.
(Pause for silent prayer.)
Brothers and sisters, *Assurance (Unison)*
    we know that we are not worthy to stoop down before our Lord,
    or even to untie the thong of his sandals.
Yet Jesus comes and washes us with his baptism,
    and fills us with his own Holy Spirit.
Jesus comes, not to punish, but to forgive,
    and to save, and to breathe new life into our lost souls.
Brothers and sisters, we have sinned against God,
    and against the Son of God;
    yet God has forgiven us, Christ has baptized us,
    and God's own Spirit fills us with new life.
Therefore, let us no longer live like the sinners we were,
    but like the new people under God that we have become,
    now and forever. **Amen!**

___ Commissioning and Blessing

Benediction

The beginning of the good news is this,
    Jesus Christ comes baptizing with the Holy Spirit.
Though we are unworthy to stoop down before him
    and untie the thong of his sandals,
    Jesus Christ, the Son of God, comes.
Let us prepare the way
    and make his paths straight. **Amen.**

Hymns and Choruses

(The asterisk [*] indicates hymns or choruses that are addressed to God and can be used as prayers.)

___ "A Charge to Keep I Have"
___ "Blessed Be the God of Israel"
___ "Come, Ye Sinners, Poor and Needy"
___ "Depth of Mercy"
___ "Herald, Sound the Note of Judgment"
___ "Heralds of Christ"
___ "On Jordan's Banks the Baptist's Cry"
___ "Prepare the Royal Highway"
___ "Prepare the Way, O Zion"
___ "Prepare the Way of the Lord"
___ " 'Tis the Old Ship of Zion"
___ "The Advent of Our God"
___ "There's a Voice in the Wilderness Crying"
___ "Today Your Mercy Calls Us"
___ *"What Is the Crying at Jordan"

Reading the Scripture

___ Recruit two people to read the lesson. A man and a woman would provide the greatest variety in the sound of their voices. Have the woman read verses 1-2a. Then the man can read verses 2b-3. Then the woman reads verses 4-6 and the words, "He proclaimed" from verse 7 (if you are using the New Revised Standard Version). Finally, the man concludes by reading verses 7-8.

___ See the first suggestion under "Drama and Movement."

Responses to the Word

___ Have the worshipers join in confessing their sins, and then lead them through the reaffirmation of their baptismal vows.

___ Have the worshipers join in the prayer of confession and assurance of pardon printed above.

___ Preach three mini-sermons with a different response after each one. Base the first mini-sermon on verse 1, that assures the worshipers that Jesus is the beginning (a new Genesis?) of hope and life. Have the people respond with an affirmation of hope or by singing a song of hope. Verses 2 and 3 are the foundation of a second mini-sermon on the roots or heritage of the Christian's hope. Call upon the people to read the Bible every day to understand and be strengthened by the foundation upon which their faith is built. A hymn about affirming the truth of the scriptures or a prayer of commitment to reading the scriptures would be an

16

appropriate response. Verse 4 reveals the way to move toward the hope and life proclaimed in verse 1. After a mini-sermon on repentance, call the people into a confession of their sin. Conclude by assuring the people the Christ does come with our new beginning.

Drama and Movement

___ Call out the congregation's puppeteers to portray the gospel lesson. Make sure that the puppets are large enough to be seen from the back pews. Have a person step out in front of the puppet stage to read the lesson. As he reads verse two, they could drop a long rolled-up scroll and let it roll across the floor. After this visual, read the prophecy of Isaiah (which actually includes Malachi 3:1 as well). When the words in verse 4, "John the baptizer appeared," are read, the puppet representing John can ham up his entrance onto the puppet stage. At the end of verse 4, John could launch into a fire and brimstone type sermon to the congregation about how much they need to repent and be baptized to have their sins forgiven. The reader might have to interrupt John to continue with verse 4. Other puppets could approach John the baptizer. As each one gets near John, he grabs them and pushes them under water. (Keep the water out of sight behind the puppet stage). A handful of blue confetti thrown into the air would represent the splash of each puppet's baptism. Sound effects could be added as well. Then as verse 6 is read, John could model his camel hair coat and his leather belt. He could eat a locust puppet, and chase after a wild-acting bottle of honey. Then when verse 7 is read, John could get serious and speak the words himself. As he says, "I have baptized you with water," in verse 8, another handful of confetti could be tossed into the air (with another splash sound effect?). But then John again gets serious when he says, "But he will baptize you with the Holy Spirit." If desired, the puppet play could easily be extended through verse 12 to represent Jesus being baptized in John's splashing water. A dove puppet could be hung from a fishing pole (keep the pole out of sight) to descend from heaven. The dove could also push Jesus to drive him out into the wilderness (or, if the comedy wouldn't ruin the message, Jesus and the dove could get into a toy car and drive into the wilderness.)

___ A single dancer could add a beautiful interpretation to the reading of the lesson. Another dimension could be added if the lesson was sung by a soloist familiar with chanting.

Visuals

___ Ask some of the craftspeople in the congregation to make a large cloth banner to hang across the front of the sanctuary. Use cloth paint to add these words on the banner, "The beginning of the good news of Jesus Christ, the Son of God." They can use colors that blend with the rest of the sanctuary.

___ Have a small group of seamstresses prepare a set of paraments. Use blue (alternate color for Advent) cloth to represent the Jordan River, and have the seamstresses applique a leather design that looks like a pair of sandals. This design could be displayed on the lectern. The pulpit hanging could have seven (number for the Holy Spirit) drops of water appliqued to it, representing Christ's baptism of water and Spirit. These drops of water could be formed from cloth or could be large tear-shaped baubles of glass or plastic. Then

17

have the seamstresses lay a tapered strip of black cloth in the center of the altar table covering. Strips of white cloth should be appliqued to the black strip to make it look like a road running from the congregation to the cross. If the congregation has a cross hanging over the altar table, the black cloth road could run right up to the cross by attaching it to the bottom of the cross. The black cloth road could flow down over the altar table and across the chancel floor and even down a center aisle between the pews. It should widen as it approaches the congregation to give the effect of distance. Of course, the cloth should be kept straight, like the path John calls upon the people to prepare.

Anthems and Special Music

Prepare the Way of the Lord — J. Berthier — Unison w/opt. instruments, cantor — GIA
Prepare the Way of the Lord — J. H. Laster — SATB — CPH
Prepare the Way of the Lord — W. Warren — SATB w/clarinet — GIA
Prepare the Way of the Lord — W. Rowen — SATB w/keyboard — SP
Prepare the Way, O Zion — H. Willan — SS w/keyboard — from *Carols for the Seasons* — CPH

Organ and Other Keyboard Music

Blessed Be the God of Israel (Forest Green) — A. Carter — found in *Seasons*, vol. 1 Advent/Christmas — PA
Come, Ye Sinners Poor and Needy (Restoration) — found in *3 Folk Hymn Improvisations* — A. Travis — MSM
Prepare the Royal Highway (Bereden väg för Herran) — found in *11 Compositions for Organ*, vol. V — C. Ore — CPH

THIRD SUNDAY
IN ADVENT

Revised
 Common: John 1:6-8, 19-28
Episcopal: John 3:23-30
Lutheran: John 1:6-8, 19-28

Note: We bow in worship before a God who not only sends a Messiah, but sends a Messiah who is a light to us; and not only sends a Messiah who is a light to us, but even sends a witness to point us to the light, so that we do not miss it or the Messiah who brings it. We bow before a God whose love has no bounds.

Jesus Christ;
The True Source of Light.

Angie Latta

Printed Resources

John 1:6-8, 19-20

___ Greeting

Ldr: "There was a man sent from God, whose name was John.
    He came as a witness to testify to the light."
Cng: **O God, let us hear John's witness,**
    and see the true light of the world.
Ldr: "This is the testimony given by John...
    Among you stands one whom you do not know,
    the one who is coming after me;
    I am not worthy to untie the thong of his sandal."
Cng: **O God, save the world and save us from unknowing,**
    open our eyes, our minds and our hearts
    to the true light of the world.

___ Prayer

Almighty God, remind your church
    that despite all the Christmas cantatas, programs, and parties,

the candlelight services, food baskets, and Christmas caroling,
we are not the Messiah, we are not the light.
We are not Elijah, nor even the prophet.
We are simply a voice.
We are here to testify to the true light,
who enlightens everyone,
and who comes into this world.
We are a voice crying out in the wilderness.
We are your church, O God,
yet we cannot bestow the Holy Spirit,
and our baptism cannot transform lives.
And of the one who can,
we are not worthy to untie the thong of his sandals.
Christmas is not about us, God,
but about the one who brings the Holy Spirit.
It is about the one whose baptism saves and transforms,
the one who is the true light enlightening everyone.
Christmas is your church's voice crying out and saying
that one comes who is the Messiah, the Savior of the world.
May our Christmas voice sound loud and clear,
now and forever. Amen.

___ Commissioning and Blessing

John was a witness testifying to Jesus Christ our true light.
"So are you to be my witnesses," says our Lord,
"crying out in this day's wilderness,
'Make straight the way of the Lord.' "
And as you witness to the light of the world,
may Christ's light shine brightly in and through you,
now and forever. **Amen.**

John 3:23-30

___ Prayer

O God, we feel like John,
who called himself "friend of the bridegroom,"
and who rejoiced in standing beside Jesus
and in listening to Jesus' glorious voice.
Especially at this time of year,
Jesus' voice sounds strongly all around,
and it is a delight to hear
the beauty and goodness of what he says.
Families and friends reach out to one another,
bridging the separation of distance and old hurts.

Strangers pause in their busyness
    to offer help and hope to those in need.
Children are honored and welcomed
    in the exclusive halls of "important matters."
Giving is venerated and acclaimed,
    while getting is discredited and devalued.
While they work, believers hum carols of nativity
    adding faith and love to their works.
Your churches ring out their testimonies to the night,
    and Jesus' light shines in the darkness through them.
Evil and hatred stand out in bitter contrast,
    and human hearts turn from such ugly choices.
Friendship and love, joy and peace,
    become the standards centering the human family.
Yes, God, it is so good to stand beside the bridegroom,
    and to feel his strong arms tenderly embrace us.
To hear Jesus call us his bride,
    quiets every fear and enlivens every hope,
    because his love is stronger than death
    and remains unwavering longer than all eternity.
Yes, God, it is no wonder that John rejoices
    in standing beside this bridegroom
    and listens to his beautiful voice.
And it is no wonder that we, your church,
    pledge our undying faith and love, O God,
    to your only Son, now and forever. Amen.

Hymns and Choruses

(The asterisk [*] indicates hymns and choruses that are addressed to God and can be used as prayers.)

John 1:6-8, 19-28

___ "Christ Is the World's Light"
___ "Give Me the Faith Which Can Remove"
___ "God Hath Spoken by the Prophets"
___ "Hark! A Thrilling Voice Is Sounding"
___ "Heralds of Christ"
___ "Herald, Sound the Note of Judgment"
___ "On Jordan's Bank"
___ "There's a Voice in the Wilderness Crying"
___ "What Is the Crying at Jordan"

John 3:23-30

___ "Christ Is the World's Light"
___ *"Christ, Whose Glory Fills the Skies"
___ *"Fairest Lord Jesus"
___ "God Hath Spoken by the Prophets"
___ *"Jesus, Joy of Our Desiring"
___ "Jesus, Name above All Names"
___ "Jesus! the Name High Over All"
___ "No Other Name"
___ *"Of the Father's Love Begotten"
___ "Ye Servants of God"

Reading the Scripture

John 1:6-8, 19-28

___ Recruit two people to read the gospel lesson. Assign their parts in this way:
    Reader 1 - verses 6-7
    Reader 2 - verse 8
    Reader 1 - verse 19
    Reader 2 - verse 20
    Reader 1 - verse 21a (And they asked him, "What then? Are you Elijah?")
    Reader 2 - verse 21b (He said, "I am not.")
    Reader 1 - verse 21c ("Are you the prophet?")
    Reader 2 - verse 21d (He answered, "No.")
    Reader 1 - verse 22
    Reader 2 - verse 23
    Reader 1 - verses 24-25
    Reader 2 - verses 26-27
    Reader 1 - verse 28

John 3:23-30

___ Recruit three people to read the gospel lesson. The first reader reads verses 23-26a. The second reader becomes the voice of John's disciples in verse 26b. The first reader says, "John answered," from verse 27. Then the third reader becomes John's voice in verses 27-30.

Responses to the Word

___ If there are people desiring baptism prior to Christmas, this would be a good Sunday to celebrate this sacrament.

___ Ask those who are willing to promise to invite at least one new person or family to attend the Christmas services with them to stand. Then ask those who stand, "Will you promise to invite at least one new person or family to attend the Christmas services with you? If so, answer, 'I will.' " The people standing might even be requested to lay their hands on their Bibles before they answer the question.

Drama and Movement

John 1:6-8, 19-28

___ Recruit six people to speak different parts in the gospel lesson. A seventh person is needed to read the lesson. Several extras (perhaps a youth Sunday school class) are needed to act as if they are being baptized. As the reader reads verses 6-8, the person designated to speak John the Baptist's words enters. (John is the only one who needs to be in costume.) The extras get up from their seats in the pews and surrender themselves to John's baptism. As the reader moves into verses 19-28, the other five actors and actresses stand from where they have been sitting in the pew and ask these questions to John: (1) "Who are you?" (2) "What then? Are you Elijah?" (3) "Are you the prophet?" (4) "Who are you? Let us have an answer for those who sent us. What do you say about yourself?" Finally, John, who has silently shaken his head to all their questions, stops baptizing and speaks the words recorded in verse 23. The reader continues with verse 24, but is interrupted by the fifth questioner in verse 25 who asks (5) "Why then are you baptizing if you are neither the Messiah, nor Elijah, nor the prophet?" John speaks the words in verses 26-27. The reader finishes reading verse 28, and John and his newly baptized followers exit together.

Visuals

John 1:6-8, 19-28

___ If the congregation's seamstresses prepared a set of paraments as suggested for the Second Sunday in Advent, then ask them to make two changes for this Sunday. They can still use the lectern covering with the leather sandals on the lectern. But the pulpit covering should be changed to a hand pointing toward the altar table. The altar table covering should be changed to a cover with some bright light symbol on it. A huge sun symbol might be used, or perhaps a large burst of bright yellows, whites, and reds.

John 3:23-30

___ Recruit three people to dress up as a bride, bridegroom, and a friend of the bridegroom. Photograph these three, and copy the photo for a bulletin cover. Black and white photos reproduce best on copiers.

___ Borrow three dressmaker forms, a wedding gown and veil, and two tuxedos from a bridal shop. Put the gown and tuxedos on the three forms, and pose them somewhere in the front of the sanctuary. Some flowers or live plants might be used to add color to the scene.

Anthems and Special Music

(John 1:6-8, 19-28)
Lo, I Am the Voice of One Crying in the Wilderness — H. Schütz — SSATTB w/opt. organ — GS
The Wilderness — S. S. Wesley — SSATB w/organ — NOV
The Word of God is Source and Seed — D. Hurd — Unison w/keyboard — from *With One Voice* — AF
The Word Was Made Flesh — M. Reger — SATB unaccompanied — CPH
This is the Record of John — O. Gibbons — SAATB w/tenor solo, organ — LG
Word of God, Come Down on Earth — J. Ahle — SATB w/keyboard — from *Hymnal Supplement 1991* — GIA

Organ and Other Keyboard Music

(John 1:6-8, 19-28)
Christ is the World's Light (Christe Sanctorum) — R. Baker — RME
God Hath Spoken by the Prophets (Ebenezer or Ton-y-botel) — found in *Seven Hymn Preludes in a New Style* — W. Swenson — HWG
On Jordan's Bank (Peur Nobis) — Variations on Puer Nobis — M. Burkhardt — MSM

(John 3:23-30)
Christ is the World's Light (Christe Sanctorium) — see above
Fairest Lord Jesus (St. Elizabeth) — G. Hancock — HWG
Jesu, Joy of Our Desiring — J. S. Bach — found in various collections

FOURTH SUNDAY IN ADVENT

Revised
  Common: Luke 1:26-38
Episcopal: Luke 1:26-38
Lutheran: Luke 1:26-38

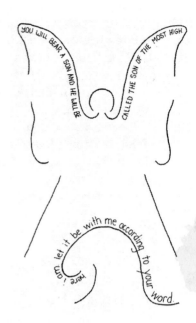

*Note: Because nothing will
be impossible to God, we
happily surrender ourselves
to God, so that we can be part
of doing the impossible.*

Printed Resources

___ Greeting

Ldr: Greetings, favored ones! The Lord is with you.
Cng: **What do you mean?**
Ldr: Mary has conceived by the Holy Spirit,
        and bears a son who will be great.
        He will be called the Son of the Most High,
        and God will give to him the throne of his ancestor David.
        He will reign forever,
        and there will be no end to his kingdom.
Cng: **Here we are, Lord. We are your servants.**
        Let it be according to your word.

___ Prayer

Ldr: God of Christmas,
        God of the faithful who trust your messengers,
        God of those who cannot believe their ears,
        we love your impossible doings.
Cng: **Nothing will be impossible with you, O God.**
Ldr: You send your angels to ordinary people,
        to announce your extraordinary plans
        for impossible things that are about to happen.
Cng: **Nothing will be impossible with you, O God.**
Ldr: You merge your Spirit with that of humanity,
        so that your kingdom might begin in a virgin's womb,
        and your Son might reign from David's throne forever.

Cng: **Nothing will be impossible with you, O God.**

Ldr: You send holiness to win a profane world,
    you pour out joy to fill those barren of all hope,
    you allow your humble children to serve your mighty ways.

Cng: **Let your Spirit, your kingdom, your Son,**
    do the impossible again, O God.
    Make our world holy.
    Fill our barrenness with the joy of new life.
    Accept our service for your impossible purposes,
    now and forever. Amen.

___ Litany of Faith

Ldr: When Mary heard she was to give birth to God's Son,
    she asked how it could be.
    So the angel Gabriel told her of Elizabeth,
    who had been barren and now was also about to give birth.
    Gabriel said,

Cng: **Nothing will be impossible with God.**

Ldr: Long before, when Sarah laughed
    at the idea that she and Abraham
    would have a child in their old age,
    the Lord asked,

Cng: **Is anything too wonderful for the Lord?**

Ldr: When besieged Jerusalem was about to be captured,
    and the Israelites thought they would lose everything,
    Jeremiah heard God tell him to buy a field,
    because God would return the Israelites to their land.
    And the Lord told Jeremiah,

Cng: **See, I am the Lord, the God of all flesh;**
    is anything too hard for me?

Ldr: When the disciples heard
    that it is easier for a camel
    to go through the eye of a needle
    than for a rich man to enter the kingdom,
    they wondered if anyone could be saved,
    and Jesus answered,

Cng: **For mortals it is impossible,**
    but for God all things are possible.

Ldr: When Jesus was questioned
    whether he could cast out an unclean spirit
    that threatened to destroy a boy,
    Jesus answered,

Cng: **All things can be done for the one who believes.**

Ldr: When Jesus told his disciples
    about faith the size of a mustard seed

being able to move mountains,
he said,

Cng: **Nothing will be impossible for you.**

Ldr: God calls us,
Jesus leads us,
and the Holy Spirit empowers us.
Nothing will be impossible for us.

Cng: **Here we are, your servants, O Lord.**
Let the impossible be achieved
by your power and our obedience,
now and forevermore. Amen.

___ Commissioning and Blessing

Ldr: In the name of the Father, Son and Holy Spirit,
you are sent out to announce
that Jesus Christ, Son of the Most High,
comes to each man, woman and child,
no matter how humble or how barren,

Benediction with the gift of eternal life and love.

Ldr: Nothing will be impossible to God,
and nothing will be impossible to you
as you serve our wonderous Lord.

Cng: **Here am I, the servant of the Lord;**
let it be with me according to your word.

Ldr: Amen!

Cng: **Amen and amen!**

Hymns and Choruses

(The asterisk [*] indicates hymns or choruses that are addressed to God and can be used as prayers.)

___ "Bless the Name of Jesus"
___ "From East to West"
___ "Gabriel's Message Does Away"
___ "Jesus! Name of Wondrous Love"
___ "Lo, How a Rose E'er Blooming"
___ "No Other Name"
___ "Nova, Nova"
___ "Praise We the Lord This Day"
___ *"Redeemer of the Nations, Come"
___ *"Savior of the Nations, Come"
___ "Sing of Mary, Pure and Lowly"
___ "That Boy-Child of Mary"
___ "The Angel Gabriel From Heaven Came"

___ "The First One Ever"
___ "The Word Whom Earth and Sea and Sky"
___ "There's Something About That Name"
___ "To a Maid Engaged to Joseph"
___ "To the Name of Our Salvation"
___ "Ye Who Claim the Faith of Jesus"

Reading the Scripture

___ If the first suggestion under "Drama and Movement" is being used, select one person to read the entire gospel lesson.

___ Recruit three people to read the lesson. One can read the narrative, one the words of the angel, and one the words of Mary.

Responses to the Word

___ Use the litany of faith printed above.

___ Use the prayer printed above following the sermon.

___ Have the choir, a soloist, or an ensemble sing songs celebrating Mary's submission to God's will. Then have the congregation join in singing hymns that celebrate this too.

Drama and Movement

___ Have an amateur photographer experiment shooting slides of various angels. These could be figurines or pictures of angels, but the final slide should look like the angel is in the air and speaking to Mary on the ground. Choose the one slide that best portrays this. Project this slide onto the front wall of the sanctuary for the reading of the gospel lesson. Have a teenage girl dress as Mary. She should strike a pose that looks like she is conversing with the angel that is projected onto the wall above her. One slide should be used for the entire reading, and Mary should freeze her pose throughout the reading.

___ Have an adult group prepare three or four brief skits that portray people on the receiving end of shocking announcements. For example, a mother and father are watching television when their daughter comes in with an announcement. "Hi, Mom. Hi, Dad. I've got some great news! I'm pregnant! But don't worry, I was secretly married six months ago. He's a wonderful man, but he's in this country illegally. So, I'm going with him when he returns to his own country. We don't want to start off our marriage on the wrong foot. I've got to go to the courthouse now, so that they can put a rush on my passport application. We're leaving next week. I'll tell you more later. Bye." Use the reaction of the receivers of such announcements to set the stage for the congregation to really hear the shocking announcement that the angel Gabriel makes to Mary in the gospel lesson.

___ Choose two of the congregation's young people to act out the parts of Mary and the angel. Have them dress their parts and speak the words recorded in the gospel.

___ Two dancers could interpret the words of the gospel lesson as it is read.

___ Find one of the many paintings of the annunciation. Have a person with a video camera capture the painted image on film. Show this video as the gospel lesson is read. The camera might begin with recording the entire scene. Then the camera could close in on the angel as the angel explains to Mary what is about to happen. If a dove is pictured in the scene, then this detail should be the focus as the angel talks about the Holy Spirit. Mary should be the focus as the lesson draws to a conclusion.

Visuals

___ Ask some of the congregation's members to go through various art books at the local library to find pictures of famous paintings of the annunciation. Use an opaque projector to project these paintings onto large sheets of paper. People with just a little artistic talent can trace the paintings and reproduce the colors on the paper. Frame these reproductions with cardboard frames and hang them around the sanctuary.

___ Have someone use black ink to trace a photograph of an annunciation painting. Then reproduce the tracing for the front of the worship bulletin.

___ Drape the altar table with blue cloth. This color is traditionally associated with Mary, and can represent her presence. Have a craftsperson in the congregation make a large papier-mâché angel. Place this angel on or near the altar table to represent Gabriel's presence.

Anthems and Special Music

A Dove Flew Down from Heaven — H. Schroeder — SATB w/flute, 2 violins — CPH
And Mary Said to the Angel — H. L. Hassler — SATB unaccompanied — CPH
Angelus ad Virginem — Carter — Unison/SATB — EB
Ave, Maris Stella — E. Grieg — SSAATTBB unaccompanied — AE
Carol of the Annunciation — M. Dale — Unison w/keyboard — CG
For All the Faithful Women — D. Potter — Unison w/keyboard — from *With One Voice* — AF
Gabriel's Message — F.A. Jackson — SATB w/organ — from *Three Advent Carols* — PA
Mary and the Angel — A. Lindstrom — SATB unaccompanied — AF
O Mary Blest, the Chosen Shrine — T. Keesecker — SATB w/keyboard — MSM
The Angel Gabriel from Heaven Came — A. Prower — SATB w/organ — CPH
The Angel Gabriel — R. Arnatt — SATB unaccompanied — AF
The Angel Gabriel — J. R. Howell — 2-part treble w/harp or keyboard — BH
The Annunciation — Harvey — SATB — SC
The White Dove — J. Brahms — SATB unaccompanied — BH
Through Gabriel — Nicholas — SSAATTBB — EB
Sing of Mary, Pure and Lowly — S. Chavez-Melo — Unison w/keyboard — from *Hymnal Supplement 1991* — GIA
Young Mary Lived in Nazareth — J. Pinson — Unison w/keyboard — from *Songs of Rejoicing* — SPC

Organ and Other Keyboard Music

Lo, How a Rose e'er Blooming (Es ist ein Ros') — found in *11 Chorale Preludes* — J. Brahms — KAL

Savior of the Nations, Come (Nun komm, der heiden heiland) — found in *25 Chorale Preludes* — H. Walcha — CFP

The Angel Gabriel from Heaven Came (Gabriel's Message) — M. Mason — AF

CHRISTMAS
EVE/DAY

Revised
 Common: Luke 2:1-20* or
              John 1:1-14+
Episcopal: Luke 2:1-14 (15-20)*
              or John 1:1-14+
Lutheran: John 1:1-14+

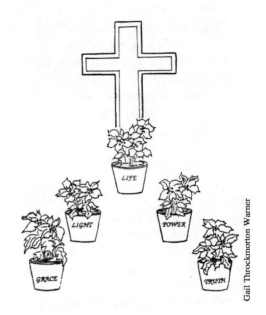

*Note: What has come into
being in Christ is life, and this
life is our light. Those who
believe and follow his light
receive the power to become
children of God.*

* See Christmas Eve/Day in *Worship Workbook For The Gospels, Cycle A,* for Luke 2:1-20
and Luke 2:1-14 (15-20).
+ See the Second Sunday after Christmas for more resources relating to John 1:1-14. (Also
see Second Sunday after Christmas, Cycle A.)

Printed Resources

___ Greeting

Ldr: Jesus Christ is the Word from God
        who becomes flesh and blood.
Cng: **God of beginning,
        God who sends life,
        God who names us your children,
        we have gathered here to worship you.**
Ldr: Jesus Christ is the light from God
        who enlightens everyone.
Cng: **Word with God,
        Word in the beginning,
        Word who brings life,
        we have gathered here to worship you.**
Ldr: Jesus Christ is the grace and truth from God
        who embraces all who receive him.
Cng: **Will of God shining in darkness,
        Will of God giving power,
        Will of God who gives new birth,
        we have gathered here to worship you.**

31

Ldr: Jesus Christ is one with God,
      who is God, who is the Word of God, who is the Will of God.
Cng: **Holy God, Holy Word, Holy Will,**
      we receive you, we believe you,
      we worship you, we praise you,
      we glorify you, we bless you,
      we bow down before you,
      forever thanking you
      for our new birth as your children.

___ Great Thanksgiving Prayer

Ldr: The Lord be with you.
Cng: **And also with you.**
Ldr: Lift up your hearts.
Cng: **We lift them up to the Lord.**
Ldr: Let us give thanks to the Lord our God.
Cng: **It is right to give our thanks and praise.**
Ldr: Lord, it is good to take time to thank you
      for the gift of life.
      In the beginning, you
      and the one John calls "the Word"
      called all life into being.
      Our lives have their origin
      in that act of divine will,
      and that beginning moment reveals our purpose
      and direction for every moment since then,
      as well as every moment yet to come.
      And so,
      with your people on earth
      and all the company of heaven
      we praise your name and join their unending hymn:
Cng: **Holy, holy, holy, God of power and might,**
      heaven and earth are full of your glory.
      Hosanna in the highest.
      Blessed is he who comes in the name of the Lord.
      Hosanna in the highest.
Ldr: "The Word" who was with you in the beginning
      has indeed come to us in your name, O Lord.
      We know "the Word" as Jesus of Nazareth, our Christ.
      John was the first to testify to Jesus' light,
      and countless millions more have added
      their own testimonies to John's,
      sometimes at the cost of their lives.
      This "Word" has become flesh and lived among us.
      We have seen his glory,

a glory that can only come from one like you, Lord.
And because we have accepted Jesus
as the source of our lives
and the light in our darkness —
because we have believed in him —
Jesus has given us a glory like his own.
Now we too are called your children, O Lord,
and what a glory and joy this is!
But not everyone knows Jesus.
Not everyone has accepted him, or believed in him.
Yet, in grace and truth, Jesus lays down his life,
to win all people to the light of your love, O God.
On the night in which he gave himself up for us,
Jesus took bread, gave thanks to you, broke the bread,
gave it to his disciples, and said:
"Take, eat; this is my body which is given for you.
Do this in remembrance of me."
And so,
in remembrance of these your mighty acts in Jesus Christ,
we offer ourselves in praise and thanksgiving
as a holy and living sacrifice,
in union with Christ's offering for us,
as we proclaim the mystery of faith.

Cng: **Christ has died; Christ is risen; Christ will come again.**

Ldr: Just as "the Word" became flesh to live among us,
so let these elements of bread and wine
become the body and blood of our Savior, Jesus Christ.
As we receive these holy gifts,
let us also receive your Holy Spirit through them.
Let your "Word" become part of our flesh.
Then use us to testify to the true light
that has come into our world,
and let our witness draw all your children
into your great family of love.
Through your Son Jesus Christ,
with the Holy Spirit in your holy church,
all honor and glory is yours, almighty Father,
now and forever.

Cng: **Amen.**

___ Commissioning and Blessing

The true light which enlightens everyone has come into the world.
Now let this true light of Jesus Christ shine through you,
    and the darkness will not overcome it, now or ever.

And may the glory that we have seen in Jesus Christ,
    also be seen in the grace and truth of your witness,
    in the name of God our Father,
    in the name of God whose Word has become flesh,
    in the name of God's light that overcomes darkness. **Amen.**

Hymns and Choruses

(The asterisk [*] indicates hymns or choruses that are addressed to God and can be used as prayers.)

___ "Christ Is the World's Light"
___ *"Christ, Whose Glory Fills the Skies"
___ *"Eternal Light, Shine in My Heart"
___ "God Hath Spoken by the Prophets"
___ "Hark! the Herald Angels Sing"
___ "I Want to Walk as a Child of the Light"
___ "Joy to the World"
___ "Morning Has Broken"
___ *"O Savior of Our Fallen Race"
___ *"O Word of God Incarnate"
___ "Of the Father's Love Begotten"
___ *"Send Your Word"
___ "The Great Creator of the Worlds"
___ *"Word of God, Come Down on Earth"

Reading the Scripture

___ Read the gospel lesson responsively with the congregation divided into two parts for their responses.

Ldr: "In the beginning was the Word,
Lft: **and the Word was with God,**
Rgt: **and the Word was God.**
Ldr: He was in the beginning with God.
Lft: **All things came into being through him,**
Rgt: **and without him not one thing came into being.**
Ldr: What has come into being in him was life,
Lft: **and the life was the light of all people.**
Rgt: **The light shines in the darkness, and the darkness did not overcome it."**
All: (Sing the "Gloria Patri")
Ldr: "There was a a man sent from God, whose name was John.
Lft: **He came as a witness to testify to the light,**
Rgt: **so that all might believe through him.**
Ldr: He himself was not the light,
Lft: **but he came to testify to the light.**

Rgt: **The true light, which enlightens everyone, was coming into the world."**
All: (Sing the "Gloria Patri")
Ldr: "He was in the world,
Lft: **and the world came into being through him;**
Rgt: **yet the world did not know him.**
Ldr: He came to what was his own,
Lft: **and his own people did not accept him.**
Rgt: **But to all who received him, who believed in his name, he gave power to become children of God,**
Ldr: who were born, not of blood
Lft: **or of the will of the flesh**
Rgt: **or of the will of man, but of God."**
All: (Sing the "Gloria Patri")
Ldr: "And the Word became flesh and lived among us,
Lft: **and we have seen his glory,**
Rgt: **the glory as of a father's only son, full of grace and truth."**
All: (Sing the "Gloria in Excelsis")

Responses to the Word

____ Have the people join in singing "Of the Father's Love Begotten." Then as the singing continues, invite people to come forward to the altar rail to pray quietly to God.

____ After a sermon on John's witness to the light of Christ, ask those who believe that "Jesus is the Word of God become flesh and is the source of life and light to all who believe" to raise their hands. Point out that by doing this they are also witnessing just as John witnessed. Then ask those who not only believe, but who have also accepted Jesus as their life and light to remain seated and sing the hymn "Christ Is the World's Light." Ask those who have not yet accepted Jesus to consider the testimony of those who are singing. When the hymn is finished, invite those who have yet to accept the life and light of Jesus Christ to bow before this Savior and accept him now. Have them silently repeat in their hearts the words of a prayer of acceptance that the pastor can provide. After praying, give those who have just accepted Jesus a chance to raise their hands in testimony of their own belief and acceptance. Follow with another hymn of celebration.

Drama and Movement

____ Use mimes to interpret the reading of the gospel lesson.

Visuals

____ Recruit one or two of the congregation's textile artists to create banners and/or paraments. Use bright yellows, oranges, golds, and silvers to portray the words, "The light shines in the darkness," and "We have seen his glory." These might be like a sunburst or explosion of light on a patchwork of dark background.

___ Arrange five white poinsettias like stairsteps leading up to the cross. Put a note in the bulletin that these five poinsettias represent five of the gifts that Christ brought into the world — life, light, power, grace and truth.

___ Gather some of the congregation's best artists. Have them paint a mural on a large sheet of canvas (available in fabric stores). On the left side of the canvas, have the artists paint a bright ball of light to represent the "Word." Perhaps they could use the Greek letters forming "Logos," and shape them into this ball of light. From this light all kinds of creatures and plants come spilling out, as if from the moment of creation. These creatures and plants spread across the canvas toward the right. On the right side of the canvas, the same bright ball of light (formed from the Greek letters of "Logos") seems to descend into this spreading stream of life. From that point two distinct streams continue on across the mural. The idea is to paint the history of life. Life comes out of the "Word." Later the "Word" comes into the stream of life, and some believe and follow the light of the "Word." Others do not believe and do not follow the light.

Anthems and Special Music

(Luke 2:1-20)
See Christmas Eve/Day in *Worship Workbook For The Gospels*, *Cycle A*

(John 1:1-14+)
Celebration of Light — D. Wood — Unison or SATB w/organ, cong., opt. handbells — SMP
Gates of Heav'n — A. Hoddinott — SATB w/organ — PA
Verbum caro factum est — Anonymous/A. Kaplan — SATB unaccompanied — BBL
I Am the Alpha and the Omega — K. Nystedt — SSATTBB unaccompanied — CPH
In the Beginning Was the Word — C. Jennings — SATB w/handbells — AF
In the Beginning Was the Word — M. Robinson — Solo for med. high voice w/keyboard — from
    Eleven Scriptural Songs — COB
The Word Is Living — M. Card — SATB w/opt. keyboard — from *Songs of Rejoicing* — SPC
The Word of God is Source and Seed — D. Hurd — Unison w/keyboard — from *With One Voice* —
    AF
The Word Was Made Flesh — H. Willan — SSA — from *We Praise Thee II* — CPH
The Word Was Made Flesh — M. Reger — SATB unaccompanied — CPH
Thus the Word Was Made as Flesh — H. L. Hassler — SSATTB — BBL
We Saw His Glory — E. Mauersberger — SA w/keyboard — from *A Second Morning Star Choir
    Book* — CPH
When Came in Flesh — G. Guest — SATB and treble and tenor solos w/organ — from *Two Advent
    Carols and a Lullaby* — PA
Word of God, Come Down on Earth — J. Ahle — SATB w/keyboard — from *Hymnal Supplement
    1991* — GIA
You Are Our God, We Are Your People — D. Hoekema — Unison w/keyboard — from *Songs of
    Rejoicing* — SPC

Organ and Other Keyboard Music

See Christmas Eve/Day in *Worship Workbook For The Gospels*, *Cycle A*

FIRST SUNDAY AFTER CHRISTMAS

"and they offered a sacrifice"

"a pair of turtledoves"

Revised
  Common: Luke 2:22-40
Episcopal: John 1:1-18*
Lutheran: Luke 2:22-40

Note: Our rising or falling is determined by our response to the one whom Simeon and Anna saw presented in the temple as a child.

---

* See Christmas Eve/Day for John 1:1-18.

Printed Resources

___ Greeting

Ldr: Simeon saw Mary and Joseph bringing Jesus to the temple,
       and he prayed to God saying,
       "My eyes have seen your salvation."
Cng: **We too, Lord, have seen with our eyes,**
       have heard with our ears,
       and know with our hearts and minds
       that Jesus Christ is the Messiah, our salvation from death.
Ldr: Anna saw Mary and Joseph's child,
       and she began praising God,
       knowing that Jesus brought the redemption she awaited.
Cng: **Merciful God, you have kept your promises**
       and have sent Jesus to pay the debts of our sin.
       Blessed be your name, O Lord,
       and welcome is the Messiah you send to us.

___ Prayer

(To be prayed by the pastor)
    Almighty God, Luke shows Jesus obeying your law from the days of his birth to the hours of his death. As your law required, Jesus was circumcised and then dedicated to you as the firstborn. He grew and became strong with your wisdom and your favor. In his twelfth year, the point of entry into the adult world, Jesus is again seen in the temple speaking with scholarly adults. At the age of thirty, when rabbis can take up their calling, Jesus

began his ministry. Jesus was constantly in the temple on sabbath days, as was his custom, Luke tells us. Always Jesus fulfilled the law. Never did he circumvent or destroy that precious gift that you gave us through Moses.

(To be prayed by the congregation)

Almighty God, Jesus fulfilled both the letter and the spirit of your law. Help us to follow Jesus' example. Transform our hearts so that we can joyfully choose the paths of obedience and discipline, instead of bypassing and avoiding them as obstacles to our willful pleasures.

(To be prayed by the pastor)

Unchanging God, Luke shows us Simeon and Anna living obedient and righteous lives that are rewarded by seeing your promises kept. Those who are led by your Spirit, and live in righteousness worshiping you day and night, are able to recognize what others cannot comprehend. Their obedience and spiritual disciplines clear their eyes to behold your most precious gifts.

(To be prayed by the congregation)

Unchanging God, teach us to live lives that are open to you. As your Spirit rests on us, let us hear your voice speaking to us. Lead us into paths of righteousness and devotion to you. Open us to the prayer that never ceases, and to the worship that continues day and night. Strengthen us as we fast from the world's excesses. And fill our mouths with songs recounting your faithfulness, and our lips with praise for your promises kept, now and forever. Amen.

___ Commissioning and Blessing

Just as Simeon and Anna pointed to Jesus,
    so are you to point to our Messiah
    with your words and your deeds.
And, until our consolation and redemption returns,
    may the Holy Spirit of God rest upon you. **Amen.**

___ Commissioning and Blessing

May the Holy Spirit of God rest upon you,
    so that you may both recognize the Messiah
    and guide others to the world's consolation and redemption.
In the name of the Lord our God,
    the Holy Spirit of God,
    and the Messiah of God. **Amen.**

Hymns and Choruses

(The asterisk [*] indicates hymns or choruses that are addressed to God and can be used as prayers.)

___ "A Stable Lamp Is Lighted"
___ "All Hail to You, O Blessed Morn"

38

___ *"Canticle of Simeon"
___ "From East to West"
___ "Go Now in Peace"
___ "Hail to the Lord Who Comes"
___ "He Is Born"
___ "Joy to the World"
___ *"My Master, See, the Time Has Come"
___ *"Nino Lindo" ("Child So Lovely")
___ "O Zion, Open Wide Thy Gates"
___ *"Virgin-Born, We Bow Before Thee"

Reading the Scripture

___ Recruit three people to read the gospel lesson. A youth or young adult should read verses 22-24 (if these are being included in the lesson). An older man should read verses 25-35, and an older woman should read verses 36-38. The youth or adult should conclude the reading with verses 39-40.

___ Let the congregation join in reading the gospel lesson by reading every other verse of the lesson from pew Bibles (or have the lesson printed in the worship bulletin). The pastor or a liturgist can begin the reading, and continue to alternate with the congregation.

___ Two storytellers (perhaps one man and one woman) could recite the stories contained in this gospel lesson. The first could tell the story about Simeon, and the other could tell the story about Anna.

Responses to the Word

___ After a sermon about the salvation that God has prepared for all people and about the cost that is associated with this salvation, invite the worshipers to accept this cost and to commit themselves to the Savior who brings it. This could be done by allowing people to come forward to the altar rail to pray, or by providing a printed prayer for them to use in the pew.

___ As suggested in "Drama and Movement," have five people act out the lesson. This can follow the reading of the lesson and a sermon about it. Let the actors move in silence. If desirable, Simeon could break the silence by speaking the words of verses 29-32. Even better, Simeon could sing the words, using the hymn "My Master, See, the Time Has Come" or the "Nunc Dimittis."

___ After a sermon pointing out that Luke states five times in this lesson that Jesus' parents did everything required in the law of the Lord for the proper raising of their son, invite the parents in the congregation to renew their pledges to raise their children in the light of this example. They could be asked to stand and answer once again the question that is posed to many parents in the baptism of their infants. They could even be asked to come forward to once again present their children before the Lord, as they reaffirm their earlier commitments.

United Methodist[1]:

> *Will you nurture these children in Christ's holy church,*
> *that by your teaching and example they may be guided*
> *to accept God's grace for themselves,*
> *to profess their faith openly,*
> *and to lead a Christian life?*

Episcopalian[2]:

> *Will you be responsible for seeing that the child you present*
> *is brought up in the Christian faith and life?*
> **I will, with God's help.**
> *Will you by your prayers and witness help this child grow*
> *into the full stature of Christ?*
> **I will, with God's help.**

Lutheran[3]:

> *In Christian love you have presented these children for Holy Baptism. You should, therefore, faithfully bring them to the services of God's house, and teach them the Lord's Prayer, the Creed, and the Ten Commandments. As they grow in years, you should place in their hands the Holy Scriptures and provide for their instruction in the Christian faith, that, living in the covenant of their Baptism and in communion with the Church, they may lead godly lives until the day of Jesus Christ. Do you promise to fulfill these obligations?*

United Church of Christ[4]:

> *Will you encourage these children*
> *to renounce the powers of evil*
> *and to receive the freedom of new life in Christ?*
> **We will, with the help of God.**
> *Will you teach these children*
> *that they may be led to profess*
> *Jesus Christ as Lord and Savior?*
> **We will, with the help of God.**
> *Do you promise, according to the grace given to you,*
> *to grow with these children in the Christian faith,*
> *to help these children*
> *to be faithful members*
> *of the church of Jesus Christ,*
> *by celebrating Christ's presence,*
> *by furthering Christ's mission in all the world,*
> *and by offering the nurture of the Christian church*
> *so that they may affirm their baptism?*
> **We do, with the help of God.**

Drama and Movement

____ Recruit five people to act out this lesson. A middle-aged man is needed as Joseph and a teenage girl to be Mary. A baby is needed for Jesus. A man and a woman in their seventies or eighties are needed to portray Simeon and Anna. A narrator is needed to read the lesson. If desirable, Simeon could speak his own lines.

Visuals

___ Have an artist create two banners. One should show Simeon holding the Christ-child in his arms, and the other should show Anna. One of Anna's hands should point to the child in Simeon's arms, and her other hand should be lifted up in praise to God. Their clothing could be decorated with symbols associated with these two people, or these symbols could be placed at the feet of the figures. Symbols for Simeon could include: eyes, a light, and a sword, as well as symbols for the Holy Spirit that rested on him. Symbols for Anna could include: a single wedding band, the temple, and the lips with which she had fasted, prayed, praised God and spoken about the Christ-child.

___ Those churches reading verses 22-24 could have their textile artists create two banners. One banner would contain two turtle doves or pigeons, and the other banner would contain a scroll with the words "The law of the Lord."

___ Churches reading verses 22-24 could have two live pigeons (or turtle doves if they can be found and legally caged temporarily) in bird cages sitting near the altar table.

___ Have a photographer in the congregation take a slide photograph of an old man holding a baby. Project this slide onto the front wall of the sanctuary as a silent testimony to the truth proclaimed by Simeon.

Anthems and Special Music

(Luke 2:22-40)
Child of Bethlehem — J. Ward — med. solo w/keyboard — from *Songs of Rejoicing* — SPC
Herr, nun lässest du deinen diener (Lord, Now Lettest Thou Thy Servant) — D. Buxtehude — Tenor
    solo w/2 violins, organ — BAR
Herr, nun lässest du deinen, Diener im Friede fahren (Lord, Now Lettest Thou Thy Servant) — H.
    Schütz — Bass solo w/ 2 violins, continuo — HAN
In Peace and Joy I Now Depart — D. Busarow — SATB w/Junior Choir and opt. keyboard — CPH
Nunc Dimittis — K. Nystedt — SAB — AF
Nunc Dimittis — F. Thorne — Solo for high voice w/organ — GS
Nunc Dimittis — C. Wiggins — Unison w/organ — AF
Nunc Dimittis — H. Willan — SSA — from *We Praise Thee II* — CPH
Nunc Dimittis — H. Willan — SATB — OUP
Oh, Sleep Now, Holy Baby — Hispanic Folk/J. D. Robb — Unison w/keyboard, guitar — from *With
    One Voice* — AF
Simeon's Song — A. Gretchaninof/C. Hanson — SSAATBB unaccompanied — CP
Song of Simeon — L. Bourgeois — Unison and descant w/keyboard — from *Songs of Rejoicing* —
    SPC
Song of Simeon — O. Gibbons — Unison or SATB w/opt. keyboard — from *Songs of Rejoicing* —
    SPC

(John 1:1-18)
See Christmas Eve/Day

Organ and Other Keyboard Music

All Hail to You, O Blessed Morn (Wie schoen leuchtet) — found in *Choral Improvisations for Organ for Ascensiontide and Pentecost*, Op. 65, vol. 4 — S. Karg-Elert — EBM

He is Born (Il est ne) — found in *Suite of Organ Carols* — R. Hudson — AF

Joy to the World (Antioch) — found in *Nativity Suite* — W. Held — CPH

SECOND SUNDAY AFTER CHRISTMAS

Revised
  Common: Matthew 25:31-46*
Episcopal: Luke 2:41-52
Lutheran: John 1:1-18+

Note: There is a time to sit listening and asking questions in our Father's house, and there is a time to go out and be obedient.

"All the nations will be gathered before Him, and He will separate the people one from another as a shepherd separates the sheep from the goats. He will put the sheep on His right and the goats on His left."
—Matthew 25:32-33

Angie Latta

* See Christ the King Sunday in *Worship Workbook For The Gospels, Cycle A* for material on this text.
+ See Christmas Eve/Day for John 1:1-18.

Printed Resources

___ Greeting

Ldr: When Jesus was twelve years old,
      his parents could not find him.
      So Mary and Joseph returned to Jerusalem,
      and found Jesus in the temple.
Cng: **We still find you in the temple, Lord.**
Ldr: Though only twelve,
      Jesus sat talking with the teachers in the temple.
      They were all amazed at his understanding and his answers.
Cng: **We too are amazed at the simplicity and the depth**
      of your words, O Lord.
      Teach us again, Rabbi of the heart,
      and bless us with your wisdom and favor.

___ Prayer

Like Jesus, we must be in your house, heavenly Father.
   We hunger for the discussions of your Word.
   We ache with the desire to please you with righteousness.
   We long for communion with you,
   and we only live when we lift up your praise.

Accept us into your house today, Father of grace and love,
   and let our souls be at home with you forever. Amen.

___ Prayer

Help us, Father, to allow others to grow toward you.
When we are anxious about their safety,
   calm our fears with the peace that comes from trusting you.
When we do not understand what they do or say,
   help us to treasure in our hearts
   the marks of their spiritual journeys.
When they do not conform to family custom,
   but strike out in unexpected directions,
   give us patience, while you lead them to wisdom.
And, as we follow the example of Mary and Joseph
   for our behavior in all these things,
   may those for whom we pray
   embrace Jesus as their guide and savior.
And may your favor be upon them,
   and upon us,
   for only then will any of us know peace. Amen.

___ Commissioning and Blessing

Ldr: You claimed Jesus at his Bethlehem birth, Father,
Cng: **And you have claimed each of us at our beginnings too.**
Ldr: You drew Jesus to you as he grew in wisdom and years,
Cng: **And you draw us closer to you as we grow in our faith.**
Ldr: Then you sent Jesus out in obedient ministry.
Cng: **In the same way, Father, send us to minister,**
   obeying your inspiration and instruction.
Ldr: In the name of Father, Son and Holy Spirit,
   leave this sabbath place,
   and return to serving God in the workplace;
   and may God's favor be upon you, today and every day.
Cng: **Amen.**

Hymns and Choruses

(The asterisk [*] indicates hymns or choruses that are addressed to God and can be used as prayers.)

___ *"Blessed Jesus, at Thy Word"
___ *"Jesus, We Want to Meet"
___ *"Lord of All Hopefulness, Lord of All Joy"

44

___ *"O God of Youth"
___ "O Sing a Song of Bethlehem"
___ "Once in Royal David's City"
___ *"Praise to the Holiest in the Height"
___ "Sing of Mary, Pure and Lowly"
___ "We Have Come into His House"
___ "We Would See Jesus"
___ "When Jesus Left His Father's Throne"

Reading the Scripture

___ One good storyteller could step in front of the congregation and relate this wonderful story to the worshipers in a very meaningful way.

___ The congregation can enter into dialogue with this text by singing individual verses of the chorus "Alleluia." Have a person begin reading the gospel lesson, and then pause after reading verse 47. At this point the congregation sings the first verse of "Alleluia." Then the reader continues until verse 49 is read. Again the reader pauses and the congregation sings the second verse of "Alleluia" (He's my Savior). The reader then finishes reading the gospel lesson, and the congregation sings the final verse of "Alleluia" (I will praise him).

Responses to the Word

___ This would be a good text for the beginning of a confirmation or membership training class for the youth of the congregation. After reading the gospel lesson and preaching a sermon on it, the pastor could invite the youth (or candidates for membership) to covenant with God and the congregation. Their covenant would be to grow in wisdom in their Father's house.

___ After a sermon proclaiming the trust that Mary and Joseph demonstrated in God and in their unique Son, invite the worshipers to pray the second prayer printed above. Follow this by asking the people to join in singing one of these hymns: "Children of the Heavenly Father," "Give to the Winds Thy Fears," "Trust and Obey," "Through It All," or "Be Still, My Soul."

Drama and Movement

___ Have the youth in the congregation act out this gospel story and the story in 1 Samuel 2 that serves as a model for Luke's story. Have them emphasize some of the obvious parallels of these two stories: the boy Samuel and the boy Jesus in the temple, the two boys both finding their future in the Lord's service, both boys growing in stature and favor with the Lord and the people, and most of all both boys destined to replace servants who have not been faithful in serving the Lord. The preacher can then use the way these two stories rub against one another to get at the message that Luke is preaching.

Visuals

___ Recruit some of the better artists in the congregation to cut out life-size figures from cardboard. Have them paint these figures to look like old Jewish scholars gathered in discussion with the twelve-year-old Jesus. Place these figures in a front corner of the sanctuary, or in an unused part of the choir loft, where the congregation can see them as they worship. Figures of Mary and Joseph hurrying to the scene can be posed in another area of the sanctuary.

___ Have someone who can sketch go to the public library to secure a picture of Albrecht Durer's woodcut of "Christ Disputing with the Doctors." See *Durer: The Complete Engravings, Etchings and Woodcuts*, by Karl Adolf Knape (New York: Harry N. Abrams, Inc., 1965) for a reproduction. This person can then sketch (or trace) Durer's wonderful interpretation portraying the wide variety of responses to the youthful Jesus. Other intrepretations have been portrayed by various artists, including Rembrandt. This sketch or tracing can be used for a worship bulletin cover and for a sermon illustration.

Anthems and Special Music

(Matthew 25:31-46)
See Christ the King Sunday in *Worship Workbook For The Gospels, Cycle A*
Before Him — K. Nystedt — Unison w/organ — from *A Third Morning Star Choir Book* — CPH
Come Ye Blessed — J. Prindle — low, med., or high solo w/piano — from *Seventeen Sacred Songs* — GS
Entreating Hands — F. Russell — Unison w/keyboard — from *Songs of Rejoicing* — SPC
For the Fruit of All Creation — W. Rowan — Unison w/keyboard — from *Songs of Rejoicing* — SPC
Whatever You've Done — A. M. Bush — Unison w/keyboard — from *Songs of Rejoicing* — SPC

(Luke 2:41-52)
Sing of Mary, Pure and Lowly — S. Chavez-Melo — Unison w/keyboard — from *Hymnal Supplement 1991* — GIA
My Son, Wherefore Hast Thou Done This To Us? — H. Schütz — Trio for SAB w/2 violins, continuo — CPH
The Blessed Virgin's Expostulation — H. Purcell — low or high solo w/piano — from *Sacred Songs* — INT

(John 1:1-18+)
See Christmas Eve/Day

Organ and Other Keyboard Music

Blessed Jesus, At thy Word (Liebster Jesu) — J. S. Bach — found in *Golden Treasury of Organ Music*, vol. 2 — OD
Lord of All Hopefulness (Slane) — found in *Five Preludes on Familiar Hymns* — H. Hopson — HF
Once In Royal David's City (Irby) — D. Willcocks — found in *The Oxford Christmas Organ Book* — OUP

EPIPHANY DAY

Revised
 Common: Matthew 2:1-12*
Episcopal: Matthew 2:1-12*
Lutheran: Matthew 2:1-12*

Gail Throckmorton Warner

*Note: Wise people still seek
our Savior, but for those who
are not so smart, our Savior
goes seeking them.*

* See Epiphany Day in *Worship Workbook For The Gospels, Cycle A* and *Worship Workbook For The Gospels, Cycle C* for more material on this text.

Printed Resources

___ Greeting

Ldr: Bethlehem-born king of kings,
      your people have come to worship you.
Rgt: **Star-marked Savior, we bow before you.**
Lft: **Desire of prophecy and prayer, we offer you our worship.**
Rgt: **Downfall of Herods everywhere, we bow before you.**
Lft: **Joy of wise men and women, we offer you our worship.**

___ Prayer

Our holy Father, Creator of all life,
    we join our brothers and sisters in bowing before your Son.
Like the poor shepherds and the wealthy magi,
    we, both rich and poor together, bow before Christ.
Like countless saints and sinners through the ages,
    we, men, women and children, bow before Christ.
Like the magi who came from other lands and other religions,
    we, former Jews and Muslims, Hindus and Buddhists,
    animists and atheists, secularists and new ageists,
    and all those others who have recognized
    a true king and savior, bow before Christ.
We surrender ourselves to Christ's rule over us,
    we lay all our treasures at our Savior's feet,
    and we beg you to anoint us with the name "Christian"
    for now and all eternity. Amen.

47

___ An Invitation to Offer Gifts

Like the magi,
    who knelt down and paid homage to Jesus,
    let us now open our own treasure chests
    and offer our gifts to the Savior of the world.

___ Commissioning and Blessing

God provides many signs to lead us to our salvation.
    May you follow them as faithfully as did the magi,
    may God protect you from the treachery of evil people,
    and may Christ reign over you now and forever.
Amen.

Hymns and Choruses

(The asterisk [*] indicates hymns or choruses that are addressed to God and can be used as prayers.)

___ "Angels from the Realms of Glory"
___ *"As with Gladness Men of Old"
___ "Bright and Glorious Is the Sky"
___ "Brightest and Best of the Stars of the Morning"
___ "De Tierra Lejana Venimos" ("From a Distant Home")
___ "Earth Has Many a Noble City"
___ "Hail to the Lord's Anointed"
___ "Holy Is He"
___ "In the Bleak Midwinter"
___ *"King of Kings"
___ *"Nino Lindo" ("Child So Lovely")
___ "O Chief of Cities, Bethlehem"
___ *"O Morning Star, How Fair and Bright"
___ *"O One with God the Father"
___ "On This Day Earth Shall Ring"
___ "Sing We Now of Christmas"
___ "The First Noel"
___ "The People Who in Darkness Walked"
___ "There's a Song in the Air"
___ " 'Twas in the Moon of Wintertime"
___ "We Three Kings"
___ *"We Worship and Adore You"
___ "We Would See Jesus"
___ "What Star Is This, With Beams So Bright"
___ "When Christ's Appearing Was Made Known"
___ *"When I Look into Your Holiness"
___ *"Worthy, You Are Worthy"

Reading the Scripture

___ Have one of the young people in the congregation memorize the scripture lesson. He or she comes forward, stands facing the worshipers, and recites the text from memory. When the young person reaches verse 6, he or she could unroll a scroll and read the prophecy of Micah from the scroll. Then, at verse 7, the young person continues reciting the text from memory.

Responses to the Word

___ Make this a Sunday when people are encouraged to give special gifts to the Lord. Announce this well ahead of the day, so people can consider what they will give. Invite the people to lay their gifts on the altar table. Modern gifts could include: volunteering a year's service to a food pantry or soup kitchen; a revised will that has included a bequest to the church or a mission project; a gift of stock to support a missionary or a scholarship fund; giving a homemade quilt or old jewelry or other valuables to be auctioned off with the proceeds going to a special church project; volunteering a year of singing in the choir, teaching Sunday school, or cleaning the church building; and whatever else people could imagine.

___ See the first suggestion under "Visuals."

Drama and Movement

___ Scan recent newspapers and magazines for three well-known figures who have publicly bowed before Christ and have opened up their treasures to Christ's use. (If you want, go back into history rather than use contemporary persons.) Then recruit members of the congregation to portray these people and reenact their acts of worship as testimonies to the congregation.

Visuals

___ Ask the youth in the congregation to make a lot of crowns from whatever materials can be gathered. Have the youth hand out these crowns to the people as they enter the sanctuary. Each worshiper should wear his or her crown during the service. Use the sermon to remind worshipers that we come as kings who exercise control over our own lives and sometimes even control over the lives of others. Yet, we surrender this control to the one who is born king of kings. Then let the worshipers come forward and lay their crowns at the base of the altar table or a manger. They may want to leave their offerings (gifts) with their crowns too.

___ Use three floral arrangements on or around the altar table. Make them three different colors to represent the three gifts of the magi to the Christ child.

Anthems and Special Music

See Epiphany Day in *Worship Workbook For The Gospels, Cycle A*
Little Baby Jesus — L. Braen — Unison w/keyboard — from *Songs of Rejoicing* — SPC
Thou Son of God — D. Robinson — SATB w/keyboard — from *Songs of Rejoicing* — SPC

Organ and Other Keyboard Music

Angels from the Realms of Glory (Regent Square) — found in *Sing and Rejoice*, vol. V — G. Krapf
        — SMP
In the Bleak Midwinter — A. O. Gibbs — CPH
'Twas in the Moon of Wintertime (Une Jeune Pucelle) — Variations on "'Twas in the Moon of
        Wintertime" — S. Fiess — MSM

BAPTISM OF
THE LORD

Revised
  Common: Mark 1:4-11
Episcopal: Mark 1:7-11
Lutheran: Mark 1:4-11

*Note: The baptism of Christ
is a gift that is given to those
being initiated into the community that Jesus created in
his own baptism.*

Printed Resources

___ Greeting

Ldr: John the baptizer appeared in the wilderness,
    proclaiming a baptism of repentance,
    for the forgiveness of sins.
Cng: **Almighty Father, repentance does not come easy to us.**
Ldr: Jesus came after John,
    is more powerful than John,
    and baptizes with the Holy Spirit.
Cng: **Beloved Jesus, use your power to transform us.**
Ldr: At Jesus' baptism, the heavens were torn apart,
    the Spirit descended like a dove upon Jesus,
    and God's voice was heard coming from above.
Cng: **Holy Spirit, make us pleasing to our Father.**

___ Prayer of Confession and Assurance of Pardon

Holy God, whom Jesus pleases,
    like the droves of people who sought John in the wilderness,
    we are an unholy people who are not pleasing in your sight.
We have much to confess.
    Even now our repentance is too half-hearted and insincere.
    We want to please you,
    but we do not want to be uncomfortable while we do it.
    We love you when it is easy,
    but we betray you when love demands sacrifice.

We love those who love us, but not always.
  Often we abuse and step on others
  to satisfy our desires and achieve success.
  Many of the politicians we elect reflect our sinfulness,
  as they protect themselves and neglect our nation.
  We have murdered native peoples to take their possessions,
  and now repulse other immigrants to protect our spoils.
We have raped our environment for profit and material comfort,
  and we have stolen from generations still unborn.
Our sinfulness has scarred our children,
  who flood our streets with violence, drugs and other madness.
We idolize media stars and sports figures,
  and heap contempt on teachers and leaders of faith.
O God! It is too much for us!
  Drown our sins again in Jordan's waters!
  Scrub us clean with your forgiveness!
  Tear apart the heavens and send down your Spirit upon us!
  Let your beloved Son lead us again to ways that please you.
Save us, O God,
  or we will be lost forever.
(Continue in silent prayer.)
Brothers and sisters,
  John said that he baptized with water,
  but one was coming who will baptize with the Holy Spirit.
In the name of our holy and righteous God, I proclaim to you
  that this one has already come
  and is Jesus Christ, God's beloved Son.
And now, even as we bow in prayer,
  heaven has already opened,
  and the gentle Spirit of God descends upon you.
I echo the voice from heaven when I say to you,
  "Your sins are forgiven and your repentance is accepted,
  now lift up your hearts to your salvation."
Our hearts, our minds, our souls and our strength
  are yours, O God, Father, Son and Holy Spirit.
  May our surrender be pleasing in your sight,
  now and forever. Amen.

___ Commissioning and Blessing

In the beginning, our Creator spoke
  and the heavens and the earth came into being,
  and God saw that it was good.
At Jesus' baptism, God spoke again
  and commissioned Jesus as our salvation,
  and to resurrect us to our former goodness.

52

Now listen to God's voice
and accept the salvation that Jesus offers,
and let God's goodness be known in the world. **Amen.**

Hymns and Choruses

(The asterisk [*] indicates hymns or choruses that are addressed to God and can be used as prayers.)

___ *"Christ, When for Us You Were Baptized"
___ "Come, Let Us Use the Grace Divine"
___ "Depth of Mercy"
___ *"From God the Father, Virgin-Born"
___ "Hail to the Lord's Anointed"
___ " 'I Come,' the Great Redeemer Cries"
___ *"Praise and Thanksgiving Be to God"
___ *"Spirit of Faith, Come Down"
___ "Spirit Song"
___ "The Sinless One to Jordan Came"
___ *"This Is the Spirit's Entry Now"
___ *"Thy Holy Wings, O Savior"
___ " 'Tis the Old Ship of Zion"
___ "To Jordan Came the Christ, Our Lord"
___ "We Know That Christ Is Raised"
___ "When Christ's Appearing Was Made Known"
___ "When Jesus Came to Jordan"
___ "When Jesus Went to Jordan's Stream"

Reading the Scripture

___ Recruit five children to memorize and recite this text. The first recites verses 4-5. The second recites verse 6 and the words "He proclaimed..." from verse 7. The third recites verses 7-8. The fourth recites verses 9-10 and the words "And a voice came from heaven..." from verse 11. The fifth child concludes verse 11. Practice with these children until they can tell the story naturally, instead of the usual rapid-fire, impossible-to-understand recitations that are common to so many children's programs.

___ See the suggestion under "Drama and Movement" below.

Responses to the Word

___ Use the prayer of confession and assurance of pardon printed above to follow a sermon that calls the people to repentance.

___ Several weeks ahead of this day, announce the opportunity for people to be baptized or to have their children baptized. Let the baptism of those who come forward be part of the response to God's Word. Then let the whole congregation immerse themselves in the memories of their own baptisms by the pastor walking around the seated worshipers and sprinkling water toward them with his or her hand. As the pastor does this, the pastor can repeat these words, "Remember your baptism, and be thankful." An organist or other instrumentalist might accompany the pastor's words by quietly playing a baptismal hymn in the background. When the pastor completes the circle of the worshipers, they can join in singing the hymn that has been played quietly thoughout the ritual.

Drama and Movement

___ Ask two dancers in the congregation to interpret the gospel lesson. The first dancer could interpret the words about John, and the second could interpret the words about Jesus.

___ Have your congregation's drama group or a thoughtful Sunday school class prepare a monologue for one person to present in worship. In this monologue Jesus is deciding whether or not he should be baptized by John. Jesus could have just ignored this radical relative who really understood very little about Jesus. Did the baptism mark the end of Jesus' carpentry and commission him for the beginning of ministry? Did it mark the end of obeying and caring for parents in order to begin a life of obeying God and caring for all the world's peoples? Was Jesus' baptism a way to identify with the sin and suffering of other people? Did Jesus choose baptism as an example for others to follow? Just why did Jesus submit to John's baptism? Follow this monologue with the reading of the gospel lesson.

Visuals

___ Recruit the congregation's textile artists to make a huge banner composed of three panels. The panel on the left shows John the baptizer stooping down to untie the sandals of Christ. The middle panel shows Christ, with one foot extended to John and the other foot standing in the Jordan River. The panel on the right shows Jesus in the Jordan River and the Holy Spirit appearing as a dove descending out of heaven toward Jesus. No words are necessary.

___ There are many classic paintings of the baptism of Christ. Ask one of the people in the congregation who enjoys sketching to go to the local library to find an art book containing one of these paintings. When this person finds a work he or she likes, then this person can copy or trace the painting onto a sheet of paper. (Tracing is easier if the page is laid on a sheet of glass with a light source under the glass.) Then this sketch of a classic interpretation of Jesus' baptism can be reproduced for a worship bulletin cover. It could also be worked into other media, like a banner, a work of stained glass, a mural, and so on.

Anthems and Special Music

See Baptism of Our Lord in *Worship Workbook For The Gospels*, Cycle A
Jesus Came from Nazareth — B. Neswick — 2-part w/organ — AF

54

Organic and Other Keyboard Music

From God the Father, Virgin-Born (Deus turorum militum) — D. Schack — found in the *Concordia Hymn Prelude Series*, vol. 5 — CPH

Thy Holy Wings (Bred dina vida vingar) — found in *Thy Holy Wings* — J. Ferguson — AF

We Know that Christ is Raised (Engelberg) — Voluntary on *Engelberg* — C. Callahan — MSM

SECOND SUNDAY AFTER THE EPIPHANY

Revised
 Common: John 1:43-51
Episcopal: John 1:43-51
Lutheran: John 1:43-51

Angie Latta

Note: Following Christ is the same as seeing heaven opened and the angels of God ascending and descending upon our Savior.

Printed Resources

___ Greeting

Ldr: We have found the Savior!
 The one expected and foretold by the Old Testament
 is Jesus, son of Joseph from Nazareth.
 Come and see.
Cng: **Lord, people have wondered**
 whether anything good can come out of such a place.
Ldr: Jesus knows your hearts.
 Come and see.
Cng: **I need for someone to know me,**
 from my outward behavior to the depths of my soul.
Ldr: Jesus knows every moment of your life,
 and can lead you into an amazing future.
 Come and see.
Cng: **Almighty God, I realize Jesus really knows me.**
Ldr: You will see greater things than this.
 In fact, you will see heaven opened,
 and angels ascending and descending upon Jesus.
 Come and see.
Cng: **I will come to see such a sight,**
 and I will bow down before Jesus,
 my teacher, my king, and the very Son of God!

___ Prayer

Father of All Blessing,
   when Jacob slept, he dreamed of a ladder
   where angels ascended and descended from heaven.
   He named the place Bethel,
   thinking it to be the house of God, and the gate of heaven.
Now, Father, you have blessed us
   by sending your Son into the world.
   Jesus is a dream come true,
   as he becomes the living gate of heaven,
   and opens that blessing to all who believe him.
The resurrected Jesus is our Bethel,
   and as his earthly body, we are your house, O God.
   Let us become a blessing to all the world,
   and may our spiritual offspring
   become as numerous as the stars in the heavens. Amen.

___ Prayer of Confession

Lft: **"Can anything good come out of Nazareth?" Nathanael asked.**
Rgt: **The same question echoes throughout our land today, Lord.**
Lft: **Can anything good come from the urban ghetto?**
Rgt: **Can anything good come from the rural sticks?**
Lft: **Can anything good come from south of the border?**
Rgt: **Can anything good come from the frozen north?**
Lft: **Can anything good come from a Black man?**
Rgt: **Can anything good come from a White man?**
Lft: **Can anything good come from a man?**
Rgt: **Can anything good come from a woman?**
Lft: **Can anything good come from old people?**
Rgt: **Can anything good come from today's youth?**
Lft: **On and on the same old question spews from our mouths.**
Rgt: **Can anything good come from bigots like us, Lord?**
Lft: **The greatest treasure on earth came out of Nazareth.**
Rgt: **What other great treasures await the opening of our eyes?**
Lft: **We are a shallow and narrow-minded people, Lord.**
Rgt: **And here we bow before an all-embracing God,**
      who cares nothing for our artificial boundaries.
Lft: **We are a sinful people, Lord.**
Rgt: **Forgive us, O God.**
Lft: **Let the depth, and breadth, and height of your love**
      melt our icy hearts.
Rgt: **Let your bias to accept without restriction,**
      and to welcome without reservation,
      reform our bondage to the prejudices of ignorance.
Lft: **Let your Nazareth-child pry open our closed minds,**

Rgt: **And give us new eyes to see your good**
      in all our brothers and sisters.
(Continue in silent prayer.)
Ldr: Jesus knew Nathanael before Philip called him,
      and Jesus saw into Nathanael's heart, and said,
      "Here is truly an Israelite in whom there is no deceit!"
      In the same way, Jesus sees into your hearts,
      and finds the good in you.
      Jesus forgives what you have been,
      and calls you to become a new person,
      serving and loving God,
      with all your heart, all your soul, and all your mind.
(The worshipers join in singing the hymn "Lord, I Want to Be a Christian.")

___ Commissioning and Blessing

Jesus found Philip
    and said to him, "Follow me."
Philip found Nathanael
    and told him about Jesus.
And someone found you
    and told you about our Savior.
Whom will you find,
    and what will you tell him about Jesus?
May the Holy Spirit guide you to that person,
    may the love of Jesus win that person's heart,
    and may the grace of God draw him into the kingdom. **Amen.**

Hymns and Choruses

(The asterisk [*] indicates hymns or choruses that are addressed to God and can be used as prayers.)

___ "Christ Is the King"
___ "Forward Through the Ages"
___ "Freely, Freely"
___ "Hark, the Voice of Jesus Calling"
___ *"Help Us Accept Each Other"
___ *"Here Comes Jesus"
___ *"I Am Thine, O Lord"
___ "I Love to Tell the Story"
___ "Isn't He"
___ "Jesus Calls Us"
___ *"Jesus, Lord, We Look to Thee"
___ "Jesus Sinners Will Receive"
___ *"Lord, Speak to Me"

___ *"Lord, Speak to Us, that We May Speak"
___ *"O Christ, Our Light, O Radiance True"
___ *"O God, Empower Us"
___ "O Zion, Haste" ("Publish Glad Tidings")
___ "Rise Up, O Men of God"
___ "Rise Up, O Saints of God"
___ "We Are Climbing Jacob's Ladder"
___ *"You Are My God"

Reading the Scripture

___ Recruit four readers to read the dialogue in this gospel lesson. One should be the narrator, and the other three can read the words of Jesus, Philip and Nathanael.

___ Add puppets to the above suggestion, and children can become interested in what appears uninteresting to most little people.

Responses to the Word

___ After a sermon on prejudice, have the people join in the prayer of confession printed above.

___ After a sermon on Jesus' words "Follow me" and Philip's words "Come and see," have the congregation sing them as part of the chorus "Alleluia." The chorus' usual verses of "Alleluia," "He's my Savior" and "I will praise him" are very open to other additions. After "He's my Savior," sing the words, "I will follow." After "I will praise him," sing the words, "Come and see."

___ After the gospel lesson and sermon, commission the worshipers to go out and invite others to "come and see" Jesus. Give all a toy building block to carry in their pocket or purse as a reminder that this is how Jesus builds the church.

___ Issue an altar call that invites the worshipers to come forward to the communion rail to meet Jesus, just as Nathanael once was invited to "come and see."

Drama and Movement

___ Gather a group of people who enjoy doing dramatic skits. Ask them to create three skits that model modern versions of Philip's witnessing. They could build their witnessing skits around witnessing to a family member, witnessing to one of the congregation's C & E's (those members who only attend at Christmas and Easter), and witnessing to a total stranger they meet at the shopping mall. Creating three skits that model witnessing will be fairly easy. The hard part will be to show how Jesus wins each person, as he won Nathanael in the gospel lesson. The pastor may want to preach on this, rather than having it acted out with skits.

___ Give the worshipers a glimpse of their heritage by reminding them of the countless "Philips" who have continued throughout twenty centuries to echo the invitation to "Come and see" Jesus. Have several people each choose one person from the twenty centuries of the church's history, and present a brief monologue that reveals how each of these people have echoed Philip's words. Persons like Augustine, Francis of Assisi, Clare of Assisi, Martin Luther, Susanna Wesley, Mother Teresa, Billy Graham, and more are the ones who have carried Philip's words through the centuries for us to hear "Come and see" today.

Visuals

___ Have the congregation's banner makers prepare two banners. The first can portray Jesus calling Philip with the words, "Follow me." The second can portray Philip calling Nathanael with the words, "Come and see."

___ Arrange a large display of flowers with a toy ladder worked into the middle of it. Place several angels (perhaps from the Christmas decorations) on the ladder and in the flowers.

___ Have an artist work with the words "You will see greater things than these" to create an interesting bulletin cover or a banner, in the way he draws the letters and words on the page or banner.

Anthems and Special Music

Come, Follow Me — J. Leavitt — SAB w/organ and oboe — GIA
Day by Day — M. How — 3-part w/keyboard — RSCM
Day by Day — Sanders — SATB — RD
Let Us Ever Walk with Jesus — P. Manz — Unison w/keyboard — MSM
Who Was the Man? — K. K. Davis — Unison w/keyboard — CG

Organ and Other Keyboard Music

I Love to Tell the Story (Hankey) — found in *11 Compositions for Organ*, set V — C. Ore — CPH
Lord, Speak to Us That We May Speak (Canonbury) — found in *Worship Service Music for the Organist* — A. Jordan — BP
Rise Up, O Saints of God (Festal Song) — found in *Twelve Hymn Preludes on Familiar Tunes* — S. Bingham — HWG

THIRD SUNDAY
AFTER THE EPIPHANY

Revised
  Common: Mark 1:14-20
Episcopal: Mark 1:14-20
Lutheran: Mark 1:14-20

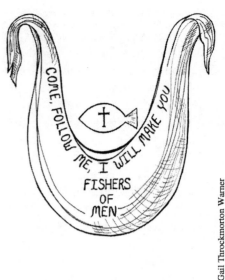

Gail Throckmorton Warner

*Note: Jesus still calls people
to follow. And some still drop
everything to obey.*

Printed Resources

___ Greeting

Ldr: Jesus Christ, the Son of God, has come among us!
Cng: **The time is fulfilled, and the kingdom of God has come near!**
Ldr: Repent, and believe in the good news.
Cng: **There is new life, new hope,**
    and a new chance to be faithful through Christ.

___ Prayer

Lft: **Jesus, blessed revelation of God,**
    you gave up your glory and power in heaven
    and sacrificed a quiet carpenter's life on earth,
    in order to publicly proclaim the good news.
Rgt: **You called ordinary people, like fishermen,**
    to tell others that the kingdom has come near.
    To follow you they gave up generations of family tradition
    and sacrificed a secure future with their loved ones.
Lft: **All this was done in obedience to God,**
    and in a real love for all God's children,
    so that they might know the good news,
    that the time is fulfilled and the kingdom has come near.
Rgt: **This wonderful kingdom of God you proclaim is both**
    already here, and almost but not yet here.
    You wrap us in its fullness when we need it most,
    and you delight us with the news that more is yet to come.
Lft: **In those precious but fleeting times when we understand,**
    we see God lancing our ugly moments to drain their poison,

61

and recognize God magnifying moments of beauty
to mold and shape us for the kingdom that is still coming.

All: **God-revealer and ruler of the kingdom that has come near,**
we bow before you,
surrendering our own lives
and answering your call to proclaim the good news,
to cast our nets far and wide,
in real love for God and all of God's children,
until time is complete
and the kingdom fills heaven and earth. Amen.

___ Commissioning and Blessing

(Use the refrain from the hymn "Where He Leads Me" for the congregation to sing the first response below. Note the shift from third person to second person. Then use the words of the second response for a new verse to the hymn. Use the familiar tune of a trifold "Amen" for the congregation to sing the third response.)

Ldr: Jesus says to you, "Follow me."

Cng: (singing) **Where you lead me I will follow,**
where you lead me I will follow,
where you lead me I will follow;
I'll go with you, with you all the way.

Ldr: "Follow me and I will make you fish for people," Jesus says.

Cng: (singing) **I'll leave my nets to follow you,**
I'll leave my nets to follow you,
I'll leave my nets to follow you,
I'll go with you, with you all the way.

Ldr: "Because you answer my call," says our Lord, Jesus Christ,
the blessing of God will be upon you
and the company of God's mighty people will surround you,
both here in the world
and in the kingdom that has already come near.

Cng: (singing) **Amen. Amen. Amen.**

(The congregation could break into a strong and joyful hymn, such as "Marching to Zion." As the congregation continues singing, begin a procession out of the sanctuary. Lead the procession with a cross, then the Bible, then acolytes with lit torches, then the worship leaders, then the choir, then invite the congregation to join in following the procession right on out into the street or parking lot, and then on into the nearby community.)

Hymns and Choruses

(The asterisk [*] indicates hymns or choruses that are addressed to God and can be used as prayers.)

___ "Christ Is the King, O Friends Upraise"
___ *"Dear Lord and Father of Mankind"

___ "God Is Working His Purpose Out"
___ "Hail to the Lord's Anointed"
593 *"Here I Am, Lord"
398 "Jesus Calls Us"
___ *"Lord God, Your Love Has Called Us Here"
___ "Rescue the Perishing"
___ "Rise Up, O Men of God"
___ "Rise Up, O Saints of God"
___ *"Send Me, Lord"
664 "Sent Forth by God's Blessing"
___ "Sois la Semilla" ("You Are the Seed")
___ *"Thy Kingdom Come, O God!"
___ "Thy Kingdom Come, On Bended Knee"
___ *"Tu Has Venido a la Orilla" ("Lord, You Have Come to the Lakeshore")
338 "Where He Leads Me"
___ *"Your Kingdom Come"
___ *"Your Kingdom Come, O Father"

Reading the Scripture

___ This would be a good text for someone to memorize and then share in a regular conversational voice with the congregation.

___ Have a person read the text as suggested under "Drama and Movement."

___ Divide the reading into three parts. The pastor can read the first part, verses 14-15. Then the left side of the congregation can read the second part, verses 16-18. The right side of the congregation finishes by reading verses 19-20. (The second and third parts could also be divided between the choir and the congregation, or between men and women.)

Responses to the Word

___ After a sermon on Jesus' call to the worshipers to become fishers of people, have the congregation pray the prayer printed above. Then move into the commissioning and blessing printed above to conclude the service with a procession of disciples going out to carry out the commitments they have just made.

___ Conduct an altar call after a sermon that focuses on Jesus' announcement of the kingdom and call for people to repent and believe.

___ Have three people share moments from their lives when they have recognized the kingdom of God breaking in upon them. Then lead the worshipers in the prayer printed above.

___ Have the worshipers join in singing "A Mighty Fortress Is Our God," especially verse four, where the phrase "Let goods and kindred go" appears.

Drama and Movement

___ Recruit four dancers to take the parts of Jesus, Simon, Andrew, and Zebedee. Have them interpret the text as it is read, with the accompaniment of a musical instrument.

___ Read the gospel lesson, then have different people recite these brief parables to peel away the layers of time that have hidden the meaning of the gospel.

— *I asked a fellow how often he went fishing. "Sometimes every day, but never less than three or four times a week." Then I thought about how often I go fishing as a disciple of Christ. I figured about three or four times a year I ask someone to come to church with me. When I suggested this frequency to my fisherman friend, he said, "Shoot, that ain't fishin'. That's just keepin' the dust washed off your hooks."*

— *I watched a lady baiting her hook with a worm. Her face was all scrunched up like she had the devil himself in her hands. When I asked why she was behaving that way, she said, "I hate putting worms on my hook, but I love fishing. So, I do what I have to do, to do what I love to do." I asked her if she would like to talk to some Christian friends of mine who had never learned that lesson in the church.*

— *I saw a man seining a stream for minnows the other day. I asked if he would use them for bait. "No," he said, "I love the minnows as much as the big fish." That made me wonder whether I really loved all the people in the church, or if I consider some expendable in trying to catch bigger and more important fish.*

— *A man was watching his wife pull in a beautiful, big bass, when their daughter came running to them. "Joey fell in the creek!" she shouted. Both parents immediately dropped their poles and the fish. A split second later, they were both in the creek lifting their son back onto the shore. I think Christians ought to be like that, ready to drop everything at a second's notice, so they can save someone drowning in sin.*

— *I was talking with a young man while he fished, when a gorgeous young woman walked by the pier where we were sitting. The young man took one look at her and said, "Now there's a keeper!" He handed his fishing pole to me, and went off after the woman. Later on, I heard the young man had married the woman, and he still hasn't asked for me to return his fishing pole. I guess the disciples figured Jesus was a keeper like that too.*

Read the gospel lesson a second time to let the worshipers reflect more deeply on its meaning.

Visuals

___ Have the congregation's banner makers create a set of banners to hang in the sanctuary that depict people in modern professions being called to follow Christ. Some examples could include farmers being told, "Follow me, and I will have you planting the Word of God." Doctors and nurses could be told, "Follow me, and I will make you healers of people's souls." Firefighters could be told, "Follow me, and I will have you extinguishing the fires of hell." Add other professions that are representative of the people in the congregation.

___ Have someone who enjoys flower arranging work a toy boat and some nets into a floral arrangement for the front of the sanctuary. Flowers could be used to fill the nets to represent the fish that are being caught up in God's kingdom.

Anthems and Special Music

As One Unknown — W. Held — SATB w/keyboard — AF
Lord, Here I Am — S. Paulus — SATB w/keyboard — AMSI
You Have Come Down to the Lakeshore — C. Gabarain — Unison hymn w/keyboard — found in
    With One Voice — AF
I Danced in the Morning — American Shaker/S. Carter — Unison w/keyboard — from *Hymnal
    Supplement 1991* — GIA
I Danced in the Morning — J. Ferguson — SATB w/organ — GAL

Organ and Other Keyboard Music

Dear Lord and Father of Mankind (Repton) — found in *Two Preludes on English Hymn Tunes* — R.
    Hobby — MSM
Jesus Calls Us (Galilee) — found in *Twenty Hymn-Tune Preludes*, set 1 — C. S. Lang — OUP
Sent Forth By God's Blessing (The Ash Grove) — found in *Sent Forth By God's Blessing* — R.
    Powell — AF

FOURTH SUNDAY
AFTER THE EPIPHANY

Revised
  Common: Mark 1:21-28
Episcopal: Mark 1:21-28
Lutheran: Mark 1:21-28

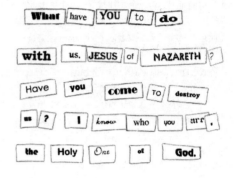

Note: In times like these, when people search for authority that can be trusted, we turn to the teaching of Jesus Christ. And we are not disappointed.

Printed Resources

___ Greeting[5]

Ld1: When Jesus was tempted by Satan in the wilderness,
      he showed that his authority
      was from a higher, greater source.
Ld2: When Jesus called Simon and Andrew, James and John,
      they recognized his authority
      and followed immediately.
Ld3: Even the unclean spirits recognized Jesus' authority.
      At his command the spirits immediately left their victims.
Cng: **And we also recognize and honor Jesus' authority.**
      Holy One of God, command us, so we may obey.
      Teach us, so we may please God.

___ Prayer for Illumination

Jesus of Nazareth, Holy One of God,
   astound us again with your teaching.
Cast your authority over our spirits,
   make us clean, pure and pleasing
   to our holy God. Amen.

___ Litany on Jesus' Teachings[6]

Ld1: Brothers and sisters, Jesus taught as one having authority, and not as the scribes.
Ld2: Big deal! People who can't do, teach.

Rgt: **But Jesus' teaching is not just empty words.**
His words are full of authority and power.

Lft: **Jesus, our Teacher, said, "Peace! be still!"**
And the wind and waves stopped threatening his disciples.

Rgt: **He said, "Little girl, get up!"**
And Jairus' dead daughter got up, alive again.

Lft: **Jesus blessed five loaves and two fish,**
and fed more than five thousand hungry people.

Ld1: And Jesus cast out the unclean spirit
that interrupted his teaching in Capernaum's synagogue.

Ld2: Unclean spirit, you say?
Nobody believes in demons and unclean spirits any more!

Rgt: **Call them what you will,**
but our world is still plagued with evil forces.

Lft: **People suffer addiction to drugs and alcohol,**
tobacco and sex, and all kinds of such evil powers.
These unclean spirits take over and destroy people's lives.

Rgt: **And the unclean spirits of hatred, revenge and bigotry**
have thrown entire nations into war against each other.

Lft: **And the unclean spirits of greed, consumerism and envy**
have raped our environment and destroyed life
for generations to come.

Ld1: Jesus' teaching is not like the scribes.
His teaching is full of authority and power.

All: **When we live according to Jesus' teaching**
the unclean spirits in our world are cast out,
and our lives can be lived fully, as God intended.

Ld2: Jesus, teach us!

All: **And let us live according to the light of your words. Amen.**

___ Commissioning and Blessing

By the authority of his word,
     Jesus casts out the unclean spirits.
Submit your desires to his power,
     obey his teaching;
because the love of Jesus Christ
     has already cleansed you
     and made you holy. **Amen.**

Hymns and Choruses

(The asterisk [*] indicates hymns or choruses that are addressed to God and can be used as prayers.)

___ *"Blessed Jesus, at Thy Word"

___ *"Break Now the Bread of Life"
___ *"Break Thou the Bread of Life"
___ *"Heal Me, Hands of Jesus"
___ "How Blest Are They Who Hear God's Word"
___ *"O Word of God Incarnate"
___ *"Silence, Frenzied, Unclean Spirit"
___ *"Thy Word Is a Lamp"
___ "We Would See Jesus"
___ *"Your Word, O Lord, Is Gentle Dew"

Reading the Scripture

___ Recruit two people to read the lesson. Divide the reading between them as follows:

Ld1: They went to Capernaum: and when the sabbath came, he entered the synagogue and taught.

Ld2: They were astounded at his teaching, for he taught them as one having authority, and not as the scribes.

Ld1: Just then there was in their synagogue a man with an unclean spirit, and he cried out, "What have you to do with us, Jesus of Nazareth? Have you come to destroy us? I know who you are, the Holy One of God."

Ld2: But Jesus rebuked him, saying, "Be silent, and come out of him!"

Ld1: And the unclean spirit, convulsing him and crying with a loud voice, came out of him.

Ld2: They were all amazed, and they kept on asking one another, "What is this? A new teaching — with authority! He commands even the unclean spirits, and they obey him."

Ld1: At once his fame began to spread throughout the surrounding region of Galilee.

___ Ask one of the youth in the congregation to memorize this story. Practice with this young person so he or she can bring the story to life as he or she tells it to the worshipers.

___ Another way to divide the reading separates and lets the worshipers hear the two stories that Mark has joined together. Have the first person read verses 21-22. The second person should read verses 23-26. Then the first concludes the lesson by reading verses 27-28.

Responses to the Word

___ Invite the worshipers to join into a special Bible study program or challenge them to form new Sunday school classes to study the teachings of Jesus. An alternative to starting something new would be to have people from the congregation's Bible study groups and Sunday school classes invite the worshipers to join their group or class.

___ Invite the worshipers to sing hymns such as "Blessed Jesus, at Thy Word," "Break Thou the Bread of Life," or "Thy Word Is a Lamp."

____ Challenge the congregation to begin reading the Bible together. Give them a list of passages to read each day, and then use these readings to shape the worship services and sermons each Sunday. Home Bible study groups can focus on these passages, too.

Drama and Movement

____ Recruit two readers and have them read the gospel lesson as outlined in the first suggestion under "Reading the Scripture" printed above. Have a liturgical dancer portray the man with an unclean spirit. The dancer rushes into the sanctuary, interrupting the reader just like the man in the lesson. Let the first reader speak the words of Jesus in verse 25. The dancer convulses as the spirit leaves him, and the reading goes on as suggested above, with the dancer reflecting the healing that has just happened.

____ Ask a group of youth or adults to present dramatizations of all four of Mark's exorcism accounts. Besides this gospel lesson, the texts are found in 5:1-20, 7:24-30 and 9:14-29. The preacher could then address all four of these events.

Visuals

____ Ask one or more of the teachers in the congregation to prepare a display of things associated with teaching. They can borrow these from a local school or gather them from people in the congregation. Items to be displayed can be a mortar board, textbooks, chemistry supplies, a computer, a globe, charts and so on. A cross should rise out of this arrangement. A ribbon-banner on the cross can proclaim the words, "A new teaching — with authority."

____ A sketch of the items suggested above could be used for a worship bulletin cover.

Anthems and Special Music

He is the Way — R. Proulx — SATB w/organ — GIA
The Secret of Christ — R. Shephard — SATB unaccompanied — RSCM

Organ and Other Keyboard Music

Break Thou the Bread of Life (Bread of Life) — found in *Twelve Hymn Settings for Organ* — D. N. Johnson — SHM
O Word of God Incarnate (Munich) — found in *Hymn Preludes for the Liturgical Year*, vol. VIII — F. Peeters — CFP
Your Word, O Lord is Gentle Dew (Af Himlens) — found in *Interpretations*, Book II — D. Cherwien — AMSI

FIFTH SUNDAY
AFTER THE EPIPHANY

Revised
  Common: Mark 1:29-39
Episcopal: Mark 1:29-39
Lutheran: Mark 1:29-39

Note: Moderns get upset at the thought of Simon's mother-in-law being healed, and then starting immediately to work serving her son's guests. But really, would you want to be sick in bed when the most important person who ever lived came to your home?

Angie Latta

Printed Resources

___ Greeting

(The response sung below is from the hymn "Jesus, We Want to Meet." Another hymn that could be used would be "When Jesus the Healer Passed Through Galilee." Both of these hymns can be found in *The United Methodist Hymnal*, and are arranged with the words divided between a soloist and the congregation, which makes singing these less familiar hymns much easier.)

Ldr: When people first learned Jesus could heal
     whole cities gathered around him.
Cng: (Sing verses 1 and 2.)
Ldr: And when Jesus went out to a deserted place for prayer
     everyone searched for him.
Cng: (Sing verses 3 and 4.)

___ Prayer

Our Father,
    we hear about people flocking to Jesus,
    being healed of their many diseases,
    and we cannot help but be envious.

We have prayed to you about some of our loved ones,
    and they still are without healing.
Remind us again, Father,
    that Jesus was not sent to settle down in Capernaum
    and become the local healing-man.
Help us remember that Jesus was not here
    to keep people alive in this world,
    and that even Jesus suffered people's taunts
    because he could not save himself
    and come down from the cross.
Keep us steady in the truth
    that there are bigger and more important things
    than just being healthy in this world.
We will stay the course,
    trusting you with our lives
    and the lives of our loved ones, forever. Amen.

___ Commissioning and Blessing

Ldr: "Let us go on to the neighboring towns,"
      Jesus told the disciples,
      "so that I may proclaim the message there also."
      Brothers and sisters,
      if we are going to follow Christ,
      then we need to go to our neighbors,
      to other towns, and around the world,
      with the message of Jesus Christ.
Cng: **We go, in the name of our living Lord.**
Ldr: May the power of God,
      the love of Jesus,
      and the communion of the Holy Spirit
      go with you.
Cng: **Amen.**

Hymns and Choruses

(The asterisk [*] indicates hymns or choruses that are addressed to God and can be used as prayers.)

___ "Carry the Light"
___ "Every Time I Feel the Spirit"
___ *"Heal Me, Hands of Jesus"
___ *"Heal Us, Emmanuel, Hear Our Prayer"
___ "How Shall They Hear the Word of God"
___ *"I Am the God That Healeth Thee"
___ *"I'm Forever Grateful"

___ *"It's Me, It's Me, O Lord"
___ *"Jesus' Hands Were Kind Hands"
___ *"Lord, Teach Us How to Pray Aright"
___ *"My Prayer Rises to Heaven"
___ *"O Christ, the Healer"
___ "O For a Thousand Tongues to Sing"
___ "Open Your Ears, O Faithful People"
___ "Rise, My Soul, to Watch and Pray"
___ "Rise, Shine, You People"
___ *"Send Me, Lord"
___ "Serenity"
___ "Sweet Hour of Prayer"
___ "Take Time to Be Holy"
___ "We've a Story to Tell to the Nations"
___ *"When Jesus the Healer Passed Through Galilee"
___ *"Word of God, Come Down on Earth"
___ *"Your Hand, O Lord, in Days of Old"

Reading the Scripture

___ Recruit three people to read this gospel lesson. The first should read verses 29-31, the second verses 32-34, and the third verses 35-39.

___ See the second suggestion printed under "Drama and Movement" below.

Responses to the Word

___ Offer the worshipers a healing service. Use the four traditional acts of healing: (1) prayer, (2) anointing with oil, (3) laying on of hands, and (4) holy communion. Services for healing can be found in the *The Book of Common Prayer* and *The United Methodist Book of Worship*. If healing services have never been offered to the congregation, then take some time to explain what will be done as part of the service. It is also important to lay a good biblical and theological foundation for the worshipers to understand God's healing work. With these preparations accomplished, invite the worshipers to come forward to the communion rail to receive healing for themselves or to pray for the healing of another.

___ Challenge the worshipers to pray the following prayer pledge:

Lord, I'm going to be more like Jesus.
    I'm going to seek out deserted places
    where you and I can talk.
When temptation makes an offer I can't refuse,
    I'll come running to you.
    No wild beast will keep us apart.
When others search after me,
    to make demands on my time,

I'm going to spend time with you,
   so you can shape and direct all I do.
When the cares of the world wear me down,
   I will seek you out,
   and find my rest
   in your unflagging strength.
When I need a change of direction,
   I'll climb to you in prayer,
   to let your transfiguring glory
   provide the vision that sets my new course.
When I need to forgive another,
   I'm heading for you,
   who first forgives me.
When I need to get closer with other people,
   I will seek your communion
   that bonds me to all your children.
And when you ask me to do the impossible,
   I'll be praying in my own Gethsemane,
   where you can take a humble servant
   and change the impossible into a new reality.
Lord, I'm going to be more like Jesus.
   I'm going to seek out deserted places
   where you and I can talk. Amen.

Drama and Movement

___ A group of young adults could have a lot of fun preparing a skit about the healing of Simon's mother-in-law. It could include just the three verses relating this event, or could flow into a presentation of the rest of this gospel lesson too.

___ A group of liturgical dancers could provide a beautiful interpretation of this lesson as it is read.

Visuals

___ Does your community have an artist who could do a serious work of art for your church? Commission this person to create a painting or sketch of the many sick people being brought to Jesus for healing. This work of art could be displayed in the church, or loaned (or donated) to a local museum, library or other civic organization where many people could see this witness to Jesus' power. If the artist did not object, a documentary could be done on video. This would be a way to bring the work to the attention of the community as it is shown on local access cable television. People from the church could explain why they commissioned such a work, and how they have experienced Jesus' healing power. The congregation working to raise funds for the commission could be shown. The artist could discuss various decisions that went into the work. And the community would hear a congregation's witness to Jesus. And besides, the final work of art would be a powerful presence in the service of worship where this gospel lesson is being read.

___ It could be a real discussion piece if the floral arrangement for this service contained many wilted, broken or dying flowers. Mix these with healthy flowers of many types and colors. Arrange the healthy flowers around a cross. Then, further from the cross, add the wilted, broken and dying flowers. The beautiful, healthy flowers represent people already healed by Jesus. The other flowers represent the sick being brought to Jesus for healing. Dare we use flowers that others would throw away? Are we not supposed to bring our best to God? Or is this like Jesus gathering people around him that others would throw away?

Anthems and Special Music

At Even, When the Sun Did Set — S. D. Wolff — SAB w/organ — CPH

Organ and Other Keyboard Music

Lord, Teach Us How to Pray Aright (Song 67) — found in *113 Variations on Hymn Tunes* — G. Thalben-Ball — NOV
O Christ the Healer (Distress) — R. Powell — found in *Hymn Preludes for Communion*, vol. 1 — CPH
O For A Thousand Tongues to Sing (Azmon) — Partita on *Azmon* — P. Bouman — CPH

SIXTH SUNDAY
AFTER THE EPIPHANY

Revised
  Common: Mark 1:40-45
Episcopal: Mark 1:40-45
Lutheran: Mark 1:40-45

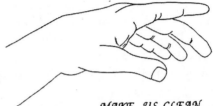

MAKE US CLEAN

Gail Throckmorton Warner

*Note: We all know the posi-
tion, kneeling before God and
begging to be made clean
again. What we do not know
is how God can continue to
cleanse those who have been
there so many times. But
thanks to God's eternal
mercy, we still feel that healing touch.*

Printed Resources

___ Greeting

Ldr: When the leper came and kneeled before Jesus,
     begging for help,
     Jesus stretched out his hand and touched him.
     "Be made clean," Jesus told the tortured soul,
     and the leper was made clean.
Rgt: **Lord, we bow before you.**
Lft: **We beg your help.**
Rgt: **Touch us.**
Lft: **Make us clean.**
Rgt: **Make us fit subjects for your kingdom.**
Lft: **And let us sing your praises on earth.**

___ Prayer

Lord, the orders have been changed,
  why don't we ever listen?
When Jesus told people who saw his miracles,
  "Say nothing to anyone,"
  the people could not keep silent.
  They told everyone!

75

So, Lord,
  why is it now that Jesus says,
  "Go into all the world and proclaim the good news,"
  that silence has suddenly become our strong point?
  Now we don't tell anyone!
What's with us, Lord?
  Will you ever be able to teach us
  to obey a command that is not two thousand years
  out of date?

___ Prayer of Confession and Assurance of Pardon

Holy God,
  we come before you covered with leprosy.
Our bodies show no sores,
  but our minds and hearts ooze
  with the sins we have committed.
Like lepers, we cry out to you,
  "Unclean! Unclean!"
Like lepers, we are cut off
  from you, our holy God.
Take pity on us, merciful God,
  and let Jesus once again
  stretch out his hand and touch us.
If you choose, Jesus can make us clean.
  His forgiveness can heal our innermost being.
Make it so, holy God,
  and we will proclaim your mercy throughout the land.
(Continue in silent prayer.)
Even today, God still chooses to make you clean.
  In the name of Jesus Christ, I say to you,
  "Your sins are forgiven. Be clean!"
Brothers and sisters, right now, right here,
  Jesus is stretching out his hand
  and touching each one of you.
Know that the forgiveness he proclaimed from the cross
  has cleansed your souls.
Now go and let your thanksgiving be known
  by living holy lives,
  in the name of our holy God,
  the holy Savior
  and the Holy Spirit. **Amen.**

___ Commissioning and Blessing

The world is full of untouchable lepers,
    but Christ sends you out to change the world.
Stretch out your hands to the unclean people around you.
    Touch them with the love of Jesus Christ.
And our almighty and all-holy God
    will work miracles of healing for everyone you touch. **Amen.**

Hymns and Choruses

(The asterisk [*] indicates hymns or choruses that are addressed to God and can be used as prayers.)

___ "God Loved the World"
___ "He Touched Me"
___ *"Heal Me, Hands of Jesus"
___ *"Heal Us, Emmanuel, Hear Our Prayer"
___ *"Help Us Accept Each Other"
___ *"I Call on Thee, Lord Jesus Christ"
___ "Jesus' Hands Were Kind Hands"
___ *"O For a Thousand Tongues to Sing"
___ *"O God, Whose Will Is Life and Good"
___ "Rescue the Perishing"
___ *"When Jesus the Healer Passed Through Galilee"
___ *"When the Church of Jesus"
___ *"Your Hand, O Lord, in Days of Old"

Reading the Scripture

___ This is the kind of scripture passage that lends itself to easy memorization by a youth or adult, who can then tell the story to the congregation. This is much more effective than just reading, if the storyteller really tells the story. This is not just a recitation of memorized verses. The person chosen to tell the story should be able to tell it as easily as he or she can tell you about what he or she saw on television last night.

Responses to the Word

___ Recruit people before the service to offer a prayer for different types of people who are isolated in today's society. After a sermon on the isolation of today's "lepers" and how Christ reached out and touched the lepers in his day, have the people recruited earlier offer their prayers. These prayers could be for people such as: victims of abuse, people with AIDS, people on welfare, illegal immigrants, mentally challenged people, very elderly people, people in prison, homosexuals, and so forth. This might be followed with a challenge to the congregation to begin a new ministry to one or more of these groups of modern "lepers."

___ Invite some people to share how they are ministering to modern-day "lepers" in the name of Christ.

___ Offer a healing service for people who feel isolated from others. People's relationships with one another often are in more desperate need of healing than are their bodies.

___ Invite the worshipers to pray the prayer of confession printed above. Then celebrate their new condition by singing the hymn "He Touched Me."

Drama and Movement

___ Two liturgical dancers or two mimes could provide a very nice interpretation of this gospel lesson.

___ Gather a group of adults to plan and present a skit on applying the lesson in this gospel passage to how Christians should treat modern-day "lepers."

Visuals

___ Ask one of the congregation's banner makers to prepare a banner with the words, "And people came to him from every quarter." The banner could project a view looking over Jesus' shoulder. Thousands of people can be seen gathered around him. The figures could be very stylized, especially in the distance, in order to fit a lot of the figures on the one banner.

___ Recruit a member of the congregation to make a flower arrangement that incorporates two birds (artificial or live ones in cages), cedarwood, crimson yarn and sprigs of hyssop (a mint-like plant with blue flowers) or some substitute that looks a bit like it. These are the items that a leper is to bring to the Lord when his or her leprosy is examined by the priest for declaring the leper cleansed (Leviticus 14:1-9). White flowers might be worked into the arrangement to represent cleansing, and to add beauty. If you want to go further, add the offering that is to be made when the leper returns a final time (Leviticus 4:10-32). This includes three lambs, a half bushel of flour, and a container of oil. Poor lepers could substitute two turtledoves or pigeons for two of the lambs, and give only a quarter bushel of flour. Sound like a fun flower arrangement? Put a note in the worship bulletin to explain what it is all about for the sake of the worshipers.

___ If some people are invited to share how they are ministering to modern "lepers," suggested above, then be prepared to project some slides or videotape of the ministry.

Anthems and Special Music

At Even, When the Sun Did Set — S. D. Wolff — SAB w/organ — CPH
For I Went With the Multitude — P. Aston — SATB unaccompanied — NOV
O Lord, We Believe — R. Kreutz — SATB unaccompanied — WLSM

Organ and Other Keyboard Music

No music could be found on this Gospel text.

SEVENTH SUNDAY AFTER THE EPIPHANY

Revised
  Common: Mark 2:1-12
Episcopal: Mark 2:1-12
Lutheran: Mark 2:1-12

Note: To be forgiven and have our guilt lifted from our shoulders is about as great as a gift can be. No wonder such crowds gathered around Jesus.

Your sins are forgiven!

Printed Resources

___Greeting

Ldr: Men and women, children and youth, young and old,
        we are looking for people who have sinned.
Cng: **I have sinned, many times.**
        My life has been crippled by sin.
Ldr: Then you have come to the right place.
        We are here so that you may know
        that the Son of Man, our Lord Jesus Christ,
        has authority on earth to forgive sins.
Cng: **Lord, have mercy upon us.**
        Christ, have mercy upon us.
        Lord, have mercy upon us.

___Prayer (Based on Mark 2:1-12 and Psalm 139)

Merciful Lord,
    you saw into the heart of the paralyzed man
    and you knew the sin that crippled him.
    You saw the questioning and criticisms
    lurking in the hearts of the scribes.
    And you see the right and wrong, the faith and the doubts,
    that confuse and contort our own hearts.
For it was you who formed our inward parts;
    you knit us together in our mothers' wombs.

Where can we flee from your presence?
    Even the darkness is not dark to you.
But we do not flee from you.
    We turn to you,
    you who knows us, forgives us, and loves us still.
We turn to you
    to heal the sin that paralyzes us,
    to answer the questions that hold us back,
    and to form our hearts to praise you once again.
We do praise you, Lord,
    for we are fearfully and wonderfully made.
    Wonderful are your works, merciful Lord. Amen.

___Commissioning and Blessing

The world is full of people too sick,
    or too full of sin,
    to seek out Christ on their own.
Brothers and sisters, we are the Church,
    We are the ones who can help the sinful and the sick.
    With our faith and our support we can bring them to Christ.
In the name of God, let's go to work,
    and may the blessing of God go with you. **Amen.**

Hymns and Choruses

(The asterisk [*] indicates hymns or choruses that are addressed to God and can be used as prayers.)

___ "Amazing Grace"
___ "Chief of Sinners though I Be"
___ "Come, Sinners, to the Gospel Feast"
___ "Come, Ye Sinners, Poor and Needy"
___ *"Dear Lord and Father of Mankind"
___ *"Depth of Mercy"
___ *"Grace Greater than Our Sin"
___ *"Hark, the Voice of Jesus Calling"
___ "He Touched Me"
___ *"Heal Me, Hands of Jesus"
___ "How Can We Sinners Know"
___ *"Lord Speak to Us, that We May Speak"
___ *"O Christ, the Healer"
___ *"Once He Came in Blessing"
___ *"Pass Me Not, O Gentle Savior"
___ "Rise, Shine, You People"
___ "Spirit Song"

___ *"To You Omniscient Lord of All"
___ *"When in the Hour of Deepest Need"
___ "When Jesus the Healer Passed Through Galilee"

Reading the Scripture

___ Find a good storyteller to relate this marvelous gospel story, with its interesting combination of healing and the forgiveness of sin.

___ Recruit the help of the choir and congregation for reading this gospel lesson. Ask one choir member to read the lesson, and the rest of the choir to speak Jesus' words as the lesson is read. The choir will need to practice this at their regular rehearsal. Then, at the beginning of the worship service (or the beginning of the scripture reading), tell the congregation that their help is also needed for reading the day's gospel lesson. Ask them to say the words, "We have never seen anything like this!" at the end of the reading. You might want to have them practice saying their line at least once. Give them some hand signal to cue them when they are to say their line. The choir member who is reading the lesson can give this signal to the congregation.

Responses to the Word

___ After a sermon on Jesus' authority to forgive sin, have the worshipers join in a traditional prayer of confession. If the congregation is not too large, the worshipers could gather at the front of the sanctuary, kneel before the Lord, and join in a printed prayer. Follow this with a generous time for silent prayers of confession. Then the pastor can announce, in the name of Jesus Christ, the forgiveness of the worshipers' sins.

___ A week or more in advance, ask some members of the congregation to prepare to share how their lives were healed when Jesus forgave their sins. Have them give these testimonies after the scripture reading.

Drama and Movement

___ Recruit the youth group to act out the gospel lesson.

___ Ask a group of young adults to prepare and present a skit that shows a contemporary person paralyzed by his or her sin. Let this group struggle with the question of how such a person would be forgiven and healed by Christ today.

Visuals

___ Ask a family with several young children to arrange five dolls in the front of the sanctuary. Ask them to arrange the dolls so that four of them appear to be carrying the fifth on a stretcher. Doll-size flower arrangements might be used to draw worshipers' eyes to this scene.

___ Ask a creative member of the congregation to prepare a banner depicting people lowering the paralyzed man through the roof to be healed by Jesus. Four figures can project above the top of the banner. Strings run from their hands to a mat holding a man being lowered into the middle of the banner. Jesus and other figures can be sitting at the bottom of the banner, and can be looking at the approaching man. Use the banner itself to represent the house.

___ Ask an artistic person to prepare a black-line sketch to be copied for a worship bulletin cover. The sketch should show a leaping figure holding a rolled mat over his head. The words "Your sins are forgiven" are added to finish the bulletin cover.

Anthems and Special Music

Blessed is He Whose Unrighteousness is Forgiven — T. Tomkins — ATB — from *Anthems for Men's Voices, Vol. 1* — OUP
I Danced in the Morning — J. Ferguson — SATB w/organ — GAL
I Danced in the Morning — American Shaker/S. Carter — Unison w/keyboard — from *Hymnal Supplement 1991* — GIA
I Will Arise and Go To Jesus — M. Shaw — SATB — GS
Now In This Banquet — M. Haugen — Cantor w/keyboard, opt. congregation — GIA
The Man on the Bed — A. Lovelace — Unison w/keyboard — CG
Three Hymns for Special Occasions — L. Betteridge — SATB w/organ — PA

Organ and Other Keyboard Music

Amazing Grace (New Britain) — found in *The King of Love* — R. Haan — SMP
Once He Came in Blessing — (Gottes Sohn ist kommen) — found in *Orgelwerke*, vol. V — J. S. Bach — CFP
Rise, Shine You People — D. Cherwien — AF

EIGHTH SUNDAY AFTER THE EPIPHANY

Revised
  Common: Mark 2:13-22
Episcopal: Mark 2:18-22
Lutheran: Mark 2:13-22

Angie Latta

Note: The Christian gospel is two thousand years old, but to someone who has not yet believed in and accepted Christ it is truly new.

Printed Resources

___ Greeting

Ld1: Be careful!
Ld2: Watch out!
Ld1: You might get a bad reputation coming to church with us.
Ld2: If you haven't noticed,
       Jesus is known for keeping bad company.
Ld1: Jesus was always eating and drinking
       with tax collectors and sinners.
Ld2: Jesus called Levi, one of Rome's tax collectors,
       and ranked him among the twelve apostles.
Ld1: You didn't really expect to find this church full of saints,
       did you?
Ld2: Look around you.
       Every member of this church has confessed to being a sinner.
Ld1: So be careful!
Ld2: Jesus came to call not the righteous but sinners.
Cng: **Jesus, we have heard you call us to this place today.**
       Our reputations are already smeared with our sin.
       We fit in here, with the rest of these sinners.
       We have come,
       so that you could set us back onto the narrow path of life.

___ Prayer

Lord, why do we rank human occupations?
Why are people who earn lots of money

ranked better than those who work just as hard,
but are not paid as well for their effort?
Why are people who work with their minds
supposed to be better than those using their muscles?
Why is it better to work at the public library
than clerking at a discount store that pays more?
Why is the supervisor given more importance
than those who actually do the work?
Even among Christians there is an occupational hierarchy.
Nurses, teachers, social workers, missionaries
and other "helping" occupations working directly with people
are given greater esteem among the Christian family.
Bankers, lawyers, and insurance agents work directly with people;
so why are these occupations less honored?
Isn't the construction worker just as important
when this provides a roof over our heads?
Or what about the factory worker who makes all the tools
that the nurses, teachers, social workers and missionaries use?
And think of the health problems we would suffer
if there were no garbage collectors.
Lord, help us pay more attention to your Son.
When Jesus called the tax collector Levi to be an apostle,
it should have put an end to all our occupational ranking.
A person's occupation does not make that person
less of a disciple to Jesus Christ.
Open us to your Holy Spirit
to direct and guide the work we do,
so that everything may be done in service to you,
our blessed Creator who first worked for us. Amen.

___ Great Thanksgiving Prayer

Ldr: The Lord be with you.
Cng: **And also with you.**
Ldr: Lift up your hearts.
Cng: **We lift them up to the Lord.**
Ldr: Let us give thanks to the Lord our God.
Cng: **It is right to give our thanks and praise.**
Ldr: It is right to give thanks and praise to you,
blessed Creator who formed us from dust
and shaped us into your own image.
And so, with your people on earth
and all the company of heaven,
we praise your name and join in their unending hymn:
Cng: **Holy, holy, holy Lord, God of power and might,**
heaven and earth are full of your glory.

Hosanna in the highest.
Blessed is he who comes in the name of the Lord.
Hosanna in the highest.

Ldr: Holy are you and blessed is your Son Jesus Christ,
who called to his side
people like Levi the tax collector.
With mercy and grace Jesus gathered sinners,
and transformed their profane and common lives
into new lives full of holiness and glory.
He took Levi's invitation to a banquet,
and transformed it
into a holy taste of the coming kingdom,
where all people find their unity in Christ's love.
At Jesus' last supper,
on the night in which he gave himself up for us,
he took bread, gave thanks to you, broke the bread,
gave it to his disciples and said:
"Take, eat; this is my body which is given for you.
Do this in remembrance of me."
When the supper was over, he took the cup,
gave thanks to you, gave it to his disciples, and said:
"Drink from this, all of you;
this is my blood of the new covenant,
poured out for you and for many
for the forgiveness of sins.
Do this, as often as you drink it,
in remembrance of me."
And so,
in remembrance of these your mighty acts in Jesus Christ,
we offer ourselves in praise and thanksgiving
as a holy and living sacrifice,
in union with Christ's offering for us,
as we proclaim the mystery of faith.

Cng: **Christ has died; Christ is risen; Christ will come again.**

Ldr: Send your Holy Spirit among the sinners gathered here.
Transform us,
and these common elements of bread and wine,
into the holy body of Jesus Christ.
Give us the blessed unity that transcends all divisions
and prepares us for the kingdom that Christ is bringing.
Through your Son Jesus Christ,
with the Holy Spirit in your holy church,
all honor and glory is yours, almighty Father,
now and forever.

Cng: **Amen.**

___ Commissioning and Blessing

The gospel of Jesus Christ is new.
    Do not try to sew this new way of life
    onto your old bad habits and practices.
Jesus Christ makes you a new person,
    and fills you with his good news
    and is making you whole again, forever.
Drink deeply of the new wine of God's love,
    Christ's salvation
    and the Spirit's power;
    and be the new person that Christ has made you. **Amen.**

Hymns and Choruses

(The asterisk [*] indicates hymns or choruses that are addressed to God and can be used as prayers.)

___ "Amazing Grace"
___ *"Bind Us Together"
___ "Come, Sinners, to the Gospel Feast"
___ "Deck Thyself, My Soul, with Gladness"
___ "Depth of Mercy"
___ "He Touched Me"
___ "I Come with Joy"
___ "I Stand Amazed in the Presence"
___ *"I Will Sing of the Mercies"
___ "In Adam We Have All Been One"
___ "In Christ There Is No East or West"
___ *"Let Us Break Bread Together"
___ *"Lord, We Have Come at Your Own Invitation"
___ *"Make Us One"
___ "Now the Silence"
___ *"O Jesus, Joy of Loving Hearts"
___ *"Pass Me Not, O Gentle Savior"
___ "Rise, Shine, You People"
___ "Softly and Tenderly Jesus Is Calling"
___ "There's Within My Heart a Melody"
___ "This Is a Day of New Beginnings"
___ "This Is the Hour of Banquet and Song"
___ "When Morning Gilds the Skies"
___ "With God as Our Friend"

Reading the Scripture

___ Recruit two people to read the gospel lesson. Then divide the reading between them as follows:

First reader: verses 13-14
Second reader: verses 15-17
First reader: verses 18-20
Second reader: verses 21-22

____ Four upper elementary children or youth can memorize the verses of this gospel lesson. Break the lesson in four parts as in the suggestion printed above. The children can tell these stories or parables to the congregation. Be careful to practice with these young people long enough to allow them to relate the stories and parables in a natural, unforced way.

Responses to the Word

____ Invite the worshipers to be made new persons in Jesus Christ. Call them into a time of silent prayer, during which they can open themselves to Christ. Follow this with a prayer by the pastor leading the worshipers into Christ's newness.

____ Celebrate holy communion. If it is possible, adapt the worship setting to allow the worshipers to gather around a table where the communion elements are served. Make a point of inviting visitors and nonmembers to participate, just as Jesus made a point of inviting the people who did not meet the requirements for eating together in his day. This may challenge the eucharistic doctrine of some denominations. Be sure to address this concern in the sermon, or in some other way.

____ Invite the worshipers to enjoy a meal prepared for them in the church's fellowship hall. This should not be a carry-in or potluck dinner, but should be served (maybe even catered) to the worshipers. A basket set out for an offering will most likely cover the cost of such a meal. (People often give more when a price is not set on the meal.) Provide entertainment that will make people laugh, sing and be happy after the meal. Remind the worshipers that as long as they have the bridegroom with them the disciples of Jesus cannot fast. Let the people celebrate the "already" dimension of the kingdom of God.[7]

____ Since Jesus' earthly ministry has ended, it would also be appropriate to recognize the "not yet" dimension of the kingdom of God. Invite those who are able to join in a fast for one day, or for one meal each day of the next week. Have them use this time to lift up their sorrow concerning Jesus' absence and to pray for his quick return.

Drama and Movement

____ Ask a group of youth or adults to prepare and present three skits. The first should show the call of Levi, the second Jesus eating with the tax collectors and sinners, and the third the controversy over Jesus' disciples not fasting. Let each of these three skits be performed in different locations in the sanctuary, and at the end of each skit the actors and actresses freeze in place, rather than exiting. When all three groups have frozen, a person steps forward and quotes Jesus' parables in verses 22-23. After a few seconds for reflection, everybody exits and the worship service continues.

___ Recruit a group of adults to act out the call of Levi and the four controversy stories that follow this in Mark's gospel. Two of these people act out the call of Levi. Then the others begin to ask Jesus critical questions (standing where they have been sitting in the pews?), as Jesus and Levi begin to walk off together. The first questioner asks why Jesus eats with sinners (2:15-17). The second questioner asks why Jesus' disciples do not fast (2:18-20). The third asks why Jesus breaks the commandment about resting on the sabbath day by picking grain to eat (2:23-28). And the fourth questions Jesus' healing on the sabbath day (3:1-6). The preacher could pick up the point of these questions and begin the sermon by sharing Jesus' answers. Then the preacher could apply this to contemporary concerns of the worshipers.

Visuals

___ Recruit someone from the congregation to prepare a display for the sanctuary. This person should start with a coat tree or dressmaker's form. From this, hang an old coat or cape with a big patch that can be easily seen from the congregation. Next to this place a small table holding a wineskin. (Someone in the congregation may have one that can be borrowed, or one may be borrowed from a community theatre's prop room. A leatherworker or shoe repairman may be able to tack together something that resembles a wineskin, too.) A bouquet of flowers may be added to the small table and/or at the foot of the coat tree.

___ Ask a group of youth to prepare a number of large posters. Have them turn the posters with the longest side being horizontal to the floor. Then paste pictures of food onto the posters to form a montage that looks like a wedding banquet spread across several tables. At the top of each poster (or table) print one or two words from this sentence, "Wedding guests cannot fast while the bridegroom is with them." An alternative to this would be to do the same thing with fabric on a series of banners.

Anthems and Special Music

In Christ No East Or West — J. Oxenham — SATB unaccompanied — SH
Let Us Break Bread Together — N. Milosevich — SATB, SATB soli w/organ — TP

Organ and Other Keyboard Music

In Christ There Is No East Or West (McKee) — found in *Fourteen Hymn Preludes* — A. Lovelace —
	AF
Let Us Break Bread Together On Our Knees — D. Woods — SMP
When Morning Gilds the Skies (Laudes Domini) — S. Saxton — found in *A Galaxy of Hymn Tune Preludes for Organ* — GAL

TRANSFIGURATION SUNDAY

Revised
 Common: Mark 9:2-9
Episcopal: Mark 9:2-9
Lutheran: Mark 9:2-9

"This is my beloved son. Listen to Him."

Note: Love is the only possible motivation for Jesus working so hard to reveal his glory to us, at the same time that he shields us from being overpowered by it.

Gail Throckmorton Warner

Printed Resources

___ Greeting

Ldr: Jesus took with him Peter and James and John.
Cng: **Like them, Lord,**
   we have heard you call us to follow you.
Ldr: Jesus led them up a high mountain.
Cng: **In our hearts**
   we are climbing that high mountain with you, Lord.
Ldr: Jesus led them up a high mountain,
   apart, by themselves.
Cng: **We are here, Lord,**
   apart from the rest of the world, by ourselves,
   but with you.

___ Prayer of Confession and Assurance of Pardon

God of dazzling glory,
   when Peter foolishly offered to build three dwellings
   for Elijah, Moses and Jesus,
   he was doing what we have so often done ourselves.
When we do not know what to say,
   when we're frightened, or angry or ashamed,
   we are apt to say anything that comes to mind,
   no matter how foolish it may be.

How we wish we could take back such misspoken words.
>   Unlike Peter's words, ours have often hurt our families,
>   or led people to actions that result in unnecessary injury.
And how many times have we filled the air with foolishness,
>   instead of keeping still to learn what you are teaching us,
>   instead of listening for the words you would put in our mouths.
We do not know how to be quiet.
>   We have forgotten how to meditate on your Word.
>   We have lost the childlike ability to enjoy your wonders,
>   and selfishly think that our adult judgment is needed
>   for your glories and mysteries to be valid in our world.
Overshadow us again with your powerful presence, O Lord!
>   Lift your strong voice above our foolish quackings!
>   Stun us into silence by once again revealing your Son's glory.
(Continue in silent prayer.)
Jesus did not reject Peter because of his foolish words.
>   Jesus simply instructed Peter and the others
>   to tell no one what they had seen on the mountain.
Then, when they came down from the mountain,
>   Jesus led his disciples toward Jerusalem,
>   where they would understand everything.
Brothers and sisters,
>   Jesus forgives us our foolish words,
>   and leads us to understanding.
Because Jesus forgives you,
>   you can follow him anywhere.
And, as you follow,
>   you will see his glory revealed again and again.
Amen.

___ Use the following ritual for a Festival of Jesus' Revealed Glory. Such a festival should proclaim and celebrate the glory of Jesus Christ that is revealed in his Galilean ministry leading up to the transfiguration. Choral or other special music may be substituted for some of the hymns listed below. A sermon may be omitted, as the Word communicates in more subtle ways in this festival. Drama, video projections, dance, and other visual interpretations may be used to make the readings communicate even more powerfully to the worshipers. The message will be more readily perceived by the congregation if one person can be used to read the introductions to the lessons and also lead the prayers that follow each lesson.

GREETING
PROCESSIONAL HYMN   "All Hail the Power of Jesus' Name"
OPENING PRAYER
God of epiphany,
>   like a trail of diamonds dropped for us to follow,
>   Jesus' ministry sparkles with the glory of your divinity.

His words flash visions of your kingdom,
    and his deeds blaze revelations of your heart.
Walk us up the transfiguration mountain again,
    and recharge the convictions of our faith
    by the fullness of Jesus' dazzling glory. Amen.

INTRODUCTION

Jesus reveals his heavenly glory in many ways.
According to Mark,
    the first revelation was at Jesus' baptism.

FIRST SCRIPTURE LESSON Mark 1:9-11

PRAYER

God of water and Spirit,
    heaven and earth found their union,
    as your heavenly Spirit plunged into earth's birthing waters
    to begin new life through Jesus Christ,
    who marries your divinity with our humanity.
Plunge us into those same waters,
    and make us one with you.

HYMN "When Jesus Came to Jordan"

INTRODUCTION

One of the simplest ways to recognize God's glory in Jesus
    is to watch how evil resists and rebuffs him.

SECOND LESSON Mark 1:21-28

PRAYER

Holy One of God,
    you have come to save us
    from all the evil
    that would possess our souls.
Cleanse and purge us with your love.

HYMN "Rise, Shine, You People" or "Jesus! the Name High over All"

INTRODUCTION

It is true that God alone can forgive sins.
    So when we see sins forgiven,
    we know that we have seen the glory of God.

THIRD LESSON Mark 2:1-12

PRAYER

God of forgiveness and love,
    in Jesus we have found one like you.
We feel your forgiveness,
    as he heals and makes us whole.
Jesus gives us new hope for ourselves,
    and another reason to glorify you, O God.

HYMN "Joyful, Joyful, We Adore Thee"

INTRODUCTION

When the dead live and breathe again in this world,

we know that we have seen the glory of God's eternal heaven
  breaking out on the face of our temporal earth.
FOURTH LESSON   Mark 5:21-23, 35-43
PRAYER
Eternal God,
  we see Jesus snatch life from death's eternal tomb,
  and it becomes impossible to keep such glorious news quiet.
HYMN   "Easter People, Raise Your Voices"
INTRODUCTION
When the hungry are fed,
  when real human needs are met in great abundance,
then we see the glory of God
  ministering among us.
FIFTH LESSON   Mark 6:34-44
PRAYER
We see your power and glory, O Lord,
  and we lay before you our meager offerings.
Receive them, we pray,
  and multiply them to do your blessed work
  in the midst of your chosen people.
OFFERING
HYMN   "Take Our Bread" or "Fill My Cup, Lord"
INTRODUCTION
Only God can contradict the laws of nature,
  and only God can command the forces of nature.
So, we bow before the glory of the divine Jesus,
  as he walks on water and commands the wind to stop its blowing.
SIXTH LESSON   Mark 6:45-51
PRAYER
In our fear and ignorance, O Lord,
  we need your calm guidance.
In our superstitions and weakness,
  we need your real strength.
In our troubles and trials,
  we need your sturdy love.
HYMN   "Stand By Me" or "How Firm a Foundation"
INTRODUCTION
When they climbed to the mountaintop with him,
  the disciples saw Jesus in all his heavenly glory.
May Jesus be transfigured before our eyes,
  as we hear the good news that reveals who Jesus really is.
TRANSFIGURATION LESSON   Mark 9:2-9
PRAYER
In awe and wonder we bow before your glory, Lord.
  In you we see everything that is beautiful,
  everything that is true,

everything that is good,
everything that is loving, hopeful and faithful.
The brightness of your light blinds us to all lesser lights.
You are our first morning ray, and our noonday sun.
  Night is ended forever.
  The new day of your promise is upon us, Lord.
Our praise goes up to you for the glorious gift of salvation
  that shines out to all of God's children. Amen.
HYMN "O Wondrous Sight! O Vision Fair" or
    "Christ, upon the Mountain Peak"
THE REVELATION CONTINUES
(Have a person read the following words.)
Jesus came down from the Mount of Transfiguration,
and set his face toward Jerusalem,
  where his glorious and powerful love
  would be revealed perfectly and completely
  in his crucifixion, resurrection, and ascension.
There, he spread his arms on a cross for each of us,
  and won our hearts with his proclamation of love.
At the end of time, we will all see his full glory again,
  when Jesus will return to reign forever
  and the pure love of God will prevail on earth as in heaven.
HYMN "Jesus Shall Reign" or "Come, Christians, Join to Sing" or
    "Christ, Whose Glory Fills the Skies"
COMMISSIONING AND BLESSING

___ Commissioning and Blessing

When Jesus came down from the Mount of Transfiguration
  he ordered his disciples to tell no one what they had seen,
  until after the Son of Man had risen from the dead.
Since then Jesus shocked the world by rising from the dead.
  Now you are commanded to tell everyone
  what you have seen and heard and felt
  in the living and transfiguring presence of our Savior.
And, as you witness, may the brightness of Christ
  lead you everywhere you go,
  direct everything you do,
  and fill every word you say. **Amen.**

Hymns and Choruses

(The asterisk [*] indicates hymns or choruses that are addressed to God and can be used as prayers.)

___ "All Hail the Power of Jesus' Name"

___ "Christ, upon the Mountain Peak"
___ *"Christ, Whose Glory Fills the Skies"
___ *"Gloria, Gloria"
___ "Glory to the King"
___ *"How Good, Lord, to Be Here"
___ "Let There Be Glory and Honor and Praises"
___ "Majesty, Worship His Majesty"
___ "O Light of Light, Love Given Birth"
___ "O Wondrous Sight! O Vision Fair"
___ "Oh, Wondrous Type! Oh, Vision Fair"
___ *"Songs of Thankfulness and Praise"
___ "Turn Your Eyes upon Jesus"
___ *"We Give You Praise"
___ *"We, Thy People, Praise Thee"

Reading the Scripture

___ Recruit three readers for this lesson. Have one read the narration of the text. A second reader can read Peter's words in verse 5, and the third reader (out of sight?) can read God's words in verse 7.

Responses to the Word

___ Have the worshipers make a praise offering to the Jesus revealed on the Mount of Transfiguration. Let them join in singing a continuous series of choruses, hymns and songs that praise the glory and greatness of Christ. The choir and other musicians could add their own special offerings to this time of praise.

Drama and Movement

___ Recruit three dancers to interpret this text as it is read. Instrumental music can be added as another layer of interpretation. This is a glorious text, and it ought to be gloriously proclaimed.

Visuals

___ Cover the altar table with a white cloth that reaches to the floor. Have the pastors and worship leaders wear white albs or pulpit robes. Pastors should wear white stoles. The pulpit, lectern, baptismal font, and other sanctuary furnishings should be white. Instead of regular banners, hang streamers of white cloth on the walls. Decorate the sanctuary with white flowers and white candles. If the choir does not have white robes, ask them to leave their robes on the hangers. They can wear white shirts (minus the ties and suit jackets) and blouses. The congregation can even be invited to wear white on this Sunday. One spot of color might be a gold *chi rho* (☧) appliqued to the altar table frontal.

___ Use three large white mums (or other large white flowers) in a floral arrangement to decorate the front of the sanctuary. Congregations with large sanctuaries might want to use three arrangements of white flowers, instead of individual flowers.

Anthems and Special Music

And As They Came Down from the Mountain — A. Hovhaness — SATB w/organ, tenor solo — CFP
Carol of the Transfiguration — G. Brandon — SA w/keyboard — BM
Christ Upon the Mountain Peak — P. Bouman — SATB w/organ — CPH
Christ Upon the Mountain Peak — C. Taylor — SATB w/keyboard — from *Hymnal Supplement 1991* — GIA
Fairest Lord Jesus — M. How — SAB — from *Twelve Easy Anthems* — RSCM
Jesus on the Mountain Peak — H. J. Gauntlett — SATB w/keyboard — from *With One Voice* — AF
Shine, Jesus, Shine — G. Kendrick — Unison w/keyboard — from *With One Voice* — AF
This is My Beloved Son — K. Nystedt — Unison w/keyboard — from *The First Morning Star Choir Book* — CPH
Transfiguration — J. Martinson — Unison and descant w/organ — PA
Tree of Life — M. Haugen — Unison w/keyboard — from *Hymnal Supplement 1991* — GIA

Organ and Other Keyboard Music

Christ, Whose Glory Fills the Skies (Ratisbon) — found in *Preludes for the Liturgical Year*, vol. VII — F. Peeters — CFP
O Wondrous Sight! O Vision Fair (Deo Gracias) — Partita on *Deo Gracias* — M. Burkhardt — MSM
Songs of Thankfulness and Praise (Salzburg) — found in *Songs of Thankfulness and Praise*, set 1 — W. Wold — MSM

---

1. *The United Methodist Book of Worship* (Nashville, TN: The United Methodist Publishing House, 1992), p. 88.

2. *The Book of Common Prayer* (Kingsport, TN: Kingsport Press for The Church Hymnal Corporation and The Seabury Press, 1977), p. 302.

3. *Lutheran Book of Worship* (Minneapolis: Augsburg Publishing House, 1978), p.121.

4. *Book of Worship: United Church of Christ* (New York: United Church of Christ Office for Church Life and Leadership, 1986), p. 137.

5. Fred Craddock, *Preaching the New Common Lectionary, Year B, Advent, Christmas, Epiphany* (Abingdon Press: Nashville, 1987), p. 142.

6. *Ibid.*, pp. 141-143.

7. Lamar Williamson, Jr., *Interpretation: Mark* (John Knox Press: Atlanta, 1983), p. 69.

ASH WEDNESDAY

Revised
  Common: Matthew 6:1-6, 16-21
Episcopal: Matthew 6:1-6, 16-21
Lutheran: Matthew 6:1-6, 16-21

Note: What reward do we seek from God? Financial security? Respect of others? Success in achieving our goals? What Jesus offers is eternal life in God's kingdom, starting now.

"*Do not store up for yourselves treasures on earth, where moth and rust consume and where thieves break in and steal...*"

* See Ash Wednesday in *Worship Workbook For The Gospels, Cycle A* for more material related to this lesson.

Printed Resources

___ Greeting

Ldr: Shhhhh. Don't attract attention from others.
     Come quietly before your Father in heaven,
     who sees in secret and will reward you.
Cng: **We are here, Father,**
     not to be praised by people
     but to praise you with our whole-hearted devotion.

___ Prayer

Holy God,
   we come not to be informed,
   but to be formed.
We come, not seeking human admiration,
   but to become fitting subjects
   of your eternal kingdom. Amen.

___ Litany on Piety

Ld1: Isaiah told us that putting on sackcloth and ashes
     is not a fast acceptable to God.
Ld2: The fast God chooses is to loose the chains of injustice,

96

to set the oppressed free,
to feed the hungry and shelter the poor,
to clothe the naked
and not turn away from one's flesh and blood.

Cng: **Lord, have mercy upon us.**

Ld1: Jeremiah told the people
that because of their sins and backsliding,
God would not hear their cries as they fasted
nor accept their offerings.

Ld2: Instead, Jeremiah warned the people
God planned to destroy them
with sword, famine and plague.

Cng: **Christ, have mercy upon us.**

Ld1: And through Zechariah, God questioned the people,
"When you fasted and mourned was it really for me?
And when you were eating and drinking
were you not just feasting for yourselves?"

Ld2: "This is what I really want," the Lord said.
"Administer true justice.
Show mercy and compassion to one another.
Do not oppress the widow, the fatherless,
the alien, or the poor.
In your hearts do not think evil of each other."

Cng: Lord, have mercy upon us.

Ld1: And Jesus said,
"Beware of practicing your piety before others
in order to be seen by them..."

Ld2: "...For then you have no reward
from your Father in heaven."

Cng: **Almighty Father in heaven,
reform our hearts,
redirect our wills.
Set us on a course of true piety
that will be seen and accepted
in the secret depths of your heart. Amen.**

___ Commissioning and Blessing

Give alms, pray and fast,
but keep your piety always directed
to your Father in heaven;
and your Father in heaven
will give you your reward. **Amen.**

Hymns and Choruses

(The asterisk [*] indicates hymns or choruses that are addressed to God and can be used as prayers.)

___ "A Charge to Keep I Have"
___ "Awake, My Soul, Stretch Every Nerve"
___ *"Before Thy Throne, O God, We Kneel"
___ *"Change My Heart, O God"
___ *"Dear Lord, Lead Me Day by Day"
___ *"Forth in Thy Name, O Lord"
___ *"I Want a Principle Within"
___ *"In My Life, Lord, Be Glorified"
___ "Let God Be God in Me"
___ *"Lord, I Want to Be a Christian"
___ *"Lord, Who Throughout These Forty Days"
___ *"Make Me a Captive, Lord"
___ *"Make Me a Servant"
___ *"My Life Is in You, Lord"
___ *"My Lord, My God"
___ *"Now Let Us All With One Accord"
___ *"O Jesus, I Have Promised"
___ *"Reign in Me"
___ *"Take Me In"
___ *"Take My Life, and Let It Be"
___ "Take Time to Be Holy"
___ *"The Glory of These Forty Days"
___ *"With All My Heart"

Reading the Scripture

Ld1: Beware of practicing your piety before others
    in order to be seen by them;
Cng: **for then you have no reward from your Father in heaven.**
Ld1: So wherever you give alms,
Ld2: do not sound a trumpet before,
    as the hypocrites do in the synagogues and in the streets,
    so that they may be praised by others.
Ld1: Truly I tell you,
Cng: **they have received their reward.**
Ld1: But when you give alms,
Ld2: do not let your left hand know what your right hand is doing,
    so that your alms may be given in secret;
Cng: **and your Father who sees in secret will reward you.**
Ld1: And whenever you pray,
Ld2: do not be like the hypocrites;

for they love to stand and pray in the synagogues
and at the street corners,
so that they might be seen by others.
Ld1: Truly I tell you,
Cng: **they have received their reward.**
Ld1: But whenever you pray,
Ld2: go into your room and shut the door
and pray to your Father who is in secret;
Cng: **and your Father who sees in secret will reward you.**
Ld1: And whenever you fast,
Ld2: do not look dismal, like the hypocrites,
for they disfigure their faces so as to show others
that they are fasting.
Ld1: Truly I tell you,
Cng: **they have received their reward.**
Ld1: But when you fast,
Ld2: put oil on your head and wash your face,
so that your fasting may be seen not by others
but by your Father who is in secret;
Cng: **and your Father who sees in secret will reward you.**

Responses to the Word

____ Conduct the Ash Wednesday service in a room separated from the sanctuary. Read the scripture, expound upon its meaning. Then invite the worshipers to go into the sanctuary one at a time, or in small groups, to pray, make their offering and begin a fast. Let the sanctuary be darkened, lighted by only a few candles. Let the time in the sanctuary by a quiet, secretive time for worshipers to be with God.

Drama and Movement

____ Recruit two people to prepare and present a dialogue. The first person is a hypocrite who goes through religious motions to gain the approval of others. The second person is a "reverse hypocrite."[1] This person goes through no religious motion so that he or she cannot be accused by others of being hypocritical. For example, consider the Sunday morning golfer who claims that he or she can be closer to God on the golf course than sitting in church. The preacher can then point the worshipers to the similarity between the two types of hypocrisy.

Visuals

____ Ask one of the creative people in the congregation to prepare an arrangement that reminds the worshipers of the lessons in today's gospel reading. This person can use a door, a trumpet, and a wash basin, pitcher and towel to lift up each of the three parts of the gospel lesson. Flowers can be used to add color and beauty to the arrangement.

Anthems and Special Music

Be Thou My Vision — R. Hunter — SATB w/keyboard — HIN
Have No Fear Little Flock — R. Johnson — SATB w/organ — AF
Treasures — R. Jorodahl — SATB w/opt. keyboard — NAK
Treasures in Heaven — J. Clokey — SATB w/keyboard, soprano solo — SB

Organ and Other Keyboard Music

O Lord, Throughout These Forty Days (Caithness) — found in *36 Short Preludes and Postludes on Well-Known Hymn Tunes*, set 1 — H. Willan — CFP
Take My Life, That I May Be (Patmos) — found in *Fourteen Organ Chorale Preludes* — T. Beck — AF
The Glory of These Forty Days (Erhalt uns, Herr) — found in *30 Little Chorale Preludes* — J. Bender — BAR

---

1. Fred B. Craddock, John H. Hayes, Carl R. Holladay, Gene M. Tucker, *Preaching the New Common Lectionary: Year B, Lent, Holy Week, Easter* (Abingdon Press: Nashville, 1984), p. 23.

FIRST SUNDAY OF LENT

Revised
 Common: Mark 1:9-15*
Episcopal: Mark 1:9-13*
Lutheran: Mark 1:9-15

Note: When we resign ourselves to joining Christ in his baptism, we also resign ourselves to joining him in being tempted and persecuted as we proclaim the good news.

* See Baptism of the Lord for resources related to verses 9-11.

Printed Resources

___ Greeting

Ldr: The time is fulfilled, and the kingdom of God has come near.
Cng: **Blessed be your name, O God!**
Ldr: Repent, and believe in the good news.
Cng: **May the repentance in our hearts, O God,**
match the words in our songs and prayers this day.

___ Greeting

Ldr: Jesus was in the wilderness forty days,
where Satan tempted him severely.
Cng: **Lord, you know our temptations,**
lend us your strength of faith.
Ldr: In that wilderness, Jesus was with the wild beasts,
and the angels waited on him.
Cng: **Lord, you know the same dangers and blessings we experience.**
Make us oblivious to the dangers,
and thankful for the blessings.

___ Prayer of Confession and Assurance of Pardon

Almighty God,
you have openly and lovingly called us to the way of life,

101

but time after time we have ignored your call.
Instead, we have listened to the dark whisperings of Satan,
    who leads us into death and eternal separation from you.
Call us again, Ever-Patient God.
    Restore us to your side, traveling on the way of life.
Forgive us, Holy God,
    for the evil we have done
    and for the good we have left undone.
Save us from the time of trial
    and deliver us from evil.
Give us the fortitude of Christ,
    who had the backbone to say "No" to temptations.
Bind us to his good destiny,
    with the unbreakable bonds of his undying love.
Only then will we be safe from all temptation.
    Only then will we enjoy walking in your way of life,
    with the peace and freedom that you desire for us.
    Only then will we be the faithful servants
    that we truly want to be.
Hear the good news preached by Jesus Christ,
    "The time is fulfilled,
    and the kingdom has come near."
In your repentance,
    believe Jesus' good news
    and receive your salvation from sin and death.
(Follow this with a hymn or special music that celebrates the good news.)

___ Commissioning and Blessing

Ldr: May Jesus Christ,
    who successfully faced the wild beasts
    and the temptations of Satan,
    make you successful
    in upholding our Christian faith
    as you are sent into the wilderness of daily living.
Cng: **Lord, make it so with us,**
    today and every day. Amen.

Hymns and Choruses

(The asterisk [*] indicates hymns or choruses that are addressed to God and can be used as prayers.)

___ "A Perfect Heart"
___ *"Forty Days and Forty Nights"
___ "Holy Is He"

___ *"I Want Jesus to Walk with Me"
___ "If You But Trust in God to Guide You"
___ *"In the Hour of Trial"
___ *"Lamb of God, Pure and Sinless"
___ *"Lord, Who Throughout These Forty Days"
___ "No Other Name"
___ "Now Let Us All with One Accord"
___ "O Love, How Deep"
___ *"O Jesus, I Have Promised"
___ *"On My Heart Imprint Your Image"
___ "Precious Name"
___ *"Savior, When in Dust to You"
___ "Spirit Song"
___ *"This Is the Spirit's Entry Now"
___ "We Will Triumph in the Lord"
___ "What a Friend We Have in Jesus"
___ "When Jesus Came to Jordan"
___ "Who Trusts in God, a Strong Abode"
___ *"Worthy, You Are Worthy"

Reading the Scripture

___ Before the scripture is read, ask three worshipers to volunteer to read. Have the first stand and read from the pew verses 9-11. Then have the second stand and read verses 12-13, and the third verses 14-15. (This type of reading encourages the congregation to carry and use their own Bibles.)

Responses to the Word

___ Offer an altar call to those who have not been successful in dealing with Satan's temptations. Give them time to pray concerning their own repentance, and then announce the good news of God's forgiveness through Jesus Christ. Follow this with a prayer of thanksgiving for this good news from God.

___ Throw a party celebrating Jesus' victory over temptation and sin. Have the congregation sing joyful hymns that proclaim Jesus' faithfulness in the face of temptation. Special music can be offered in the same vein. Helium-filled balloons, party hats and noisemakers can be given to the worshipers by members dressed as clowns. Cake and ice cream can be served in the fellowship hall after the service. The clowns could lead a parade from the sanctuary to the fellowship hall. Worshipers could be encouraged to revel in Jesus' victory with their noisemakers and shouts of joy while they parade to the fellowship hall. The clowns could conduct an award ceremony for resisting various temptations. Of course, all the awards are given to Jesus because Jesus is the only one to ever resist all temptations. (Be aware of the contrast between this response and the usual dismal ways the church begins the season of Lent. Worshipers may need help in understanding the difference, so be ready with this help.)

103

Drama and Movement

____ A mime troupe (or some volunteers recruited for just this one Sunday) could portray this lesson, without even reading the lesson out loud.

____ A childrens' Sunday school class could use puppets to tell this gospel story.

Visuals

____ Declare a family night. Have every person bring an old picture frame and a covered dish for supper. Then have everyone, children, youth and adults, prepare a picture of the Spirit driving Jesus into the wilderness. Have a variety of media available for people to choose for their work, everything from crayolas and magic markers to charcoal and oil paints. The picture frames are for framing all these works of art. Then have a group decorate the sanctuary with these framed pictures. One picture could be chosen for reproduction as the worship bulletin cover. A particularly wonderful picture might be enlarged for a mural that will remain in the sanctuary throughout Lent.

____ Ask a flower arranger in the congregation to prepare an arrangement to interpret verse 13. Will this person use forty flowers? Will wild beasts be represented by animal miniatures or by wild-looking flowers? How should angels be represented, and Satan? Let this person's imagination run free. If desired, a short paragraph about the arrangement could be printed in the worship bulletin.

____ Hang forty strips of purple ribbon or narrow bands of purple cloth in the sanctuary. This could be left hanging throughout Lent. Part of the length could be pinned up in back. Then as the days of Lent pass, mark each day by removing the pins and letting the ribbon or cloth hang to its full length. (Remember, Sundays are not counted in the forty days of Lent.)

____ Have one of the congregation's computer buffs work with a group of adults. The adults should name numerous temptations that people face. Then let the computer buff run these off as paper banners to be hung in the sanctuary. These banners will remind the congregation of all the temptations that surround them every day.

Anthems and Special Music

Like the Murmur of the Dove's Song — D. Robinson — Unison w/keyboard — from *Songs of Rejoicing* — SPC

Now Let Us All With One Accord — Attributed to F. Lewis/J. L. Hooker — Unison hymn w/keyboard — found in *Hymnal Supplement 91* — GIA

The Glory of These Forty Days — Attributed to M. Luther — Unison hymn w/keyboard — found in *With One Voice* — AF

Triune God, Mysterious Being — A. Fedak — Unison w/keyboard — from *Songs of Rejoicing* — SPC

When Jesus Came to Jordan — English Folk/R. Vaughan Williams — Unison w/keyboard — from *With One Voice* — AF

Organ and Other Keyboard Music

If You But Trust in God to Guide You (Wer nur den lieben Gott) — found in *An Organ Book* — U. S. Leupold — AF (Chantry)

Lamb of God, Pure and Sinless (O Lamm Gottes, unschuldig) — J. Pachelbel — found in *80 Chorale Preludes - German Masters of the 17th and 18th Centuries* — CFP

Savior, When in Dust to You (Aberystwyth) — found in *Two Communion Meditations* — E. Childs — HWG

SECOND SUNDAY OF LENT

"If anyone would come after me, he must deny himself and take up his cross and follow me."
—Mark 8:34

Angie Latta

Revised
  Common: Mark 8:31-38*
Episcopal: Mark 8:31-38*
Lutheran: Mark 8:31-38*

Note: Faithful discipleship means following Jesus, even when it contradicts common sense, denies our human nature, or challenges our religious beliefs.

---

* More material relating to this lesson can be found on Proper 19.

Printed Resources

___ Greeting

Ldr: Jesus taught his disciples
  that the Son of Man must undergo great suffering
  and be rejected by the elders,
  the chief priests,
  and the scribes,
  and be killed,
  and after three days rise again.
Cng: **Lord, these are harsh words in our ears.**
  They contradict our understanding of fame and success.
  Teach our hearts to receive your ways.
Ldr: Then Jesus called the crowd and his disciples and said,
  "If any want to become my followers,
  let them deny themselves
  and take up their cross
  and follow me."
Cng: **Lord, it is hard enough to hear**
  that you will suffer and be killed.
  But now you call us to deny our own natures,
  and to follow you in suffering and being killed.
  If it were not for your love, Lord, we would turn away.
  But you have captured our hearts,
  so follow you we must.

___ Prayer

Crossbearing Savior, Author of Perfect Love,
I will follow you
    up the treacherous slopes of the world's highest mountains,
    and down the deepest caves into the bowels of the earth.
I will follow you
    through howling storms that tear away every fiber of courage,
    and into miles of muck and mud congealing in endless boredom.
I will follow you
    as the weight of my own cross bears down on me,
    and even in those times when you shoulder both our crosses.
I will follow you
    as death stands before me, threatening my every step,
    and as following gets really hard in living that is too easy.
I will follow you,
    my Teacher, my Guide, my Christ.
Now, I pray, make my heart as brave as my words. Amen.

___ Commissioning and Blessing

Do not follow our Savior,
    who undergoes great suffering, rejection and death,
    unless you are willing to deny yourself
    and take up your own cross.
Because those who follow Christ
    will find a cross laid upon their shoulders.
But do follow our Savior,
    who is resurrected, ascended to heaven and comes again soon,
    if you want to forfeit your life in this world,
    in order to save your life for the new world that never ends.
Because anyone who follows Christ
    will receive new life in the glory of God's eternal love.
Let it be so with you, today and every day,
    in the name of the Father, Son, and Holy Spirit. **Amen.**

___ Commissioning and Blessing

Go out singing and shouting
    about the one of whom you've heard here today.
Do not be ashamed of Jesus our Christ,
    or of his teachings;
but proclaim Christ to all you meet:
    to the poor and the broken,
    to the successful and the influential,
    to all of God's children far and wide.

And when Jesus returns in the glory of his Father,
    Jesus will not be ashamed of you.
Thanks be to God, Father, Son and Holy Spirit. **Amen.**

Hymns and Choruses

(The asterisk [*] indicates hymns or choruses that are addressed to God and can be used as prayers.)

___ "All Depends on Our Possessing"
___ "Am I a Soldier of the Cross"
___ "'Come, Follow Me,' the Savior Spoke"
___ *"God of Grace and God of Glory"
___ "Fight the Good Fight with All Thy Might"
___ "Let Us Ever Walk with Jesus"
___ "Lift High the Cross"
___ "Must Jesus Bear the Cross Alone"
___ "Onward, Christian Soldiers"
___ "Rejoice, Ye Pure in Heart"
___ "Stand Up, Stand Up for Jesus"
___ "Take Up Thy Cross"
___ "'Take Up Your Cross,' the Savior Said"
___ "The Battle Belongs to the Lord"
___ "Where He Leads Me"
___ *"Who Trusts in God, a Strong Abode"
___ *"Your Kingdom Come, O Father"

Reading the Scripture

___ Print this text in the worship bulletin. Divide the reading between the congregation and one strong solo voice. The congregation reads verses 31-33a. The solo voice reads Jesus' words in 33b. The congregation reads 34a. Then the solo voice concludes the reading with the rest of Jesus' words.

___ Use the hymn "Am I a Soldier of the Cross" as a sung congregational response to the words of the gospel lesson. Have someone read the verses as listed below, pausing as the congregation sings the stanzas of the hymn.
    Verses 31-32
    Hymn stanza 1
    Verse 33
    Hymn stanza 2
    Verse 34
    Hymn stanza 3
    Verse 35
    Hymn stanza 4
    Verse 36-37

Hymn stanza 5
Verse 38
Hymn stanza 6

Responses to the Word

___ Use the prayer printed above for the congregation to affirm their desire to take up their crosses and follow Jesus wherever he might lead.

___ Have the congregation join in an affirmation of faith to demonstrate that they are not ashamed of their relationship with Jesus Christ.

___ Prepare a bulletin insert that the worshipers can use to respond to the challenge to take up their crosses and not be ashamed of their Christian faith. This insert would have a list of things that could be checked off by the worshiper. Then the worshipers can put their finished list in the offering plate, or bring it forward and lay it on the altar. The list could include items such as these:
1. I will write letters to editors of secular newspapers or magazines to make a Christian witness concerning some social issue.
2. I will join a group of people who are demonstrating against some action or decision that is contrary to the teachings of Christ, and will work with them to reverse the action or decision.
3. I will write poems or compose songs that proclaim the good news of Jesus Christ and work hard to get them published.
4. I will confront friends or fellow workers who tell jokes distasteful to the Christian faith, or who use the name of our Lord as a curse word.
5. I will work with young people in such a way that I can share my Christian faith with them.
6. I will tell other people about the love of Christ and encourage them to open their lives to a relationship with the living Christ.
7. I will make business decisions on the basis of my Christian faith, rather than on the basis of what will make the most money.

Drama and Movement

___ Embellish the text a little. Choose two people to act this out. One will be Jesus and one Peter. Put the two in period costumes. Let Jesus and Peter enter the sanctuary from the back. As they enter, Jesus tells the congregation about the suffering, rejection and death that must be endured by the Son of Man. These teachings could be quotes lifted from other sections of Mark's gospel, or from the other gospel writers as well. Peter visibly objects to what Jesus is revealing, and when they reach the front of the sanctuary Peter takes Jesus aside. In a stage whisper Peter tells Jesus not to say these things so openly. Jesus looks at the congregation, and loudly shouts for all to hear the words recorded in 33b-38. Then, as his words sink into people's understanding, Jesus and Peter quietly exit.

___ Let a group of adults or older youth create and present three skits that depict contemporary people denying themselves and taking up their crosses.

Visuals

___ Arrange a large bouquet of flowers for the front of the sanctuary. Take one boldly-colored flower and lay it on the table to the side and a little away from the bouquet. This can represent Jesus' rejection of Peter's way of thinking.

___ Remove the brass cross from the altar table, if there is one there, and use a life-size wooden cross at the front of the sanctuary. This could stand on the floor, be hung from the ceiling, or just be leaned against the altar table. Flowers should not be used to make the cross more attractive. Let it stand out in all its ugliness.

___Ask an artist in the congregation to prepare two murals to be hung in the sanctuary. The first should show people acting ashamed of Jesus Christ, and the second should show Christ coming in the clouds and acting ashamed of the people.

Anthems and Special Music

Weary of All Trumpeting — H. Distler — Unison hymn w/keyboard — found in *Hymnal Supplement 91* — GIA
Above the Voices of the World Around Me — A. Fedak — Unison w/keyboard — from *Songs of Rejoicing* — SPC

Organ and Other Keyboard Music

Lift High the Cross (Crucifer) — Processional on Crucifer — D. Busarow — CPH
Onward, Christian Soldiers (St. Gertrude) — found in *Six Preludes for Organ* — L. Groom — HWG
Stand Up, Stand Up for Jesus (Webb) — G. Young — found in *Contemporary Hymn Preludes* — HPC

THIRD SUNDAY
OF LENT

Revised
  Common: John 2:13-22
Episcopal: John 2:13-22
Lutheran: John 2:13-22

Note: Familiarity breeds contempt. The resurrection, sign of Christ's authority and truth, would put normal people on their knees at the sight of such a powerful miracle.

Printed Resources

___ Greeting

(The congregational responses printed below should be sung. They are from the refrain of "All Creatures of Our God and King," and can be sung to that tune.)

Ldr: People of God, now is the time
   when we worship God in Spirit and in truth.

Cng: **O praise ye! O praise ye!**
   Allelulia! Allelulia! Allelulia!

Ldr: Almighty and Holy God,
   this Sunday hour for worshiping you is not enough;
   and so we give you every hour of every day of our lives,
   as our living sacrifice offered continuously to you.

Cng: **O praise ye! O praise ye!**
   Allelulia! Allelulia! Allelulia!

Ldr: We gather in this building dedicated to you,
   but the only temple we worship
   is the one raised by your Son, Jesus Christ.

Cng: **O praise ye! O praise ye!**
   Alelulia! Allelulia! Allelulia!

Ldr: We reach up to you
   with familiar forms, prayers and songs;
   knowing they would all fall short
   if it were not for your grace reaching down.

Cng: **O praise ye! O praise ye!**
   Allelulia! Allelulia! Allelulia!

Ldr: Your house of prayer is not a place,
or a time, or a set ritual.
It is your sheltering embrace
that covers us continuously with your love.

Cng: **O praise ye! O praise ye!**
Allelulia! Allelulia! Allelulia!

(Let the congregation join in singing "All Creatures of Our God and King" at this point.)

___ Prayer of Confession and Assurance of Pardon

Almighty God, we are a sinful people.
We always want to control things —
like the Jews in Jesus' time who tried to control their lives
by placing the Temple at the center of their adoration.
Jesus threatened their temple and all their customs,
because he called upon them to worship only you,
the one who really has control over our lives.
How many times have we tried to take control from you,
by worshiping a church building, or a certain pastor,
a particular custom, or some other transient object?
And every time we do this,
we set up that thing we worship for destruction,
because you will tolerate no other gods before you.
Forgive our sinfulness, God of our beginning and our end.
Help us once again to bow down before you,
and to submit our lives and fortunes to your gentle control.
Take charge of our days. Lead us on the paths you choose.
Because neither the stones of temples nor the wood of churches
can add even one more breath to the extent of our lives.
Only you, God, can save us,
and only Christ can open the door to eternity for us.
(Continue in silent prayer.)
Take heart, brothers and sisters,
for Jesus cleansed the temple,
and Jesus has cleansed your souls.
And as a sign of his truth and power,
Jesus offers us the temple of his body,
that was destroyed and raised again in three days.
Rejoice and be glad,
because God has given Jesus control over our destinys.

___ Commissioning and Blessing

"Destroy this temple, and in three days I will raise it up"
is the sign that Jesus gave his critics.
Now go and tell others that Jesus has kept his promise.

This and all other signs point to Jesus,
   the Son of God and Savior of the world.
May you always remember Jesus' words,
   and believe the holy scriptures.
Such faith will be rewarded,
   as you are raised up at the end of time,
   in the name of the Father, Son and Holy Spirit. **Amen.**

Hymns and Choruses

(The asterisk [*] indicates hymns or choruses that are addressed to God and can be used as prayers.)

___ "All My Hope on God Is Founded"
___ *"Creator of the Earth and Skies"
___ "He Is Lord"
___ "He Is Lovely"
___ *"Hope of the World"
___ *"Jesus, We Want to Meet"
___ *"O Thou Who Camest from Above"
___ *"O Young and Fearless Prophet"
___ "Rise, Shine, You People"
___ "What Does the Lord Require"

Reading the Scripture

___ Print the gospel lesson in the worship bulletin. Divide the reading among three groups. Have a leader in front read the narrative portion. Let the congregation on the right side of the sanctuary read the words of Jesus, and those on the left read the words of the Jews. The congregation might follow this reading by singing a chorus such as "Majesty, Worship His Majesty" or singing the refrains from hymns such as "Wonderful Words of Life" or "Thy Word Is a Lamp."

Responses to the Word

___ After a sermon on how people commit idolatry by worshiping church buildings, rituals, and other trappings of religion, have the congregation join in the prayer of confession printed above.

___ After a sermon on how Jesus lays down his life as the most authentic sign possible for proving his love and heavenly authority, invite the worshipers to come to the altar rail to recommit their lives to the one who would make such a sacrifice for them.

___ Allow the worshipers time for silent reflection on whether they are using their temples (their bodies) as houses of prayer or if they are making themselves into no more than marketplaces. After the time of reflection have the worshipers join in a hymn about prayer such as "O Thou Who Camest from Above," "Come Down, O Love Divine," or "Holy Spirit, Truth Divine."

Drama and Movement

___ After the gospel reading have mimes act out the resurrection of Jesus. Use John's twentieth chapter to guide the actions. Mary Magdalene comes in and sees the stone removed from the tomb. She runs to Simon Peter and the other disciple. They run to the tomb. The other disciple looks in the tomb and sees the linen grave wrappings. When Peter arrives, he enters the tomb and the other disciple follows him. They see the tomb holds only the abandoned wrappings, and this is enough for the other disciple to believe. Peter and the other disciple return to their homes. Only Mary remains, weeping outside the empty tomb. She looks into the tomb and sees two angels. She indicates she is looking for Jesus' body. She turns and sees Jesus but does not recognize him. She indicates to him that she is looking for Jesus' missing body. If the mimes are not strict about never speaking, it would be very effective to have Jesus just say the one word, "Mary!" Realizing who Jesus is, Mary falls at his feet. Then she runs out to tell the others. Jesus exits in another direction. And the congregation understands that Jesus' promised sign has been realized.

Visuals

___ Have the people in the congregation who arrange flowers create three arrangements of similar composition. Set these three arrangements in a row in the front of the sanctuary to remind the worshipers of Jesus' prophecy that he would raise up the temple of his body three days after it was destroyed.

___ Use a cage with a pair of live doves in it to decorate in the front of the sanctuary. Put a small table beside the cage and pile coins on the table. Make a whip of cords and lay it across the table. Use live green plants and a few large stone blocks (if you can find them in your area) to complete the scene.

Anthems and Special Music

Christ Is Made the Sure Foundation — D. Wood — SATB w/organ — AP
Christ is Made the Sure Foundation — H. Purcell (adapted) — SATB w/keyboard — from *Hymnal Supplement 1991* — GIA
Jesus and the Traders — Z. Kodaly — SATB w/opt. keyboard — BH

Organ and Other Keyboard Music

All My Hope on God is Founded (Michael) — P. Bouman — found in *The Concordia Hymn Prelude Series*, vol. 32 — CPH
Hope of the World (Donne secours) — found in *Hymns for the Church Year* — R. Petrich — AF
Rise, Shine You People (Wojtkiewiecz) — found in *A New Song* — G. Krapf — SMP

FOURTH SUNDAY OF LENT

Revised
 Common: John 3:14-21
Episcopal: John 6:4-15*
Lutheran: John 3:14-21

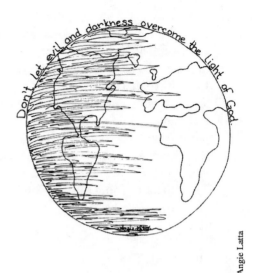

Angie Latta

Note: It is easy to give everything we have to Christ, because Christ has already given everything he had to us.

---

*See Proper 12 for material related to this text.

Printed Resources

___ Greeting

Ldr: At God's command,
       Moses lifted up a bronze serpent on a staff,
       so that people bitten by poisonous snakes
       could look at it and live.
Cng: **Blessed be the name of our God who works miracles.**
Ldr: At God's command,
       Jesus allowed himself to be lifted up on a cross,
       so that people poisoned by Satan's ways
       could look to him for salvation and life.
Cng: **Blessed be our God whose miraculous name is love.**

___ Prayer of Confession and Assurance of Pardon

Ldr: The judgment at the end of time is this,
       that the light has come into the world,
       and people loved darkness rather than light
       because their deeds were evil.
Cng: **Lord have mercy.**
Ldr: For all who do evil hate the light
       and do not come to the light,
       so that their deeds may not be exposed.
Cng: **Christ have mercy.**

115

Ldr: But those who do what is true come to the light,
     so that it may be clearly seen
     that their deeds have been done in God.
Cng: **Lord have mercy.**
(Let the congregation pray silently concerning their personal deeds of darkness.)
Ldr: God did not send the Son into the world to condemn,
     but in order that you might be saved through him.
     Repent and believe the good news concerning
     your forgiveness, salvation and new life in Christ.
Cng: **Thanks be to you, O great God of love. Amen.**

___ Prayer

Rgt: **Holy God,**
Lft: **even though we**
Rgt: **forget you,**
Lft: **deny you,**
Rgt: **resist you,**
Lft: **run from you,**
Rgt: **betray you,**
Lft: **disobey you,**
Rgt: **belittle you,**
Lft: **ignore you,**
Rgt: **fight you,**
Lft: **replace you,**
Rgt: **test you,**
Lft: **and otherwise try your tolerance;**
Rgt: **you still love us so much**
Lft: **that you give us your only Son.**
Rgt: **Thank you.**
Lft: **Thank you.**
Rgt: **Thank you.**
Lft: **Thank you.**
All: **Amen.**

___ Commissioning and Blessing

Jesus Christ has been lifted up for your salvation.
     Keep your eyes on him,
     and he will lead you on the path of life. **Amen.**

Hymns and Choruses

(The asterisk [*] indicates hymns or choruses that are addressed to God and can be used as prayers.)

___ "Christ Is the World's Light"
___ *"Eternal Light, Shine in My Heart"
___ "I Want to Walk as a Child of the Light"
___ *"Jesus, Refuge of the Weary"
___ *"Jesus, Thy Boundless Love to Me"
___ "Morning Glory, Starlit Sky"
___ "My Song Is Love Unknown"
___ *"O God, I Love Thee"
___ *"O Love Divine, What Hast Thou Done"
___ "Oh, How He Loves You and Me"
___ "Praise to the Holiest in the Height"
___ "Rise, Shine, You People"
___ "Sing, My Soul, His Wondrous Love"
___ "The Great Creator of the Worlds"
___ "There's a Wideness in God's Mercy"
___ "To God Be the Glory"
___ "What Wondrous Love Is This"
___ "When Morning Gilds the Skies"

Reading the Scripture

___ This would be a good lesson to be recited by one of the people in the congregation who is good at memorizing scripture. Have him stand near the people and speak the words of the lesson in a normal conversational tone of voice.

___ Congregations that like to have their children memorize and recite scripture could find few texts as fitting as today's lesson for this purpose. Six children could recite this lesson by dividing up the verses as follows: 14-15, 16, 17, 18, 19, and 20-21.

___ This lesson could also be read responsively, with the congregation using pew Bibles to read every other verse.

Responses to the Word

___ This would be a good Sunday to extend an invitation to people who have not yet commited their lives to Christ. This could be done with an altar call, with a raised hand while the person remains in the pew, or even in silent prayer where the worshipers can make their commitment without the public display of faith. Sometimes Christians put stumbling blocks in the path of those coming to believe in Christ because of the insistence that everything must be done publicly. Some new believers are not ready to share publicly this unfamiliar experience at first. That will come later, as their faith matures and deepens.

___ Hand out candles to the worshipers as they enter the sanctuary. Then, after a sermon on those who do and do not come to the light, invite the worshipers to come forward to light their candles from the main candles on (or near) the altar table. After their candles are lit have them form a circle to sing a hymn like "Pass It On." The pastor could conclude the worship service by talking about how Christians are meant to live in the light, and challenging the worshipers to do so with their actions in the coming weeks.

Drama and Movement

___ Gather a group of young people and adults to present two dramatic sketches. The first should go back into time and present the Numbers 21:4-9 story of Moses lifting up the serpent. The second should bring the good news of John 3:14-21 into the worshipers' contemporary world, where people are still saved from "the Serpent's" poison by looking to Jesus Christ for their salvation and life.

___ Mimes could work with the themes of light and darkness in verses 19-21. Turn out the sanctuary lights and let them tell their story with flashlights and maybe one or two good floodlights.

Visuals

___ Recruit someone from the congregation to prepare an arrangement of flowers with a tau cross (looks like the letter "T") rising up out of it. Use a rubber snake painted a bronze color (see Numbers 21:9) or dried grapevine to represent the serpent mentioned in verse 14.

___ Protestants might explore using a crucifix as one of the symbols useful in conveying the impact of this gospel lesson.

___ Have volunteers decorate the front of the sanctuary with live green plants to represent eternal life. Intersperse red roses throughout the green leaves of the live plants to represent the love of God. Put a single white rose in one of the plants to represent the Son that God gave for the sake of the world.

___ Ask one of the congregation's banner makers to prepare a large banner for this Sunday. Have this person use bright yellows and whites at one of the top corners of the banner (almost like a bright, shining sun) to represent the light that comes into the world. At the opposing bottom corner dark blues, purples and black can be used to represent the darkness that evil people prefer. Put numerous dark figures cowering in the dark lower corner of the banner. Put these figures in various postures. Some can be afraid of the light, others can be trying to push the light back, and other attitudes toward the light of God can be represented like this. Above the figures in the dark lower corner, have the banner maker place two or three figures standing erect with arms extended to the light coming from the top corner. These figures should be standing in the light to represent those who do what is true and do not mind their deeds being seen.

Anthems and Special Music

(John 3:14-21)
Also hat Gott die welt geliebt — D. Buxtehude — high solo w/2 violins, continuo — BAR
Baptized in Water — Gaelic tune/B. W. Bisbee — SATB w/keyboard — from *With One Voice* — AF

Comfortable Words — L. Betteridge — SATB w/keyboard — PA

For God So Loved the World — H. Distler — SAB unaccompanied — CPH

For God So Loved the World — R. Edwards — Unison w/keyboard — from *Songs of Rejoicing* — SPC

For God So Loved the World — D. Grotenhuis — SATB w/keyboard — MSM

For God So Loved the World — H. Schütz — SATTB — from *A Second Motet Book* — CPH

God is Love — G. George — SA — AF

God Loved the World — SATB — from *The Church Choir Book II* — CPH

God's Love — B. Burroughs — high solo w/keyboard — from *New Testament Songs* — HP

God So Loved the World — K. Bissell — Unison — from *O Come Let Us Sing* — WAT

God So Loved the World — Bruckner/Klein — SATB unaccompanied — GIA

God So Loved The World — O. Gibbons — SAATB unaccompanied — NOV

God So Loved the World — J. Goss — SATB — from *The Church Anthem Book* — OUP

God So Loved the World — F. J. Haydn/A. Lovelace — SATB w/keyboard — AF

God So Loved the World — J. MacDermid — low, med., or high solo w/keyboard — FOR

God So Loved the World — J. Stainer — available in various voicings — available with various publishers (GS)

God So Loved the World — G. P. Telemann — SAB — from *The SAB Choir Goes for Baroque* — CPH

Great God of All the Universe — J. Pinson — Unison w/keyboard — from *Songs of Rejoicing* — SPC

Sicut Moses — D. Buxtehude — high solo w/organ — BAR

The Gospel Shows the Father's Grace — M. Rottermund — SA — CPH

Truly, Truly, I Say to You — G. Krapf — Unison — CPH

(John 6:4-15)
See Proper 12

Organ and Other Keyboard Music

Jesus, Refuge of the Weary (O du Liebe meiner Liebe) — found in *Preludes on Six Hymn Tunes* — J. Engel — AF

My Song is Love Unknown (Love Unknown) — found in *Eight Hymn Preludes for Lent* — P. Stearns — HF

What Wondrous Love is This (Wondrous Love) — Variations on a Shape-Note Hymn — S. Barber — GS

FIFTH SUNDAY OF LENT

Revised
 Common: John 12:20-33
Episcopal: John 12:20-33
Lutheran: John 12:20-33

Gail Throckmorton Warner

Note: Jesus is the model for human life. Watch how he denies his own will and submits himself continually to God's will.

Printed Resources

___ Greeting
(In the congregational response printed below, "Lead Me, Lord," can be sung from *The United Methodist Hymnal*, page 473.)

Ldr: Jesus said, "Whoever serves me must follow me."
Cng: **Lead me, Lord, lead me in righteousness;**
  make thy way plain before my face.
  For it is thou, Lord, thou, Lord only,
  that makest me dwell in safety.
Ldr: And Jesus said, "Where I am, there will my servant be also."
Cng: **Lead me, Lord, lead me in righteousness;**
  make thy way plain before my face.
  For it is thou, Lord, thou, Lord only,
  that makest me dwell in safety.
Ldr: And Jesus said, "Whoever serves me, the Father will honor."
Cng: **Lead me, Lord, lead me in righteousness;**
  make thy way plain before my face.
  For it is thou, Lord, thou, Lord only,
  that makest me dwell in safety.

___ Greeting

Ld1: "The hour has come for the Son of Man to be glorified."
Ld2: "The world has gone after him!"
Cng: **Jews and Greeks, Africans and Europeans,**
  North and South Americans, Asians and Pacific Islanders,
  every people in every country on every continent,

have a church kneeling before your glory, Lord,
on this, the day you made beautiful with your faithfulness.

Ld1: "Now is the judgment of this world;
now the ruler of this world will be driven out."

Ld2: Because Jesus Christ has been "lifted up from the earth,"
and is drawing all people to himself.

Cng: **At the chosen hour, you died on the cross, Lord,**
and now you bear much fruit for the glory of God.
Your glory grows as the church follows your path,
and as we serve you, the Father honors us,
and gathers us to be kept for life eternally.

___ Prayer of Confession and Assurance of Pardon

Heavenly Father,
Jesus tells us that whoever serves him will follow him,
but we have not done this.
Often we have followed our own selfish ways,
or the ways demanded by other people who do not follow Jesus.
This disobedience has kept us from serving him.
Jesus tells us that wherever he is,
his servants will be there too.
But Jesus has gone to places and to people
that make us feel uncomfortable.
So we have not gone everywhere that Jesus has gone.
This disobedience has separated us from him.
Finally, Jesus assures us that those who serve him
will be honored by you, our heavenly Father.
But when we have not served, when we have not followed,
when we have not been there, how can you honor us?
Can you remove our shame and make the dishonorable honorable?
Will you once again show mercy, forgive and remake us?
Will you? Please.
(The people pray in silence, and then the pastor says the following.)
When Jesus was lifted up onto the cross all the world was judged,
and the ruler of this world was driven out.
Now Jesus draws all people to himself,
to follow him,
to be with him,
and to be honored by our heavenly Father,
who, in his infinite mercy,
has once again forgiven you,
and again bestowed honor upon you,
all because you are still drawn to Jesus, our Savior.
Amen.

___ Commissioning and Blessing

Those who love their life lose it,
and those who hate their life in this world
    will keep it for eternal life,
in the name of the Father, Son and Holy Spirit. **Amen.**

___ Commissioning and Blessing

Jesus said,
    "Unless a grain of wheat falls into the earth and dies,
    it remains just a single grain;
    but if it dies,
    it bears much fruit."
May his dying bear fruit in your life,
    for the sake of our God and for the coming kingdom. **Amen.**

Hymns and Choruses

(The asterisk [*] indicates hymns or choruses that are addressed to God and can be used as prayers.)

___ *"Day by Day"
___ *"Dear Lord, Lead Me Day by Day"
___ "Hallelujah! What a Savior"
___ "Here I Am"
___ "In Christ There Is No East or West"
___ "Jesus Calls Us"
___ "Lift High the Cross"
___ *"Make Me a Servant"
___ "Now the Green Blade Riseth"
___ *"O Jesus, I Have Promised"
___ *"We Would See Jesus"
___ "Where He Leads Me"

Reading the Scripture

___ Recruit two readers. The first will read the lesson. The second will provide the voice of God that sounds like thunder in verse 28b. Let this person read the words of God into a hidden microphone so that it interrupts and disturbs the contemporary followers of Jesus like it did the first followers.

___ Recruit a man and a woman to read this lesson. Divide the reading as follows:
Verses 20-22
Verses 23-24
Verse 25

Verse 26
Verses 27-29
Verses 30-32
Verse 33

Responses to the Word

____ Use the second greeting printed above as an affirmation of faith. Then follow this with a hymn such as "All Hail the Power of Jesus' Name," "Jesus Shall Reign," "Ye Servants of God," or "Jesus! the Name High Over All."

____ Use the prayer of confession and assurance of pardon printed above to follow a sermon on people not following or serving Jesus.

____ Have the congregation join in praying (by singing) a hymn like "O Jesus, I Have Promised" or "Dear Lord, Lead Me Day by Day."

Drama and Movement

____ Two liturgical dancers could interpret this text. Let one interpret the words of Jesus, and the other interpret the rest of the text.

____ Intersperse the following vignettes in the worship service so as to allow time for make-up people to age the pastor and his wife.

ACT 1

Terry: Honey, are you sure that you want to do this? These people run this town. They could destroy this church. They could destroy your ministry. Ken, they could destroy us. How much of this do you think I can take?

Ken: But they're wrong! They're nothing but a bunch of slum landlords! And what they are doing has destroyed hundreds of lives already. Children have died in those rat-holes they call apartments! How can I let these people get away with murder? How can I let them drain the last drop of hope from those poor people who have no place else to go? Those people are counting on me.

Terry: I'm counting on you too, Ken. I want to have children of my own. I want to live a normal life. I don't want to fight a war. (She puts her arms around him.) I want to raise a family. Is that too much to ask?

Ken: No, Terry. It's not too much to ask. (He stands, and looks up.) God, why does everything have to be so hard? I didn't ask for this. I just wanted to preach the gospel, visit people in the hospital, and raise my family in peace. I don't think I'm ready for all this. (They exit.)

ACT 2

Ken: (He hurries into the room where Terry is sitting.) Terry! I know why I was called to this church now!

Terry: Good! (She has second thoughts.) Er, at least I think it's good.

Ken: (He ignores her hesitation.) I was finishing my evening prayers when I heard it.

Terry: Heard what?

Ken: It was like this voice. It was all so clear. I understand everything now.

Terry: You sure it wasn't just thunder from the storm that is moving in?

Ken: Stop kidding, Terry. I'm serious.

Terry: I know you are dear. And that always frightens me.

Ken: The decision whether this church is going to live or die is being made right now. They're either going to become more and more ingrown and die, or they will learn to begin reaching out, giving themselves to others, and live on to minister for Jesus Christ.

Terry: Ken, you and I both know that these people have already made that decision. They don't want to reach out to anybody else. They like things just the way they are.

Ken: I know, and that is what I'm here to change.

Terry: Then there's a storm brewing alright, and I'm not talking about the weather outside.

Ken: (He ignores her comment.) No longer am I going to sit by quietly while Mrs. Grundy repeats for the ten thousandth time, "Charity begins at home." She hasn't got a charitable bone in her whole body. She just wants to make sure that she can control how every dime, nickel and penny is spent. And then there's our marvelous chairman of the evangelism committee, and his insistence that we not pester any unchurched people with the gospel message. "Might make them mad, and then they'll never come to our church." How he ever became the chairman of evangelism I'll never understand.

Terry: Ken, I'm not kidding. You're brewing up the makings of a terrible storm. Are you sure you heard your voice correctly?

Ken: I heard it loud and clear. Why, do you know that just last Sunday, I told the kids in the youth group that I knew some unchurched youth that they could invite to the youth meetings? They were all excited about building up the group, until I told them the names of the young people I had in mind. Then they began listing all the reasons why they couldn't stand having those kids in our youth group. Terry, the youth sounded just like the adults in this church!

Terry: I know, Ken. This church has already made up its mind.

Ken: But they will die this way. Maybe not in the next year or two, but I guarantee you they are on the path toward closing the church!

Terry: I know, but you can't change them. They've made up their minds, and if you try to change them they'll crucify you. Are you ready for that again? We've been through one war. Do you really want to do it again? Last time it got so bad they almost destroyed our marriage. Are you ready to put us on the rocks again? And this time we have our children to think of. You know how mean people can be. Are you willing to put your kids through that?

Ken: I don't know, Terry. I only know that I heard a clear voice telling me what to do. But I really don't know whether I have the strength to obey. (He listens to far-off thunder.) That really is thunder isn't it?

Terry: In more ways than one. I'm afraid we're in for another big storm, aren't we? (They exit.)

ACT 3

(The scene opens with Terry bent over, sobbing with grief. A woman stands beside her, and is trying to comfort her.)

Woman 1: Your husband is a hero. There were a lot of us standing here wishing we could do something to rescue those boys from that icy river, but your husband was the only one willing to go into that water to save them. And the way he took that rope off himself and tied it to those kids is something that I will never forget. I know that I couldn't have done it. But it saved those kids. And your husband almost made it too! For a man his age he certainly was a strong swimmer. So close. But then he just slipped under the water and disappeared. I've never seen anything so heroic in all my life.

Terry: (She speaks very quietly through her tears.) He was no hero.

Woman 1: What did you say?

Terry: (She speaks louder.) Ken was no hero. He was just an ordinary man listening to the voice of God.

Woman 1: I don't mean to disagree with you, but it seems to me that anyone who gives his life to save someone else's is a pretty heroic person.

Terry: Dying was no big deal to Ken. He had done it so many times before. (She reflects for a moment, and then continues.) The first time was probably the hardest. Those land-lords were terribly cruel to us. It nearly destroyed Ken to see how much those people had hurt me, but God picked us up and put us both   back together again. (Don enters from behind Terry while she is talking.) And after that Ken was never again afraid of death, never again afraid to risk everything.

Don: He certainly wasn't afraid to risk everything to turn our church around.

Terry: (She sees Don for the first time, and throws her arms around him.) Oh, Don, he's left me for good this time.

Don: I came as soon as I heard.

Terry: What am I going to do without him, Don?

Don: We're all going to miss him. He did a lot of good with his life.

Terry: I wish that were true, Don. The truth is that Ken did a lot of good by his dying, not his living. (She sobs again as another woman walks to her side.) I wonder what good will come from this.

Woman 2: Excuse me. I just learned that you were the wife of the man who saved my daughter. Was his name Reverend Ken Smith?

Terry: Yes.

Woman 2: What a small world. I just love that man. Do you know that this is the second time he saved my daughter's life?

Terry: What do you mean?

Woman 2: When she was just a little baby we lived in the city, and Reverend Ken forced my landlord to fix the heat in our building. That was a terribly cold winter, and I just know that my baby would never have made it through the winter if God hadn't sent your husband to get our heat turned back on. And now God sent him back to save her again. God must have some pretty important plans for my daughter to send your husband to save her twice. Well, I have to go with her to the hospital, but I just had to talk to you before we left. I know my blessing is your tragedy. But, if it's any comfort to you, my daughter and I will never, ever forget what Reverend Ken did for us. (She exits.)

Don: Terry, do you remember the scripture that Ken kept quoting?

Terry: How can I forget? "Unless a grain of wheat falls into the earth and dies, it remains just a single grain; but if it dies, it bears much fruit."

Don: Ken lived that scripture over and over, and he is still bearing fruit.

Terry: He followed Jesus every step of the way. I just hope I'm strong enough to do the same.

Don: Come on. I'll take you home. (They exit.)

Visuals

___ Recruit one of the congregation's banner makers to make a banner that shows a single grain of seed, under the ground. Above ground a huge plant that bears many grains of seed should be shown.

___ After a sermon on how Christ is glorified in being "lifted up from the earth," project slides of famous works of art depicting Christ on the cross. While projecting these, have the congregation sing various choruses such as "Majesty, Worship His Majesty," "His Name Is Wonderful," and "Turn Your Eyes upon Jesus."

Anthems and Special Music

A Great Harvest — A. Peloquin — SATB w/organ — GIA
If I Be Lifted Up — M. Blankenship — SATB w/keyboard — BP
Servants of God — E. Butler — SATB w/organ, opt. handbells — HWG
The Word of God is Source and Seed — D. Hurd — Unison w/keyboard — from *With One Voice* — AF

Organ and Other Keyboard Music

Jesus Calls Us (Galilee) — found in *Eight Hymn Preludes* — A. Lovelace — AF
Now the Green Blade Riseth (Noel Nouvelet) — C. Schalk — found in *Concordia Hymn Prelude Series*, vol. 11 — CPH
O Jesus, I Have Promised (Munich) — found in *Ten Hymn Tune Fantasies* — C. McKinley — HWG

PASSION/ PALM SUNDAY

Revised
 Common: Mark 11:1-11 or
   14:1—15:47 or 15:1-39 (40-47)
Episcopal: Mark 11:1-11a or
   (14:32-72) 15:1-39 (40-47)
Lutheran: Mark 14:1—15:47 or
        15:1-39

Note: Many follow Jesus but quickly run away when others challenge them. Shallow faith is exposed by such behavior, like the young man who left his only clothing behind in order to escape those who had arrested his Lord.

Printed Resources

___ Greeting

(Use Mark 11:1-11 as the greeting. Have someone read it dramatically, and then have children and/or the choir process into the sanctuary waving palm branches.)

___ Greeting

Ldr: On the first day of Unleavened Bread,
      when the Passover Lamb is sacrificed,
      Jesus sent his disciples into the city
      to prepare their Passover meal.
Rgt: **The room is ready.**
Lft: **The table is set.**
Ldr: We have come to commune with you, Jesus,
      to receive from you the living bread
      and the cup of your eternal blessing.
Rgt: **Hosanna to you, Lord!**
Lft: **Hosanna in the highest heaven!**

____ Prayer

Thank you, God, for the woman at Bethany.
    Her costly ointment of nard, poured on Jesus' head,
    provided a beautiful act of love.
We have caused so much grief for Jesus,
    betrayed him so many times,
    that we just wish
    it could have been us in that woman's shoes.
Thank you, God, for her foresight,
    for her sacrifice,
    for her love.
Thank you, God, that this nameless woman
    did a beautiful thing,
    for the One who did so much for us. Amen.

____ Prayer of Confession and Assurance of Pardon

Almighty God,
    fear eats away at our faith.
Like Peter,
    we swear boldly in the company of the faithful
    that we will never deny Jesus.
Then, when other believers are not around,
    we speak and act like we never knew Jesus existed.
Like the young man
    who left his clothes behind to escape Jesus' accusers,
    we are afraid of what the accusations of others might do to us.
God, we hate the fear
    that makes us hate ourselves.
We want to stand strong and true to our convictions.
    Like Jesus, we want to faithfully walk the path you set,
    even if it means the sacrifice of our lives.
God, we want to conquer the fear
    that keeps us from honoring you.
(Continue in silent prayer)
Jesus did not suffer crucifixion for saintly people.
    Jesus died for people like Peter who denied him,
    and the young man who ran away naked,
    and for you and me, who are afraid to be faithful.
    Jesus died so that fear can no longer control us.
    He died so that we can be free,
    He died so that we can walk the path God has set before us.
Sin is powerless.
    Death cannot hold us.
    Fear's enforcers are destroyed.

Jesus Christ has set us free!
     Go, and live boldly the godly lives
     with which we can honor our Savior and God.
Amen.

___ Commissioning and Blessing

"Truly this man was God's Son!"
     We must live in the way Jesus has shown us.
     We will live, because Jesus has died for us.
Amen.

Hymns and Choruses

(The asterisk [*] indicates hymns or choruses that are addressed to God and can be used as prayers.)

The service of palms
___ *"All Glory, Laud, and Honor"
___ *"All Hail, King Jesus"
___ *"Alone Thou Goest Forth, O Lord"
___ *"Here Comes Jesus"
___ *"Hosanna"
___ "Hosanna in the Highest"
___ "Hosanna, Loud Hosanna"
___ "In the Name of the Lord"
___ *"Jesus, Lord to Me"
___ "Mantos y Palmas" ("Filled with Excitement")
___ "Lift Up Your Heads, Ye Mighty Gates"
___ "Rejoice, Ye Pure in Heart"
___ *"Ride On! Ride On in Majesty!"
___ *"You Are My God"

The passion
___ *"Ah, Holy Jesus"
___ *"Alas! and Did My Savior Bleed"
___ "Behold the Lamb"
___ "Cross of Jesus, Cross of Sorrow"
___ "Go to Dark Gethsemane"
___ "He Never Said a Mumbalin' Word"
___ "I Stand Amazed in the Presence"
___ "It Happened on That Fateful Night"
___ *"Jesus, I Will Ponder Now"
___ "Lamb of Glory"
___ *"Lamb of God, Pure and Sinless"
___ *"O Crucified Redeemer"

_____ *"O Love Divine, What Hast Thou Done"
_____ *"O Sacred Head, Now Wounded"
_____ *"O Sorrow Deep"
_____ "Oh, How He Loves You and Me"
_____ *"Thank You, Lord"
_____ " 'Tis Finished! The Messiah Dies"
_____ *"To Mock Your Reign, O Dearest Lord"
_____ "Were You There"
_____ "What Wondrous Love Is This"
_____ "When I Survey the Wondrous Cross"

Reading the Scripture

_____ Select a few of the congregation's best public readers. Let one read the narrative of the passion story, and another read Jesus' words. The remaining readers take the parts of other people who speak during the story. Except for the narrator and the person reading Jesus' words, the readers can take the part of more than one person in the story. The lesson should be read with the same energy and feeling as when it was first experienced. *The New Handbook of the Christian Year* (Nashville: Abingdon) by Hoyt L. Hickman, Don E. Saliers, Laurence Hull Stookey, and James F. White has the entire text already broken into the various readers' parts.

_____ See the second suggestion under "Drama and Movement."

Responses to the Word

_____ Use the prayer of confession and assurance of pardon printed above.

_____ If you use the second suggestion under "Drama and Movement," follow the reading and dance with silence. Then move from the silence to a strong soloist singing a song of praise to Jesus Christ. The service could end with this, allowing the worshipers to go home carrying thoughts about what Jesus has done for them.

Drama and Movement

_____ Set a committee to work on finding a horse (people who raise horses will not allow colts to be ridden), or use the more traditional donkey. Have someone in biblical costume feeding this animal in the front of the sanctuary as worshipers arrive. It would present no problem with the service if the children are allowed to pet the animal. Then have a "disciple" come in from the back of the sanctuary. This person comes forward and unties the animal. The dialogue recorded in 11:5-6 provides the words for the actors' dialogue. The animal is led out. Then the music begins, and "Jesus" rides in. The choir can follow shouting the words recorded in 11:9-10, or they can be singing an enthusiastic Palm Sunday hymn. The children and others can throw palms on the floor in front of the procession. Have the congregation join in singing, or go directly into a prayer (like the first one printed above). Then have someone read 11:11. Then "Jesus" looks around the sanctuary and exits. The person feeding the animal at the beginning of the service can lead it out of the sanctuary at this point.

___ Recruit several dancers. Let them take the roles of the characters in the longer gospel lesson from chapters 14 and 15. As the lesson is read, the dancers move silently, carrying the worshipers' eyes along with their ears and, hopefully, their hearts. Keep the props simple, or use none at all, letting the worshipers' imaginations provide the props. The dancers should dress in albs or other simple costumes, rather than trying to take on the costumes of the biblical period. This allows a dancer to take the role of more than one character in the story, although the dancer who depicts Christ should not take on any other role. Use the biblical words, the dancers' movements and the worshipers' imaginations to recreate the scene of Jesus' passion. This can be a very powerful experience and does not need to be followed by a sermon. The long reading is sermon enough.

Visuals

___ Decorate the sanctuary with palms. Florists usually rent tubs for this occasion. Purple ribbons may be used to tie two or more palms together to attach them to walls or pews. If the passion narrative is being read as part of the service, then add a cross to one or more of the palm arrangements. The combination reminds us that the two events are very much connected.

___ Hang narrow banners of purple cloth. Pin palm branches to the cloth.

___ To represent the passion of Christ, make an arrangement using some of the following articles: unleavened bread, an alabaster jar, money, a dipping bowl, a cup, a ceramic (or other material) rooster, a sword, a club, a linen loincloth, a blindfold, a flogging whip, a purple cloak, thorns twisted into a crown, a cross, a sign with the words, "The King of the Jews," a sponge on a stick, and a linen burial cloth. By reading Mark 14-15, other articles might by identified for inclusion in the arrangement.

Anthems and Special Music

(Mark 11:1-11)
Holy, Holy, Holy — F. Mendelssohn — SATB/SATB unaccompanied — HIN
Hosanna, Blessed is He That Comes — C. Gregor/E. Wienandt — SATB w/keyboard — JFB
Hosanna, Son of David — L. Sateren — SATB unaccompanied — AF
Hosanna to the Son of David — O. Gibbons — SSAATB unaccompanied — ECS
Lift Up Your Heads, O Gates — R. Dirksen — SATB w/keyboard — from *With One Voice* — AF
Little Grey Donkey — N. Sleeth — Unison w/oboe, percussion — CG
Lord, Hosanna in the Highest — S. Glarum — SATB or SAB w/keyboard — GS
On Calvary's Hill — R. Wetzler — SATB — AF
Shout the Glad Tidings — D. Williams — SS or SA — AF
The Royal Banners Forward Go — Bruckner/Peck — SATB unaccompanied — CPH
When Jesus Left His Father's Throne — English folk melody/R. Vaughan Williams — SATB w/
    keyboard — from *Hymnal Supplement 1991* — GIA

(Mark 14:1—15:47)
Gethsemane — G. Young — SATB w/organ — BFW
How Blest is He That Comes — A. Fedak — SATB w/organ — CPH
My Song is Love Unknown — J. Ireland — Unison w/keyboard — from *With One Voice* —AF

(Mark 15:1-39)
A Purple Robe — R. Hopp — SATB w/keyboard — from *Songs of Rejoicing* — SPC
O Sacred Head, Now Wounded — H. L. Hassler/J. S. Bach — SATB w/keyboard — from *Hymnal Supplement 1991* — GIA
There Was Great Darkness — C. Gounod/R. Hines — SAB w/opt. keyboard — AF
The Seven Last Words — D. Pinkham — SATB w/tenor and bass solo, organ and tape — ECS
To Mock Your Reign — W. Rowan — Unison w/keyboard — from *Songs of Rejoicing* — SPC
Two Spirituals — R. E. Jones — SATB and baritone solo — PA

Organ and Other Keyboard Music

All Glory, Laud, and Honor (Valet will ich der geben) — A Palm Sunday Processional on "All Glory, Laud and Honor" — J. Bender — CPH
Alas and Did My Savior Bleed (Martyrdom) — found in *Three Lenten Preludes*, set 2 — R. Hobby — MSM
When I Survey the Wondrous Cross (Rockingham Old) — found in *Ten Hymn Preludes in Trio Style* — D. Harris — HWG

HOLY THURSDAY/
MAUNDY THURSDAY

Revised
  Common: John 13:1-17, 31b-35*
Episcopal: John 13:1-17* or Luke 22:14-30
Lutheran: John 13:1-17, 31b-35*; Mark 14:12-26

4 So he got up from the meal, took off his outer clothing, and wrapped a towel around his waist. 5 After that, he poured water into a basin and began to wash his disciples' feet, drying them with the towel that was wrapped around him.
—John 13: 4-5

Angie Latta

Note: The glory of Jesus is in giving his life for others. Our glory is in recognizing that our lives depend upon Jesus' gift and representing Jesus' love for others.

---

* See Holy Thursday in *Worship Workbook For The Gospels, Cycle A* and *Worship Workbook For The Gospels, Cycle C* for more material relating to this lesson.

Printed Resources

___ Greeting

Ldr: The glory of Jesus is seen
         as he gives himself on the cross.
Cng: **And the glory of God is seen
         in the glory of God's gift to humankind.**
Ldr: "Little children," Jesus said,
         "I give you a new commandment,
         that you love one another."
Cng: **Just as Jesus has loved us,
         we also should love one another.**
Ldr: By this everyone will know
         that you are Jesus' disciples.
Cng: **Glorious God, let the love of Jesus
         be our gift to others.
         This will be our glory.**

___ Add this line to the beginning of the hymn, "Let Us Break Bread Together on Our Knees":
    Let us wash feet together on our knees;
    Let us wash feet together on our knees.

_____ Prayer of Confession and Assurance of Pardon

Ldr: God of mercy and love,
        when Judas went out that door
        a part of each one of us went with him.
Cng: **We have all betrayed Jesus**
        in one way or another.
Ldr: And when the disciples sat unmoving at the table,
        each waiting for the other to wash their feet,
        a part of each one of us sat there with them.
Cng: **We have all sat unmoving,**
        waiting for someone else
        to do what we should be doing ourselves.
Ldr: And when Peter
        did not want Jesus to wash his feet,
        a part of each one of us joined him in that rejection.
Cng: **We have all resisted the new hierarchy of Jesus,**
        where those who are greatest
        become loving servants to all.
(Continue in silent prayer.)
Ldr: Even though Jesus' disciples betrayed him,
        had no heart for serving others,
        and resisted his example,
        Jesus' glory shines
        because he still loved them
        and gave his life for them.
        And now, children,
        just as Jesus washed the first disciples,
        he washes you and removes all of your sin.
Cng: **If our glorious Teacher and Lord**
        can do this for us;
        then we can take up his example
        of bowing down in service to others.
Ldr: By this everyone will know
        that you are disciples of Jesus Christ,
        if you have love for one another.

_____ Commissioning and Blessing

Know that Christ still bends down
    to wash your feet every day.
Receive his cleansing love,
    and be thankful.
And lift your praise to the gates of heaven,
    as you follow his example here on earth,
    in the name of Father, Son, and Holy Spirit. **Amen.**

Hymns and Choruses

(The asterisk [*] indicates hymns or choruses that are addressed to God and can be used as prayers.)

___ *"For Perfect Love So Freely Spent"
___ "Go Forth for God"
___ *"Jesu, Jesu"
___ *"Jesus, Lord, We Look to Thee"
___ *"Lord, We Have Come at Your Own Invitation"
___ *"Lord, Whose Love Through Humble Service"
___ "Love Consecrates the Humblest Act"
___ *"Love Divine, All Loves Excelling"
___ "Of the Glorious Body Telling"
___ "Sent Forth by God's Blessing"
___ *"Strengthen for Service, Lord"
___ "The Church of Christ, in Every Age"
___ "There's a Spirit in the Air"
___ *"When the Church of Jesus"
___ "Where Charity and Love Prevail"

Reading the Scripture

___ Intersperse one person's reading of the gospel lesson with the congregation's singing of the hymn, "Jesu, Jesu." The reading and singing should alternate as follows:
   Verses 1-5
   Stanza 1
   Verses 6-17
   Stanzas 2-3
   Verses 31b-35
   Stanzas 4-5

Responses to the Word

___ Celebrate holy communion as suggested under "Drama and Movement" below.

Drama and Movement

___ Recruit twelve people to work with the pastor. Dress all thirteen to look like Jesus and his disciples. Have these people gather around the communion table. (If the church's table is not suited for this, then set up another table in the chancel so that the thirteen can gather around it.) As communion is being served, the pastor washes the feet of the people gathered around the table. Two of the "disciples" at the table serve the communion elements to the rest of the congregation, who file up to the table to receive it. After the people at the table have all had their feet washed, then they receive the elements.

Visuals

___ Ask an artist in the congregation to prepare two life-size silhouettes from cardboard cut-outs. The silhouettes should be of Peter and Jesus, where Jesus is washing Peter's feet. An alternative to cardboard cut-outs would be to project the silhouettes onto a sanctuary wall. This visual should remain throughout the worship service.

___ Ask someone who does calligraphy to prepare a worship bulletin cover with a cross and the words, "Having loved his own ... he loved them to the end."

Anthems and Special Music

(John 13:1-7)
See Maundy Thursday in *Worship Workbook For The Gospels*, *Cycle A*
We Come to the Hungry Feast — R. Makeever — Unison w/keyboard, guitar — from *With One Voice* — AF

(Mark 14:12-26)
An Upper Room — A. Sherman — Unison or 2-part w/keyboard — AMSI
An Upper Room With Evening Lamps Ashine — D. Music — SATB w/opt. organ — MSM
Eat This Bread — J. Berthier — SATB w/solos, opt. keyboard — from *Hymnal Supplement 1991* — GIA
Hymn of the Last Supper — V. Demarest — med. solo w/keyboard — from *Choice Sacred Songs* — OD
This is My Body — E. Bonnemere — Unison w/keyboard — from *With One Voice* — AF
When In Our Music God is Glorified — C. V. Stanford — Unison w/keyboard — from *With One Voice* — AF
When Jesus Came to Save Us — A. Fedak — Unison w/keyboard — from *Songs of Rejoicing* — SPC
When Twilight Comes — F. Feliciano — Unison w/guitar — from *With One Voice* — AF

Organ and Other Keyboard Music

Lord, Whose Love in Humble Service (Beach Spring) — found in *7 Settings of American Folk Hymns* — W. Held — CPH
Of the Glorious Body Telling (Pange Lingua) — found in *Meditations on Communion Hymns* — L. Sowerby — HWG
Where Charity and Love Prevail (Twenty-fourth) — J. Coe — found in *Concordia Hymn Prelude Series*, vol. 9 — CPH

GOOD FRIDAY

Revised
  Common: John 18:1—19:42*
Episcopal: John (18:1-40) 19:1-37
Lutheran: John 18:1—19:42* or
          19:17-30

Gail Throckmorton Warner

Note: "What thou, my Lord, hast suffered was all for sinners' gain; mine, mine was the transgression, but thine the deadly pain." (verse 2 of "O Sacred Head, Now Wounded")

* For more material related to this passage see Good Friday in *Worship Workbook For The Gospels, Cycle A.*

Printed Resources

___ Greeting

Ld1: Soldiers and officials came
     with lanterns and torches and weapons.
Ld2: "Whom do you seek?" Jesus asked them.
Cng: **They came for us, because of our sin.**
Ld1: But Jesus went with them.
Ld2: He took our place.
Cng: **Thank you, Jesus.**
Ld1: Pilate said, "I find no crime in him."
Ld2: We told Pilate to release a robber,
     rather than the Son of God.
Cng: **Jesus, the sin is ours, not yours.**
Ld1: The crowds shouted, "Crucify him!"
Ld2: And so Jesus took our place.
Cng: **Jesus, we owe you everything.**

___ Prayer

Holy Savior,
    my betrayal set Judas against you,

my denial stabbed Peter's words into your heart,
   and my lies concealed your innocence.
Because of my sinful thoughts,
   thorns pierced your scalp.
Because I have lived according to the flesh,
   the flogger's cords tore into your muscles.
The cross of my judgment
   was laid on you to carry.
My refusal to believe and accept you
   hammered nails into your hands.
My greed divided your clothing,
   and gambled for your robe.
My insults and mocking ways
   filled the mouths that taunted you.
My sin tore you from God,
   and drained your life, drop by precious drop.
The spear thrust into your side
   aimed at ending my wickedness forever.
You died my death,
   and my sin sealed your tomb.
With one great act of love
   you gathered all my shame and guilt,
   and buried it in the depths of hell.
Risen Savior,
   I stand before you naked and new.
I died in you,
   now I pray you will live in me. Amen.

___ Commissioning and Blessing

"It is finished."
   The crucifixion is accomplished.
   Scripture is fulfilled,
   and the tomb has received the only one
   for whom it was never intended.
Go now,
   knowing this is not the end,
   but the beginning of something new. **Amen.**

Hymns and Choruses

(The asterisk [*] indicates hymns or choruses that are addressed to God and can be used as prayers.)

___ *"Ah, Holy Jesus"
___ "Alas! and Did My Savior Bleed"

138

___ *"Alone Thou Goest Forth, O Lord"
___ "At the Cross Her Station Keeping"
___ *"At the Cross Her Vigil Keeping"
___ "Behold the Lamb"
___ "Beneath the Cross of Jesus"
___ "Cross of Jesus, Cross of Sorrow"
___ "Go to Dark Gethsemane"
___ "He Never Said a Mumbalin' Word"
___ "He Is Lovely"
___ "I Am Crucified with Christ"
___ *"Jesus, I Will Ponder Now"
___ *"Jesus, in Thy Dying Woes"
___ *"Lamb of God"
___ "Morning Glory, Starlit Sky"
___ *"My Tribute"
___ *"O Crucified Redeemer"
___ *"O Love Divine, What Hast Thou Done"
___ *"O Sacred Head, Now Wounded"
___ *"O Sacred Head, Sore Wounded"
___ "Oh, How He Loves You and Me"
___ "Sing, My Tongue, the Glorious Battle"
___ "The Flaming Banners of Our King"
___ "The Old Rugged Cross"
___ "The Royal Banners Forward Go"
___ " 'Tis Finished! The Messiah Dies"
___ *"To Mock Your Reign, O Dearest Lord"
___ "Were You There"
___ "When I Survey the Wondrous Cross"

Reading the Scripture

___ Conduct a service of Tenebrae (darkness). Choose several good oral readers from the congregation. Divide the reading among them as outlined below. Light fourteen purple candles and one white candle (the Christ candle) at the beginning of the service. After each section of the gospel lesson is read, extinguish one candle. Traditionally, a loud noise (made by a borrowed set of cymbals?) is made when the Christ candle is extinguished.

    read 18:1-11   then extinguish the first candle
    read 18:12-14   then extinguish the second candle
    read 18:15-17   then extinguish the third candle
    read 18:18-22   then extinguish the fourth candle
    read 18:23-27   then extinguish the fifth candle
    read 18:28-32   then extinguish the sixth candle
    read 18:33-38   then extinguish the seventh candle
    read 18:39-40   then extinguish the eighth candle
    read 19:1-3   then extinguish the ninth candle
    read 19:4-6a   then extinguish the tenth candle

read 19:6b-16a then extinguish the eleventh candle
read 19:16b-18 then extinguish the twelfth candle
read 19:19-25a then extinguish the thirteenth candle
read 19:25b-27 then extinguish the fourteenth candle
read 19:28-30   then sound a loud noise and extinguish the Christ candle
read 19:31-42

Responses to the Word

___ After a sermon on Christ's atonement of our sin, invite the worshipers to pray the prayer printed above.

___ Using either of the suggestions under "Drama and Movement," the best response from the worshipers might be to leave the sanctuary in silence.

Drama and Movement

___ Conduct a service of Tenebrae, as suggested under "Reading the Scripture." Add to the dramatic effect by doing the reading in a darkened sanctuary, where the only lights are the candles being used for tenebrae. A reading light will have to be provided for the readers. (Depending upon the laws of some states, exit lights may have to remain lighted as well.) Of course, the reading light could be eliminated if the text was memorized and spoken from memory. Even if nothing else is memorized, consider having the readers memorize 19:31-42 so that even the reading light can be turned off when the Christ candle is extinguished.

___ Recruit five dancers to work with the choir. Have the choir choose choral music that relates Jesus' crucifixion. As the choir sings, the dancers conclude the experience with four of their number lifting the limp body of the fifth over their heads. They carry "the body of Jesus" out of the sanctuary in this manner. The congregation follows the dancers out as if in a funeral procession. (The congregation needs to be told how this will happen at the beginning of the service. A couple of families in the front pew can be cued to start following the dancers as an example for the rest of the worshipers to follow.)

Visuals

___ Have a volunteer arrange lanterns, torches and weapons in the front of the sanctuary. Add a large olive branch to this arrangement. Put a note of explanation in the worship bulletin that says the arrangement recalls how a world of darkness (needing lanterns and torches) met Christ with violence (the weapons). Christ is represented by the olive branch (a symbol of peace and well-being) that also recalls that Jesus was praying on the Mount of Olives when he was arrested.

Anthems and Special Music

See Good Friday in *Worship Workbook For The Gospels*, *Cycle A*
Calvary — African-American Spiritual — SATB — from *Hymnal Supplement 1991* — GIA
The Passion According to St. John — W. Byrd — SAB/TTB speaking voice/soli — CPH
The Passion According to St. John — R. Hillert — SATB w/opt. keyboard — CPH
The Passion According to St. John — H. Schütz — SATB w/opt. keyboard — GIA

Organ and Other Keyboard Music

Ah, Holy Jesus (Herzliebster Jesu) — found in *Neumeister Collection* of J. S. Bach — ed. C. Wolff
    — BAR
Beneath the Cross of Jesus (St. Christopher) — found in *Three Lenten Preludes*, set 2 — R. Hobby
    — MSM
Were You There (Were You There) — found in *Eight Hymn Preludes for Lent* — P. Stearns — HF

EASTER DAY

Revised
  Common: John 20:1-18* or
              Mark 16:1-8
Episcopal: Mark 16:1-8
Lutheran: Mark 16:1-8 or
             Luke 24:13-49+ or
             John 20:1-9 (10-18)*

Note: Every time that people try to anoint Jesus' dead body and consign him to the tomb of history, they discover that he is not there. Jesus goes ahead of them where they will see him again, and again, and again.

* Material related to John 20:1-18 can be found on Easter Day in *Worship Workbook For The Gospels, Cycle A.*

\+ Material related to Luke 24:13-49 can be found on Easter Day in *Worship Workbook For The Gospels, Cycle C.*

Printed Resources

___ Greeting

Ld1: Who will roll away the stone sealing Jesus' tomb?
Ld2: It is very large, and heavy, and immovable...
       like death itself.
Cng: **And who will roll away the stone sealing our tomb?**
Ld1: When the women went to the tomb on the first morning...
Ld2: The stone had already been rolled back!
Cng: **Death's cold seal was broken!**
Ld1: Jesus was not in the tomb!
Ld2: Christ is risen!
Cng: **And we are resurrected with him!**
All: (The people sing the chorus, "Alleluia." On the second verse use the words "You're my Savior" and on the third verse use "I will praise you.")

____ Prayer

God of endless serendipity,
    Mary Magdalene, Mary the mother of James, and Salome
    bought spices to anoint the dead body of Jesus.
    But they never got to use them.
No one could measure the joy
    that the Magdalene and her friends must have felt,
    when they were able to use their spices
    for some purpose other than what they had intended.
You are an unimaginable and unlimited God.
    You thrill your children with blessings
    unthinkable and beyond our wildest dreams.
The fantastic, the miraculous, and the incredible
    are some of your favorite devices
    for energizing, animating, and reviving
    those who expect too little of life,
    and who no longer hope for your new possibilities.
Do it again, God. Do it always,
    in us,
    and in those yet to be gathered to your flock. Amen.

____ Affirmation of Faith

Wmn: **We trust that Mary Magdalene,**
            Mary the mother of James, and Salome
            went to Jesus' tomb on the first day of the week,
            and found the tomb empty.
        We are convinced that Jesus, who was crucified,
            rose from his tomb with new life,
            and went ahead of the disciples to Galilee.
        We trust these truths because of the women's experience,
            but even more,
            we are convinced because we have had the same experience.
        Death is empty of all power and meaning.
            No longer can a tomb frighten us into silence.
            The fear is gone, and confidence in Christ grows daily.
        Jesus still lives and goes ahead of us.
            We see Jesus in every act of love and compassion,
            in every work of justice and righteousness,
            in every tear wiped away
            in every smile restored to God's children.
        We maintain that Jesus goes ahead of us,
            So we can follow, leaving all tombs empty,
            and move ever closer to the full glory of Jesus Christ.

Men: We trust the testimony of our grandmothers and mothers,
      wives, sisters and daughters.
    Their words are true.
    Christ is alive,
      and the tomb is forever empty.
    We also know that Jesus goes ahead of us,
      and that all women and men are called to follow,
      until we see Jesus in his final glory
      at the end of time.

All: We maintain that death and tombs are empty.
    We turn our backs on them forever.
    And we will hurry toward our Galilee
      where we will see Jesus today and every day,
      thanks be to God. Alleluia!

___ Commissioning and Blessing

Ld1: Jesus is not in the tomb.

Ld2: Therefore you need not fear death.
    It no longer has any hold over you.

Ld1: Jesus is going ahead of you.

Ld2: He is preparing the way for you to follow him,
    and, as you follow, you will see him.

Ld1: Go and tell others what you have seen and heard.

Ld2: You are witnesses of a miraculous gift from God.
    Make others aware that God gives them life,
    and gives it in glorious abundance!

Cng: **Amen and amen!**

___ Commissioning and Blessing

The words "...he is going ahead of you to Galilee;
    there you will see him..."
must have brought great comfort and relief
    to Peter and the other disciples
    who had denied and abandoned Jesus.
And, knowing that we too have denied and abandoned Jesus,
    it is a comfort and relief to us
    to hear those same words,
    "...he is going ahead of you...
    there you will see him...."
Brothers and sisters, Jesus never denies or abandons us.
    Receive this truth, and live accordingly,
    in the name of the Father, Son and Holy Spirit. **Amen.**

Hymns and Choruses

(The asterisk [*] indicates hymns or choruses that are addressed to God and can be used as prayers.)

___ "Awake, My Heart, with Gladness"
___ "Celebrate Jesus"
___ "Christ Is Arisen"
___ "Christ Is Risen"
___ "Christ the Lord Is Risen Today"
___ "Christo Vive" ("Christ Is Risen")
___ "For This Purpose"
___ "Hallelujah! Jesus Lives"
___ "He Is Lord"
___ "He Is Risen, He Is Risen"
___ "He Rose"
___ "O Sons and Daughters, Let Us Sing"
___ "O Sons and Daughters of the King"
___ "On Earth Has Dawned This Day of Days"
___ "Praise the Savior, Now and Ever"
___ "The First One Ever"
___ "The Strife Is O'er, the Battle Done"
___ "Up from the Grave He Arose"
___ "Woman in the Night"

Reading the Scripture

___ Recruit three women to read the gospel lesson. Have them alternate on each verse. For example, the first woman would read verse 1, the second verse 2, the third verse 3, and then the first woman verse 4, and so on.

___ Ask one of the congregation's best storytellers to memorize this gospel lesson, and then to tell it to the congregation in the form of a story.

Responses to the Word

___ Celebrate the presence of the risen Lord by enjoying holy communion with him on this resurrection day.

___ Change the usual order of the worship service. Put the gospel lesson and sermon in the beginning of the service. Then follow these with a festival of song. Let the congregation celebrate Jesus' resurrection by singing several resurrection hymns, songs and choruses. Intersperse various pieces of special music in between the congregation's singing. Easter is a high and holy day, but it should also be a lot of fun.

___ Have the worshipers join in the above affirmation of faith.

145

Drama and Movement

___ This would be an especially good day to use dancers to interpret the gospel lesson. No props are necessary. Just three women dancers giving expression to the feelings of the first women at Jesus' tomb.

Visuals

___ Recruit people to make two banners. One should show the sun just above the horizon, and under it the tomb with the stone rolled away. If desired, add the words, "He is not here." The second banner should show the Sea of Galilee and the rolling hills that surround it. The sun could be shown high above the horizon. Christ could be shown standing beside the water. If desired, the words "He is going ahead of you" could be added.

___ Set some of the congregation's creative construction crew to work building a papier mâché wall in the sanctuary. They should form a cave in the wall, and inside the cave there needs to be a shelf carved into the "stone." Lay some white cloth on this shelf to represent Jesus' burial clothes. Set the spices brought by the women outside the cave. Decorate the area with various potted lilies, daffodils and tulips.

Anthems and Special Music

(John 20:1-18)
See Easter Day in *Worship Workbook For The Gospels*, *Cycle A*
Anthem for Easter — S. Belcher — SATB unaccompanied — PA

(Mark 16:1-8)
Alleluia, Do Not Be Amazed — M. Cooley — SATB w/organ — CPH
Anthem for Easter — S. Belcher — SATB unaccompanied — PA
Christ Has Arisen, Alleluia — Traditional Tanzanian — SATB unaccompanied — from *With One Voice* — AF
Christ Is Risen As He Said — D. Holden-Holloway — SATB w/keyboard — from *Songs of Rejoicing* — SPC
Come, Ye Sad and Fearful Hearted, He is Risen! — D. Williams — SAB w/organ — AF
Do Not Be Amazed — J. Bender — 2-part w/organ — CPH
Early in the Morning — A. van Iderstine — SATB w/organ — AMSI
He Has Risen — K. Nystedt — (S)SATB unaccompanied — from *Three Motets* — AF
Morn's Roseate Hues — G. Chadwick — SATB w/organ, bass and alto solo — PA
Now is Christ Risen — K. Nystedt — SATB w/treble instrument and handbells — AF
Song at the Empty Tomb — M. Haugen — 2-part w/synthesizer and organ — GIA
Who Rolls Away the Stone — A. Hammerschmidt — SSATB w/instruments and SSB soli — CPH

(Luke 24:13-49+)
Alleluia! Jesus Is Risen — D. Johnson — SATB w/keyboard — from *With One Voice* — AF
And They Drew Nigh — L. Sowerby — SATB w/organ — HWG
Awake, Arise, Lift Up Your Voice — T. Haweis, S. Webbe — SATB w/keyboard — from *Hymnal Supplement 1991* — GIA
Christ Is Risen! Shout Hosanna! — W. Rowan — Unison w/keyboard — from *With One Voice* — AF

146

Christ Who Alone Art Light of Day — H. Distler/L. Palmer — SAB w/organ and 2 violins — CPH
Come, O Blessed of My Father — J. Bender — 2-part w/organ — CPH
Did Not Our Heart Burn Within Us — L. Salathiel — SATB w/keyboard and bass solo — GS
He Comes to Us as One Unknown — C. H. H. Parry — Unison w/keyboard — from *Hymnal Supplement 1991* — GIA
I Want Jesus to Walk with Me — African-American Spiritual/J. J. Cleveland, V. Nix — SATB w/opt. keyboard — from *With One Voice* — AF
Motets from "Resurrexi" — G. Near — SATB unaccompanied — PA
On the Day of Resurrection — M. Sedio — Unison w/keyboard — from *Songs of Rejoicing* — SPC
Stay With Us — W. Pelz — Unison w/keyboard — from *With One Voice* — AF
The Way To Emmaus (solo cantata) — J. Weinberger — high solo w/organ — BEL

Organ and Other Keyboard Music

Awake, My Heart With Gladness (Auf, auf, mein Herz) — found in *Six Preludes on Easter Hymns* — W. Held — CPH
Christ Is Arisen (Christ ist erstanden) — found in *Seventy-nine Chorales for the Organ*, op. 28 — M. Dupré — HWG
O Sons and Daughters of the King (O Filii et Filiae) — B. Owen — found in *International Collection of Nineteenth Century Hymn Tune Preludes* — MAF

SECOND SUNDAY OF EASTER

Revised
  Common: John 20:19-31*
Episcopal: John 20:19-31*
Lutheran: John 20:19-31*

Note: We can huddle in fear. We can harbor doubts. But we can never lock out the good news that Christ has conquered sin and death for our salvation.

* More material relating to this text can be found on the Second Sunday of Easter in *Worship Workbook For The Gospels, Cycle A.*

Printed Resources

___ Greeting *call to worship*

Ld1: The first disciples told Thomas, "We have seen the Lord."
Ld2: But Thomas refused to believe
     until he had touched Jesus' wounds.
Cng: **God, save us from our own doubts.**
Ld1: Jesus appeared to Thomas and removed all his doubts.
Ld2: Then Jesus said, "Blessed are those who have not seen
     and yet have come to believe."
Cng: **God, give us faith when we cannot see.**
Ld1: Open your holy scriptures to us, O God,
     so that we can be filled with belief.
Ld2: Pour out your Holy Spirit upon us, O God,
     so that we can know. *Amen*

do Ld1 & Ld2 — & Cng as shown

___ Prayer

God of new life and hope,
  so many people's doors are locked shut,
  the inmates hiding inside because of fear.
Send your risen Son to these frightened children.
  Let them see his wounds suffered for them.
  Let them see the testimonies of his victory.

148

Resuscitate these prisoners of fear.
  Breathe your powerful Spirit into their hearts.
  Overwhelm their doubts with the hope for new life.
In the name of our risen Savior,
  we ask you to bless others as you have blessed us,
  unlocking every door that confines one of your children. Amen.

___ Commissioning and Blessing

Ldr: Now Jesus did many other signs
      in the presence of his disciples,
      which we have not had time to share in this service.
      But these have been shared so that you may come to believe
      that Jesus is the Messiah, the Son of God,
      and that through believing you may have life in his name.
Cng: **We do believe that Jesus is our Savior and your Son, O God.**
Ldr: Then peace be with you,
      and with all those with whom you share this good news.
Cng: **For peace, life and joy we give you thanks, gracious Father.**
Ldr: In the name of Father, Son and Holy Spirit, amen.
Cng: **Amen!**

___ Commissioning and Blessing

Benediction

Jesus said, "Peace be with you.
  As the Father has sent me, so I send you.
Receive the Holy Spirit.
If you forgive the sins of any, they are forgiven them;
  if you retain the sins of any, they are retained."
May it be so with you today and always,
  in the name of the Father, Son and Holy Spirit. **Amen.**

Hymns and Choruses

(The asterisk [*] indicates hymns or choruses that are addressed to God and can be used as prayers.)

___ "Awake, Arise, Lift Up Your Voice"
___ *"Breathe on Me, Breath of God"
___ "Celebrate Jesus"
___ "Christ Is Arisen"
___ *"Forgive Our Sins as We Forgive"
___ "He Is Lord"
___ "He Is Lovely"
___ "He Lives"
___ *"Holy Spirit, Ever Living"

149

___ *"Let It Breathe on Me"
___ "Look, Now He Stands!"
___ "Look There! The Christ, Our Brother, Comes"
___ *"O Breath of Life"
___ "O Sons and Daughters, Let Us Sing"
___ "O Sons and Daughters of the King"
___ *"That Easter Day with Joy Was Bright"
___ "We Walk By Faith, and Not By Sight"

Reading the Scripture

___ Read the gospel lesson responsively, with the leader reading a verse and then the congregation and then the leader and so on. Use a familiar praise chorus (one that does not have to be looked up in a hymnal) to conclude the reading.

Responses to the Word

___ After preaching a sermon focusing on worshipers receiving the Holy Spirit, the pastor can walk down the center aisle of the sanctuary. As the pastor reaches each pew, he or she pauses beside the closest worshiper. The pastor says to the worshiper, "Receive the Holy Spirit." Then the pastor takes the worshiper's hand and blows into the worshiper's palm. The pastor does this to each person within easy reach, and then asks these worshipers to pass the Spirit to those beside them. In this way, all the worshipers can experience this gift from Jesus.

___ Insert a blank piece of paper in the worship bulletin. After a sermon on forgiving the sins of others, have the worshipers write down names of people that they will forgive in the next week. Ask them to reach out to the people they will forgive in some manner. A phone call, a bouquet of flowers, a personal visit, a letter, E-mail, or any other means of saying "I forgive you" could be part of this reaching out.

Drama and Movement

___ Recruit a male dancer from the congregation to do a simple interpretation of the lesson as it is read. This person could show the marks in his hands and side. (Let these be seen in the worshipers' minds. Don't try to use makeup to imitate Jesus' real wounds.)

Visuals

___ Purchase charcoal art markers from a local artist supply retailer. Then, as the worshipers enter the sanctuary, mark a cross on the back of both their hands. Tell the people that these marks are to remind them of the wounds Jesus had in his hands, and his feet, and his side.

Anthems and Special Music

Because You Have Seen Me, Thomas — L. Marenzio — SATB — CPH

Dona Nobis Pacem — Traditional — 3-part canon — from *With One Voice* — AF

He Lives Forevermore — C. Ore — Unison w/organ — AF

Motets from "Resurrexi"— G. Near — SATB unaccompanied — PA

O That I Knew Where I Might Find Him — W. S. Bennett — SATB w/opt. organ — from *The Church Anthem Book* — OUP

O That I Knew Where I Might Find Him — A. Rowley — high solo w/keyboard — BH

Peace Be unto You — K. Nystedt — SATB unaccompanied — AF

Peace Be with You — R. Wetzler — SATB unaccompanied — AMSI

The Beatitude of John — L. Pfautsch — SATB and tenor solo w/guitar, finger cymbal, handbells — HF

There Came Jesus — J. Handl — SATB w/opt. keyboard — GIA

This Is the Day — A. M. Bush — Unison w/keyboard — from *Songs of Rejoicing* — SPC

We Walk By Faith — M. Haugen — Unison w/keyboard — from *Hymnal Supplement 1991* — GIA

We Walk By Faith and Not by Sight — S. McFarland — SATB w/keyboard — from *With One Voice* — AF

See Second Sunday of Easter in *Worship Workbook For The Gospels*, *Cycle A*

Organ and Other Keyboard Music

Breathe on Me, Breath of God (Durham) — found in *36 Short Preludes and Postludes on Well-known Hymn Tunes* — H. Willan — CFP

Forgive Our Sins as We Forgive (Detroit) — Partita on *Detroit* — D. Hurd — AF

That Easter Day with Joy Was Bright (Puer Nobis) — Variations on *Puer Nobis* — M. Burkhardt — MSM

THIRD SUNDAY
OF EASTER

Revised
 Common: Luke 24:36b-48
Episcopal: Luke 24:36b-48
Lutheran: Luke 24:36b-48

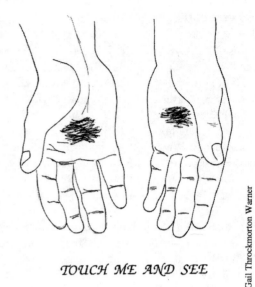

TOUCH ME AND SEE

Gail Throckmorton Warner

Note: While in our Easter joy, we too are disbelieving and wondering, but Jesus is still patiently revealing himself so that we might believe.

Printed Resources

___ Greeting

Ldr: "Peace be with you."
Cng: **And also with you.**
Ldr: After the resurrection,
      some of Jesus' first words to his friends were,
      "Peace be with you."
Cng: **We come seeking your peace, blessed Jesus.**
      Your peace is not like the world's,
      the peace you offer, Lord,
      cannot be shaken by this world's terrors.
      Fill us with this peace that defeats even death.

___ Prayer for Illumination

God of the Holy Scriptures,
    we see Jesus' example.
When tempted in the wilderness,
    Jesus resisted by calling on scripture.
In a Nazareth synagogue,
    Jesus began his ministry by reading scripture.
When a lawyer asked what must be done to inherit eternal life,
    Jesus quoted scripture for an answer.
Even as he was marched to his crucifixion,
    scripture filled Jesus' thoughts and words.
Then after his resurrection, Jesus opened the scriptures
    to show his disciples how they had been fulfilled.

God of the Holy Scriptures,
    open our minds to understanding this Word you have kept for us,
    and make us faithful disciples
    and enthusiastic witnesses to the truth of your Holy Word.
Amen.

___ Affirmation of Faith

I declare my allegiance in God,
    creator of the vast reaches of the cosmos,
    and creator of each man, woman and child on earth.
I am convinced that God came to us in Jesus Christ,
    a true human being and truly God.
    Jesus gave up his life for our salvation,
    and was put to death on a cross.
    Jesus was dead, and was buried in a borrowed tomb.
    Three days later Jesus was resurrected in body and spirit.
    The women saw his empty tomb,
    and he broke bread with two disciples traveling to Emmaus.
    Then Jesus appeared to the eleven and their companions.
    He showed them his hands and feet, and said,
    "Touch me and see;
    for a ghost doesn't have flesh and bones...."
    Then Jesus ate broiled fish in their presence.
    He opened the disciples' minds to understanding the scriptures,
    and he sent them into the world as witnesses of these things.
    Then Jesus withdrew from the disciples,
    and was carried up into heaven.
I hold that God has kept the promise
    to clothe the church with the power of the Holy Spirit.
    Now, as a disciple of Christ and a member of his church,
    I am determined to witness to the truth of all these things.
    And through my mouth, my hands, and my feet,
    Jesus continues to work wonders in this world.
    I will serve Jesus until he returns from heaven,
    in the same way that we saw him ascend there.

___ Commissioning and Blessing

The law, the prophets and the psalms had to be fulfilled.
    Jesus had to suffer
    and be raised from the dead on the third day,
and now repentance and forgiveness of sin
    is to be proclaimed in Jesus' name to all nations.
You are witnesses of these things,
    and, just as our heavenly Father promised,

power from on high is being sent upon you,
in the name of the Father, the Son and the Holy Spirit. **Amen.**

___ Commissioning and Blessing

Ldr: While they were still startled, terrified
and doubting in their hearts,
while in their joy they were disbelieving
and still wondering,
the course was set for Jesus' first disciples.
Each received new vocations in the Lord's service.
In the same way, the course for your life
while you still have fears and doubts,
while you still wonder what all this means,
has already been established.
Even though you have only just begun to understand
Jesus' crucifixion and resurrection,
you have received a new direction for your life's work.
As you take up this service to our Messiah,
our Father will give you everything you need,
even the Power from on high.
Cng: **Thanks be to God. Amen.**

Hymns and Choruses

(The asterisk [*] indicates hymns or choruses that are addressed to God and can be used as prayers.)

___ "Alleluia, Alleluia! Hearts and Voices Heavenward Raise"
___ "Celebrate Jesus"
___ "Christ Is Alive"
___ "Christ Jesus Lay in Death's Strong Bands"
___ "Christ the Lord Is Risen Again"
___ "Come, Ye Faithful, Raise the Strain"
___ "He Is Lord"
___ "He Is Risen, He Is Risen!"
___ "He Lives"
___ "I Live"
___ "Jesus Lives"
___ "Look There! The Christ Our Brother Comes"
___ "Love's Redeeming Work Is Done"
___ "O Sons and Daughters, Let Us Sing"
___ "That Easter Day with Joy Was Bright"
___ "The Day of Resurrection"
___ "The Strife Is O'er, the Battle Done"
___ "Thine Be the Glory"

___ "This Joyful Eastertide"
___ "We Walk by Faith, and Not by Sight"

Reading the Scripture

___ Have the congregation begin singing softly the chorus "Alleluia." Then, as the people continue to sing, have a person with a good reading voice read the gospel lesson. To make sure people who are hard of hearing can hear the words, have the reader use a sound amplification system.

___ Recruit two readers for this lesson. Have one read Jesus' words and the other the narrative that carries along the story.

Responses to the Word

___ Preach a sermon on the physical nature of Jesus' resurrection and the need for Jesus' disciples to be engaged in the physical world, as well as prepared for the world that is yet to come. Then have the congregation join in the affirmation of faith printed above. An alternative to the affirmation of faith would be to challenge the worshipers to take up some project for improving the environment or the physical life of an individual, or people in general.

___ Challenge the congregation to form small Bible study groups in their homes. They can invite neighbors and other friends to attend. Even two or three can form a study group. Provide the congregation with simple study materials, but make the Bible itself the main focus of the study. The congregational members should witness to the truth of what the scriptures say about Jesus Christ, and in this way fulfill Jesus' charge in verse 48. Those who will accept this challenge could hold up their hand in the worship service in order to receive a copy of the study materials. The church's ushers could pass these materials to those responding.

___ After a sermon on doubting and disbelieving, invite the worshipers to join in an affirmation of faith. Use the affirmation printed above, or another one more familiar to the people.

Drama and Movement

___ Does your congregation have one of those people who, with a little make-up and a good costume, looks just like Jesus (at least in the congregation's imagination)? Then put this person in costume. Use some professional make-up to create "wounds" for his hands and feet. Have this person greet people as they come to worship. This person should not pretend to be Jesus, but when people remark on his appearance he could reply, "I am dressed this way to remind you that Jesus appeared just like this to his first disciples. He invited them to touch him and know that the flesh and bones of his body were again full of life. Jesus really did rise from the grave, and that is the good news for us." For an extra touch this special greeter could be eating something (dried fish?).

155

Visuals

____ Have the most artistic person in the congregation work with someone who is good at sewing. Ask these two people to make a huge banner with a bigger-than-life Jesus holding out his hands to the worshipers. The figure should be as realistic as the two people can make it. Add just four words to the banner, "Touch me and see."

____ Ask some of the youth of the church who are good at sketching pictures to provide four pictures to be reproduced for the worship bulletin cover. The four pictures are: (1) Jesus' wounded hand; (2) a piece of broiled fish; (3) a scroll of the law of Moses; and (4) a dove to represent "the power from on high." Set these four pictures in a window pane type of display, or work them into a montage. Then reproduce them for the bulletin covers.

Anthems and Special Music

Alleluia! Jesus Is Risen — D. Johnson — SATB w/keyboard — from *With One Voice* — AF
Awake, Arise, Lift Up Your Voice — T. Haweis/S. Webbe — SATB w/keyboard — from *Hymnal Supplement 1991* — GIA
Christ Is Risen! Shout Hosanna! — W. Rowan — Unison w/keyboard — from *With One Voice* — AF
Peace Be Unto You — E. Elgar — Tenor solo w/keyboard — NOV
See What Love — F. Mendelssohn — SATB w/keyboard — AF
Stay With Us — W. Pelz — Unison w/keyboard — from *With One Voice* — AF

Organ and Other Keyboard Music

The Day of Resurrection (Lancashire) — R. Arnatt — found in *The Parish Organist*, part eleven — CPH
Thine Be the Glory (Judas Maccabaeus) — D. Johns — found in *Concordia Hymn Prelude Series*, vol. 10 — CPH
This Joyful Eastertide (Vruechten) — found in *Resurrection Suite* — A. Wyton — HF

FOURTH SUNDAY OF EASTER

Revised
  Common: John 10:11-18
Episcopal: John 10:11-16
Lutheran: John 10:11-18

"I have other sheep that do not belong to this fold. I must bring them also, and they will listen to my voice. So there will be one flock, one shepherd."

Note: Jesus laid down his life for us. No one took it from him. What have we laid down for Jesus?

Printed Resources

___ Greeting

Ldr: As Jesus taught the Jews he said to them,
Chr: "I have other sheep that do not belong to this fold.
I must bring them also, and they will listen to my voice."
Cng: **Merciful God, we're the "other sheep," aren't we?
O God, help us listen carefully to Jesus' voice.**
Ldr: And Jesus also said to the Jews,
Chr: "There will be one flock, one shepherd."
Cng: **Merciful God, we know Jesus laid down his life
to form one great and holy kingdom
for the descendants of Abraham
and for those outside that blessed flock.
Hear us today, as we lift up our praises and thanksgivings
to you and to our great shepherd, Jesus Christ.**

___ Prayer

**God of power and might,
    let us be like Jesus.
Make us strong enough to be gentle.
    powerful enough to forgive,
    mighty enough to stoop down in service,
    and sturdy enough to trust you for our daily bread.
Give us, God of heaven and earth,
    the power to lay down our lives for others,
    so that we can thank the One
    who laid down his life for us. Amen.**

____ Commissioning and Blessing

The good shepherd does not run away,
    but stays and cares for his sheep.
The good shepherd knows his own,
    and lays down his life for them.
You know the shepherd's voice.
    Listen to the sounds of it,
    and follow it to the salvation of your lives. **Amen.**

Hymns and Choruses

(The asterisk [*] indicates hymns or choruses that are addressed to God and can be used as prayers.)

____ *"Ah, Holy Jesus"
____ "Have No Fear, Little Flock"
____ *"I Am Thine, O Lord"
____ *"Praise and Thanks and Adoration"
____ *"Savior, Like a Shepherd Lead Us"
____ "The King of Love My Shepherd Is"
____ "The Lord's My Shepherd, I'll Not Want"
____ *"Unto Thee, O Lord"
____ "With God as Our Friend"
____ *"You Satisfy the Hungry Heart"

Reading the Scripture

____ Let someone introduce the reading of the lesson. Then have another person, who cannot be seen by the congregation, read the lesson over the sound system.

____ Have the reader dress in the manner of a contemporary sheep rancher. He or she can carry a shepherd's crook to help the congregation identify him or her as a sheep rancher. Let this person stand up in front of the congregation and tell the worshipers the words Jesus spoke about his being the good shepherd. This would be most effective if the person did this from memory. Another way would be to have the reader take a small Bible from his or her pocket, and read the lesson from this "personal" pocket testament.

Responses to the Word

____ Hold a community-wide communion service, in which the "other sheep that do not belong to this fold" join together in a holy communion with our one shepherd. We all know that Christians should be united in communion rather than being divided by human doctrines which make the eucharist much less than what Christ intended for it to be. "One flock, one shepherd" are Jesus' words that need to be heard today.

___ Invite people who have not yet come to know Christ as their shepherd to listen to his voice. Lead them in praying that Christ be their only shepherd in their hearts, minds and souls. Follow the worship service where this happens with a party in the fellowship hall. Make the "new sheep" the honored guests at the party.

___ Have a praise and prayer service honoring Jesus Christ, the good shepherd of the sheep, who laid down his life for his own.

Drama and Movement

___ Does your congregation have a creative storyteller? If so, ask this person to create a story about a big bad wolf, three little sheep (instead of pigs) and a shepherd who saves the day for the sheep. Have this person tell the story to the children in the worship service. Of course, adults are permitted to listen too.

___ Hold the worship service in a nearby sheep pasture. Let the shepherd there talk about the ways that the sheep need a shepherd. Follow this with the pastor preaching about the ways that we need Christ.

___ Let a group of mimes or a clown troupe act out this story.

Visuals

___ Recruit some volunteers to arrange a display in the front of the sanctuary. The display can be composed of several paintings of the good shepherd interspersed with bouquets of flowers. Pots of live flowers or bouquets of wild flowers might be used instead of bouquets from the florist. The good shepherd paintings might be gathered from around the church, borrowed from members, or borrowed from a Christian bookstore. Many community libraries also have various paintings to loan out.

___ Is there a sculptor or carver in the congregation or community? Ask this person to use a favorite medium to prepare a statue of the good shepherd to display in your church's sanctuary. A commission would be expected by some artisans. Others might just enjoy the chance to make a gift like this to the Shepherd who laid down his life for them. (Make sure that the statue is large enough to be effective in the sanctuary. Large sanctuaries need large statues.)

___ Have the children of the church draw pen and ink sketches (black ink copies are better) of the good shepherd with the flock. They can decide for themselves whether to include the hired hand or the wolf. Use these drawings for bulletin covers. Make as many copies of each as will be needed to serve the total congregation. Who says the bulletin covers all have to look alike?

Anthems and Special Music

See Fourth Sunday of Easter in *Worship Workbook For The Gospels*, *Cycle A*

He Gathers the Lambs — A. M. Bush — med. solo w/keyboard — from *Songs of Rejoicing* — SPC

I Am the Good Shepherd — B. Burroughs — med. solo w/keyboard — from *New Testament Songs* — HP

I Am the Good Shepherd — E. Elgar — Tenor solo w/keyboard — from *The Light Of Light* — NOV

I Am the Good Shepherd — G. Nevin — med. solo w/organ — OD

I Am the Good Shepherd — R. Wetzler — Unison w/keyboard — found in *Alleluia, I Will Sing* — AF

I Am the Good Shepherd — H. Willan — Unison w/organ — found in *Twelve Sayings of Jesus* — CPH

I Am the Good Shepherd — D. Wood — Unison w/keyboard — AF

Organ and Other Keyboard Music

Have No Fear, Little Flock (Little Flock) — found in *6 Hymn Preludes*, set 2 — J. Eggert — CPH

The King of Love My Shepherd Is (St. Columba) — found in *Two Choral Preludes II* — R. Milford — OUP

The Lord's My Shepherd, I'll Not Want (Brother James' Air) — D. Wood — SMP

FIFTH SUNDAY
OF EASTER

Revised
  Common: John 15:1-8*
Episcopal: John 14:15-21+
Lutheran: John 15:1-8*

"I am the vine and you are the branches. If a man remains in me and I in him, he will bear much fruit; apart from me you can do nothing."

Angie Latta

Note: "My Father is glorified by this, that you bear much fruit and become my disciples." How are you doing at glorifying the Father? How are we doing as a congregation?

---

*See *Worship Workbook For The Gospels, Cycle A* for more material relating to this lesson.
+See *Worship Workbook For The Gospels, Cycle A* for material relating to this lesson. None of the material printed below relates to this text.

Printed Resources

___ Greeting

Ldr: Jesus Christ is the true vine.
Cng: **And we are your branches, O Lord.**
Ldr: Every branch that bears fruit he prunes to make it bear more fruit.
Cng: **Prune us today, O Lord, so that our lives can glorify the Vinegrower.**

___ Great Thanksgiving Prayer (adapted from Psalm 80:8, Jeremiah 2:21 and 5:10, Hosea 10:1 and 14:7, Zechariah 8:12, John 15:1-8, and Revelation 14:18)

Ldr: The Lord be with you.
Cng: **And also with you.**
Ldr: Lift up your hearts.
Cng: **We lift them up to the Lord.**
Ldr: Let us give thanks to the Lord our God.
Cng: **It is right to give our thanks and praise.**
Ldr: It is right, and a good and joyful thing,
       always and everywhere to give thanks to you,
       Father Almighty, creator of heaven and earth.
       You brought a vine out of Egypt,
       drove out the nations before it,

161

and planted it in the land of your promise.
Though a choice vine, from the purest stock,
it degenerated and became a wild vine.
Time and again you sent armies through the vine-rows
stripping away the branches that were not yours.
Under your care, Israel became a luxuriant vine,
but they laid their fruit on the altars of false gods.
The more you increased their fruit,
the more altars they built to these gods.
Still, you loved the vine you had planted,
and sent prophets into the vineyard to say:
"Once again the vine shall live beneath the shadow of God."
"There shall be a sowing of peace,
and the vine shall yield its fruit,
and the skies shall give their dew."
And so, with your people on earth
and all the company of heaven
we praise your name and join their unending hymn:

Cng: **Holy, holy, holy Lord, God of power and might,**
heaven and earth are full of your glory.
Hosanna in the highest.
Blessed is he who comes in the name of the Lord.
Hosanna in the highest.

Ldr: You are a holy God, and blessed is the one you send to us.
From the root of David, under the shadow of your Spirit,
the shoot of Jesus sprouted and grew.
He is the true vine,
to which you have grafted us as his branches.
Apart from him we wither and die,
and are good for nothing but to be thrown into the fire.
But, as we abide in him, he abides in us,
and we bear much fruit that glorifies you, vinegrower God.
In Jesus, we live beneath your shadow.
Your peace is sown in our hearts,
and your heavens water us with their dews.
And all this is made possible because of the love
with which Jesus has loved us.
On the night in which Jesus gave himself up for us
he took bread, gave thanks to you, broke the bread,
gave it to his disciples, and said:
"Take, eat; this is my body which is given for you.
Do this in remembrance of me."
When the supper was over, he took the cup,
gave thanks to you, gave it to his disciples, and said:
"Drink from this, all of you;
this is my blood of the new covenant,

162

poured out for you and for many
for the forgivness of sins.
Do this, as often as you drink it,
in remembrance of me."
And so,
in remembrance of these your mighty acts in Jesus Christ,
we offer ourselves in praise and thanksgiving
as a holy and living sacrifice,
in union with Christ's offering for us,
as we proclaim the mystery of faith.

Cng: **Christ has died; Christ is risen; Christ will come again.**

Ldr: Jesus is coming again,
and when he comes his angels will gather our ripe fruit
for the glory of your eternal kingdom.
But until he comes, let us abide in Christ,
and let Christ abide in us.
Draw us beneath the shadow of your Holy Spirit,
along with these gifts of bread and wine.
Make them be for us the body and blood of Jesus,
and let them nourish us with his love and faithfulness,
that we might bear the same fruit for your glory.
Through your Son, Jesus Christ,
with the Holy Spirit in your holy church,
all honor and glory is yours, almighty Father,
now and forever.

Cng: **Amen.**

___ Commissioning and Blessing

Jesus told his disciples,
"If you abide in me,
and my words abide in you,
ask for whatever you wish,
and it will be done for you."
May you know this promise kept,
under the care of our Vinegrower-God,
now and forever. **Amen.**

Hymns and Choruses

(The asterisk [*] indicates hymns or choruses that are addressed to God and can be used as prayers.)

___ "Amid the World's Black Wilderness"
___ "Christ Loves the Church"
___ *"Forth in Thy Name, O Lord"

___ "His Name Is Life"
___ "In Him We Live"
___ *"In My Life, Lord, Be Glorified"
___ "Let God Be God in Me"
___ "Like the Murmur of the Dove's Song"
___ *"My Life Is In You, Lord"
___ "Sent Forth by God's Blessing"
___ "The Strong Name of Jesus"
___ "There's a Spirit in the Air"
___ *"We Are an Offering"

Reading the Scripture

___ Have a person read this lesson, and use the choir to provide the echoes to emphasize certain thoughts.

Ldr: "I am the true vine..."
Chr: True vine.
Ldr: "...and my Father is the vinegrower."
Chr: Vinegrower.
Ldr: "He removes every branch in me that bears no fruit."
Chr: Every branch.
Ldr: "Every branch that bears fruit he prunes to make it bear more fruit."
Ch1: More fruit.
Ch2: More fruit.
Ch3: And more fruit.
Ldr: "You have already been cleansed by the word that I have spoken to you. Abide in me..."
Chr: Abide in me.
Ldr: "...as I abide in you."
Chr: Abide in you.
Ldr: "Just as the branch cannot bear fruit by itself unless it abides in the vine, neither can you unless you abide in me."
Chr: Abide in me.
Ldr: "I am the vine..."
Chr: The vine.
Ldr: "...you are the branches."
Chr: The branches.
Ldr: "Those who abide in me and I in them bear much fruit..."
Chr: Much fruit.
Ldr: "...because apart from me you can do nothing."
Chr: Nothing.
Ldr: "Whoever does not abide in me is thrown away like a branch and withers..."
Chr: Thrown away and withers.
Ldr: "...such branches are gathered, thrown into the fire, and burned."
Chr: Thrown into the fire and burned.

164

Ldr: "If you abide in me, and my words abide in you, ask for whatever you wish..."
Chr: Whatever you wish.
Ldr: "...and it will be done for you."
Chr: Will be done for you.
Ldr: "My Father is glorified..."
Chr: Glorified.
Ldr: "...glorified by this, that you bear much fruit..."
Ch1: Much fruit.
Ch2: Much fruit.
Ldr: "...and become my disciples."
Chr: And become his disciples.
(The choir sings a doxology or a praise chorus.)

Responses to the Word

___ Develop a "shopping list" of ways that worshipers can bear fruit in their lives. Have them check at least one of the ways for them to bear fruit in the coming week, and challenge them to do so. Some possibilities for the list include:

Read the Bible to a blind person or a small child.

Let a nursing home resident dictate a letter you write to one of his or her friends or relatives.

Bake cookies and take them to a new resident on your street and invite him or her to worship with you next Sunday.

Offer your friendship to a lonely person.

Take two or three youth out to lunch. Listen to their concerns.

Take on a task to improve the environment for everyone.

Forgive somebody who has hurt you.

Compose a poem or a song praising God.

Paint a room in an elderly person's home.

Plant a garden and give the produce away.

Clean the cupboards in the church kitchen.

Enroll yourself for music lessons so that you can use the new skill to praise God.

Write a letter to the newspaper editor to lift up some issue that would concern Christ.

Offer yourself as a free babysitter to help a busy parent.

Drama and Movement

___ Gather the small children in the church. Let them color and cut out paper costumes that they can use to dress up as the vine, the branches, the fruit, and even the fire. Who should they dress up as the vinegrower? Let these children act out the words of the gospel lesson as an older child reads it.

Visuals

___ Ask someone in the congregation who owns a video camera to go around the communtiy and record people bearing fruit for God. These could be people in the congregation, or just anyone in the community. A youth group might take this on as a project. They could even present the scenes they taped in a television news show format, with the exception that they will report on good news.

Anthems and Special Music

(John 14:15-21)
See Sixth Sunday of Easter in *Worship Workbook For The Gospels*, *Cycle A*
If Ye Love Me, Keep My Commandments — I. Fischer — med. solo w/keyboard — CFE
Two Hymn Anthems — R. E. Jones — SATB w/organ — PA
Come, Thou Holy Spirit — F. Jackson — SATB w/organ — PA

(John 15:1-8)
See Sixth Sunday of Easter in *Worship Workbook For The Gospels*, *Cycle A*
Alleluia! Jesus Is Risen — D. Johnson — SATB w/keyboard — from *With One Voice* — AF
A Vineyard Grows — K. Lee Scott — SATB w/organ — MSM
As the Father Loves Me, So Have I Loved You — R. Schultz — SATB w/organ — CPH
I Am the Vine — D. Doig — med. solo — from *Everything for the Church Soloist* — HP
I Am the Vine — C. McCormick — SATB w/keyboard — found in *Anthems from Scripture* — SH
I Danced in the Morning — American Shaker/S. Carter — Unison w/keyboard — from *Hymnal Supplement 1991* — GIA
In the Beginning, before Pain and Sinning — A. Lovelace — Unison w/keyboard — from *Songs of Rejoicing* — SPC
I Received the Living God — Anonymous/D. Cherwien — Unison w/keyboard — from *With One Voice* — AF
Like the Murmur of the Dove's Song — D. Robinson — Unison w/keyboard — from *Songs of Rejoicing* — SPC
Many Are the Lightbeams — O. Widestrand/M. Haugen — Unison w/keyboard — from *Hymnal Supplement 1991* — GIA
O Blessed Spring — R. B. Farlee — Unison w/keyboard — from *With One Voice* — AF
The Vine Most Surely I Am — H. Schütz — SSATTB unaccompanied — CMP
We Have Been Told — D. Haas — Unison w/keyboard — from *Hymnal Supplement 1991* — GIA

Organ and Other Keyboard Music

Forth In Thy Name, O Lord (Song 34) — found in *113 Variations on Hymn Tunes for Organ* — NOV
Like the Murmur of the Dove's Song (Bridegroom) — found in *Four Chorale Preludes* — P. Gehring — CPH
Sent Forth by God's Blessing (The Ash Grove) — found in *Interpretations*, Book II — D. Cherwien — AMSI

SIXTH SUNDAY OF EASTER

Revised
  Common: John 15:9-17
Episcopal: John 15:9-17
Lutheran: John 15:9-17

FRIENDS
OF
CHRIST

Gail Throckmorton Warner

Note: All that Jesus told us has been done to put his joy in us. So shall we be solemn and serious today? Or shall we shout and sing our praises?

Printed Resources

___ Greeting

Ldr: Jesus loves you!
Cng: (Sing verse 1 of the hymn "Jesus Loves Me.")
Ldr: Jesus loves us!
Cng: (Sing verse 2 of the hymn, but sing "us" instead of "me.")
Ldr: Our joy is complete because Jesus loves us.
Cng: (Sing verse 3 of the hymn.)
(The refrain of the hymn can be repeated to introduce a time for chorus singing.)

___ Prayer for Illumination

God of abiding love,
  Jesus calls us friends
  because he has taught us your truth.
Tell us more, God who gives what is asked,
  so that we may grow
  in truth, service and love. Amen.

___ Prayer of Confession and Assurance of Pardon

All: **Merciful God, we do not deserve your love,**
      nor do we deserve the love of our Savior, Jesus Christ.
      We have not obeyed Jesus' commands.
      We have not loved others as Jesus has loved us.
      We have not laid down our lives for our friends.

Jesus has called us friends;
but all too often we have treated him as a stranger,
or, even worse, as an enemy.
Eternal God, we do not deserve the life you offer,
much less to be loved by you,
or to be called a friend of Jesus Christ.
Have mercy upon us, O Lord.
Have mercy upon us, blessed Jesus.
Have mercy upon us, O Lord.

(Continue in silent prayer.)

Ldr: Brothers and sisters,
   our mighty God still loves us.
   Jesus still calls us friends,
   and lays down his life that this might be so.
   Through the love and death of Jesus Christ
   you are forgiven!

Cng: **Through the love and death of Jesus Christ**
   you are forgiven!

Ldr: Let us rejoice in this, the greatest of all gifts!

Cng: **And let us obey the commands of Jesus Christ,**

Ldr: By loving one another,

Cng: **Even at the cost of our lives,**

Ldr: And bearing fruit that lasts.

Cng: **Amen!**

___ Commissioning and Blessing

Jesus said, "I have called you friends
   because I have made known to you
   everything that I have heard from my Father.
You did not choose me,
   but I chose you.
And I appointed you to go and bear fruit,
   fruit that will last,
   so that my Father
   will give you whatever you ask in my name." **Amen.**

Hymns and Choruses

(The asterisk [*] indicates hymns or choruses that are addressed to God and can be used as prayers.)

___ *"Abide with Me"
___ *"Abide with Us, Our Savior"
___ *"Help Us Accept Each Other"
___ *"I Love You, Lord"

___ *"I'm Forever Grateful"

___ "Jesus Es Mi Rey Soberano" ("O Jesus, My King and My Sovereign")

___ "Jesus Is All the World to Me"

___ "Jesus Our Friend and Brother"

___ *"Jesus, Thy Boundless Love to Me"

___ *"Joyful, Joyful, We Adore Thee"

___ *"Lord of All Nations, Grant Me Grace"

___ *"Love Divine, All Loves Excelling"

___ *"O God, I Love Thee"

___ "Oh, How He Loves You and Me"

___ "One There Is, above All Others"

___ *"The Gift of Love"

___ *"Thee Will I Love, My Strength"

Reading the Scripture

___ This is a good lesson to print in the worship bulletin (or use pew Bibles) so that the congregation can do the reading. Have the right and left sides of the congregation alternate the reading at each verse. This usually works more smoothly if there are two people in front to lead the two sides of the congregation.

___ Have one person read the gospel lesson, and have the congregation respond to the lesson by singing the hymn, "Abide with Us, Our Savior." The reading and singing alternate like this:

Read verses 9-11
Sing stanza 1
Read verses 12-13
Sing stanza 2
Read verses 14-15
Sing stanza 3
Read verse 16-17
Sing stanza 4

Responses to the Word

___ Use the prayer of confession and assurance of pardon printed above.

___ Move the worship service into the church's fellowship hall, and hold a love feast. Originating in the early church, and closely connected with the Lord's Supper, this service includes sharing food, prayer, testimonies, and singing. Communion bread, wine and grape juice are not served, because doing so would lead to confusion with the Lord's Supper. Other breads like crackers, rolls or sweet breads are usually used with water. Of course a full meal would be appropriate as well. The service is mostly a time of praise and testimony. The scriptures are read. A mixture of spontaneous and fixed prayer (such as the "Lord's Prayer" or "Be Present at Our Table Lord") are lifted up to God. Testimonies are shared spontaneously by the worshipers as they tell what God has been doing in their lives and witness to the hope and trust that they place in God for their future. Hymns, choruses, and other songs are sung. There is a lot of participation by all the worshipers, including the children and youth. A sermon is not usually part of the service, but a pastor may add his or her personal witness to what is shared spontaneously by the worshipers. Since this is not a sacramental service, it may be led entirely by laypersons. For the same reason, this may present a good format for celebrating God's love with a congregation of another denomination that would not be free to join together in celebrating the Lord's Supper. Food remaining after the meal is normally taken to people who could not be present as a way of sharing the love in the larger community. *The United Methodist Book of Worship* has a more detailed description of the love feast.

Drama and Movement

____ Use two or more dancers to interpret the words of this lesson.

____ Ask the youth in the congregation to develop and present two or three short skits that illustrate obedience to Christ's command to love.

Visuals

____ It is rather campy, but the sanctuary could be decorated with red hearts and red flowers. Some congregations could have fun with this. Heart-shaped balloons filled with helium can be attached to the pews so that they float over the heads of the worshipers. Other hearts can be attached to the walls. Worshipers can be given heart-shaped nametags. The nametags can also bear the words "Friend of Christ."

____ Hang a horizontal banner on (or under) the sanctuary's cross. The sign should read "Fruit that lasts."

Anthems and Special Music

Christ is Risen! Shout Hosanna! — W. Rowan — Unison w/keyboard — from *Songs of Rejoicing* — SPC
Give Thanks to God on High — R. Edwards — Unison w/keyboard — from *Songs of Rejoicing* — SPC
I Have Chosen You — L. Allen — SATB w/brass — BP
My Song is Love Unknown — J. Ireland — Unison w/keyboard — from *With One Voice* — AF
No Greater Love — M. Joncas — Unison w/keyboard — from *Hymnal Supplement 1991* — GIA
Of Divine Love — found in *Three Antiphonal Carols* — E. Routley — SATB w/keyboard — NOV
Ubi Caritas et Amor — J. Berthier — SATB w/keyboard and opt. instruments — from *With One Voice* — AF
You Shall be My Witnesses — J. Chepponis — SATB w/keyboard, 2 violins, flute — GIA

Organ and Other Keyboard Music

Abide With Me (Eventide) — found in *Twenty Hymn-Tune Preludes*, set 1 — C. S. Lang — OUP

Joyful, Joyful, We Adore Thee (Hymn to Joy) — J. Engel — found in *Concordia Hymn Prelude Series*, vol. 27 — CPH

Love Divine, All Loves Excelling (Hyfrydol) — found in *Ten Hymn Preludes in Trio Style* — D. Harris — HWG

ASCENSION DAY

Revised
  Common: Luke 24:44-53*
Episcopal: Luke 24:49-53* or
             Mark 16:9-15, 19-20
Lutheran: Luke 24:44-53*

"When he had led them out to the vicinity of Bethany, he lifted up his hands and blessed them. While he was blessing them, he left them and was taken up to heaven."

Angie Latta

Note: The God in the Old Testament is met again in the New Testament, and again in the faithful witness of today's disciples.

* See *Worship Workbook For The Gospels, Cycle A* for more material related to this lesson.

Printed Resources

___ Greeting

Ldr: Jesus opens minds.
Cng: **Open our minds to resurrection-thinking, O Lord.**
Ldr: Jesus blesses believers.
Cng: **Bless our witness with ascension-living, O Lord.**

___ Prayer

Father, like the first disciples,
   our understanding is in part
   and too shallow to sustain us.
   Our strength fails,
   and our witness falls silent.
Jesus said he would send what you promised.
   Let it be so.
   Clothe us with power from on high.
   Open our minds to understanding,
   and empower us to be your witnesses,
   beginning in our community
   and extending to all nations. Amen.

___ Prayer for Illumination

Ldr: ~~Awesome God of heaven and earth,~~

As Jesus opened the minds of the disciples
   to understand the scriptures. *Gracious*
~~Cng:~~ **Let our minds be opened too, ~~God.~~** *Amen*

Ldr: Jesus blessed the disciples and filled them with great joy.

Cng: **Let us also be blessed and filled with your joy, O God.**

(Read the lesson. Then have the congregation break into a joyful hymn or song, while dancers give the joy a visible expression.)

___ Commissioning and Blessing

Benediction:

In the name of the ascended Christ,
   I lift up my hands and give you our Savior's blessing.
As long as Christ is in heaven,
   may you be filled with the great joy that comes from believing;
and when Christ returns,
   may your joy be multiplied a thousandfold. **Amen.**

Hymns and Choruses

(The asterisk [*] indicates hymns or choruses that are addressed to God and can be used as prayers.)

___ *"A Hymn of Glory Let Us Sing"
___ *"All Hail, King Jesus"
___ "All Hail the Power of Jesus' Name"
___ *"All Praise to Thee, for Thou, O King Divine"
___ "Alleluia, Alleluia"
___ "Alleluia! Sing to Jesus"
___ "At the Name of Jesus"
___ "Canticle of Christ's Obedience"
___ "Christ Is Alive"
___ "Christ Is the World's Light"
___ "Crown Him with Many Crowns"
___ "Glory to the Lamb"
___ "Hail the Day That Sees Him Rise"
___ "Hail Thee, Festival Day"
___ *"Hail, Thou Once Despised Jesus"
___ "He Is Exalted"
___ "His Name Is Wonderful"
___ "Jesus Shall Reign"
___ "Look, the Sight Is Glorious"
___ *"Lord, I Lift Your Name on High"
___ "Majesty, Worship His Majesty"

173

___ *"O Lord Most High, Eternal King"
___ "Rejoice, the Lord Is King"
___ "Rejoice, the Lord of Life Ascends"
___ "See the Conqueror Mounts in Triumph"
___ "The Head That Once Was Crowned"
___ "The Lord Ascendeth Up On High"
___ "The Lord Reigneth"
___ "To Him Who Sits on the Throne"
___ "Up Through Endless Ranks of Angels"
___ "We Will Glorify"
___ "Who Is He in Yonder Stall"
___ *"You Are Crowned with Many Crowns"
___ *"You Are My God"

Reading the Scripture

___ See the prayer for illumination printed above.

___ Print the gospel lesson in the worship bulletin to be read responsively with the congregation. The leader begins by reading verse 44, and then the congregation reads verse 45. The leader reads verses 46-49. Then the congregation reads verses 50-51, the reader verse 52, and the congregation concludes with verse 53.

Responses to the Word

___ Ask your congregation's praise and worship team to prepare a musical response that lets the congregation become living echoes of the disciples described in verses 52-53. If your congregation does not have one, borrow a praise and worship team from a neighboring church that is doing a lot of contemporary music. Follow the congregation's normal pattern of worship until the gospel lesson has been read. Have the pastor briefly emphasize verses 52-53 and lay the foundation for the congregation to join the praise and worship team in worshiping and blessing God "with great joy."

___ The pastor can preach the sermon in three parts with a musical response after each part. The first part of the sermon can focus on verses 46-47, where the preacher can talk about how Jesus' forgiveness relieves us of the suffering our sin causes. The worshipers can respond by singing "Do, Lord, Remember Me" or "Something Beautiful." From here the preacher moves on to verse 48, and talks of how we are to tell others about the good news we hear in Jesus. The worshipers can respond by singing "Pass It On" or "Here I Am, Lord." (If the congregation likes choruses let them sing just the refrain of "Here I Am, Lord.") Finally, the preacher can move to verse 49, and talk about how God clothes people with power. The worshipers can respond by singing either "We Shall Overcome" or "There Is A Balm in Gilead." Let the last response flow into the singing of the refrain from "Blessed Assurance." Use this refrain like a chorus, and repeat it a few times before moving to the sending forth or next act of worship.

Drama and Movement

___ Ask a Sunday school class to research Old Testament prophecies relating to Jesus Christ. Let the class members dress as Moses, prophets, psalmists, and other Old Testament figures to recite the prophecies. Then have the gospel lesson read.

___ Have an Ascension Day parade through your community. Join with other congregations if it is possible. Use banners and dancers to add to the occassion. A float would be another way to add to the festivities. The choir, riding on a vehicle, could lead singing. Clowns could pass out modern language translations of the scriptures to onlookers. Celebrate the ascension of Christ so that the whole community hears the congregation's witness.

Visuals

___ Recruit someone in the congregation to prepare a bulletin cover sketch or a banner depicting the cross sitting or based on the words, "the law of Moses, the prophets, and the psalms must be fulfilled."

Anthems and Special Music

(Luke 24:44-53)
See Ascension Day in *Worship Workbook For The Gospels*, *Cycle A*

(Mark 16:9-15, 19-20)
See Ascension Day in *Worship Workbook For The Gospels*, *Cycle A*
Go Ye Into All the World — V. Ford — SATB w/opt. keyboard — CF
Go Ye Into All the World — C. McCormick — SATB w/opt. keyboard — found in *Anthems from Scripture* — SH
Lo, I Am With You Always — R. Peek — SATB w/keyboard — AP

Organ and Other Keyboard Music

A Hymn of Glory Let Us Sing (Lasst uns erfreuen) — found in *Five Preludes on Familiar Hymns* — H. Hopson — HF
All Hail the Power of Jesus' Name (Coronation) — J. Langlais — found in *Modern Organ Music*, Book 2 — ed. D. Willcocks — OUP
Crown Him with Many Crowns (Diademata) — C. Callahan — MSM

SEVENTH SUNDAY OF EASTER

Revised
  Common: John 17:6-19
Episcopal: John 17:11b-19
Lutheran: John 17:6-19

"So that they may have my joy"

Note: How does it make you feel to know that Jesus has prayed for us? And how do you feel when you realize that Jesus is still praying for us?

*Figures adapted from work of unknown artist in ceramic sculpture.

Printed Resources

___ Greeting

Ldr: Christ's-men, Christ's-women, come.
      You do not belong to the world, come.
      Listen, as our Savior prays for us to our God.
Cng: **Pray for each of us. Pray for all of us, Holy Jesus.**
Ldr: Come and be wrapped in the protection of our almighty God.
      Come and be sanctified in the truth.
      Come and be one with your new brothers and sisters.
Cng: **Protect and sanctify us, Holy God,**
      and make us one with each other,
      just as you and our Savior are one.

___ Prayer

Holy Father,
sometimes we feel very protected from evil,
  but sometimes we feel like we need Jesus to pray for us again.
Sometimes we feel like we are living in another world,
  and sometimes we feel too much a part of this world.
Sometimes we remember the truth Jesus shared from you,
  and sometimes we cannot even remember your name.
Father, save us from being "sometimes" people.
  Sanctify us to living full-time in your word.
For your word is our truth, and your truth is our life,
  and as your truth is lived, the joy of Christ is made complete.
Let it be so today, and in all times to come. Amen.

____ Affirmation of Faith

We declare our trust in God,
  Creator of the universe,
  and of each of us who live upon this earth.
We assert that Jesus Christ
  came from heaven to be born and raised a human with us.
  Jesus made God known, and spoke God's Word on earth.
  Those whom God gave to Jesus as believers
  were drawn into a new world that is yet to be fully realized.
  Unbelievers who remained in the old world hated Jesus,
  crucified him, and sealed his dead body in a tomb.
  But Jesus rose from the dead, appeared to believers,
  communed with them, and charged them to continue in his way.
  Then Jesus returned to God from whom he had come.
We affirm the Apostles of Jesus Christ,
  who received God's Word, and kept it in their hearts and lives.
  Because they no longer belonged to the world,
  unbelievers hated and persecuted them too.
  Though one was lost, as scripture had prophesied,
  the others held to the Word given to them.
  God sanctified them in the truth,
  and protected them from the evil one's corruptions.
  All were severely tested, and some were martyred,
  but upon their firsthand witness, God built the church.
We affirm the church,
  who through these many generations
  has received and kept the faith in God,
  and the Word of God that Jesus made known.
  God continues to protect the church,
  and to sanctify it in the truth.
  We are part of this church,
  and we pray without ceasing for the Holy Spirit of God
  to guard us and to sanctify us,
  that the joy of Jesus Christ
  may be made complete in our faith.

____ Commissioning and Blessing

Ldr: Father Above,
      in the name of Jesus Christ I pray.
      These people know your name,
      and they trust Jesus as having come from you.
      Now they no longer belong to the world.
      Because they have received your word,
      the world hates them.

Because they have received your word,
they need your protection from the evil one.
Holy Father, protect them.
Sanctify them in truth,
and make them one with each other
just as you and the Christ are one.

Cng: **Amen.**

Ldr: Brothers and sisters,
in the name of Jesus Christ I charge you.
Keep our Father's word in your hearts,
be sanctified in truthful living,
and be of one spirit with each other.
Know that evil has no power over you,
that your life is protected,
and that you no longer belong to this world.
Rejoice, and live as those who belong to God.

Cng: **Amen.**

Hymns and Choruses

(The asterisk [*] indicates hymns or choruses that are addressed to God and can be used as prayers.)

___ "A Charge to Keep I Have"
___ "Be Still, My Soul"
___ "Beams of Heaven as I Go"
___ "By Gracious Powers"
___ *"Christians, While on Earth Abiding"
___ *"Dear Lord and Father of Mankind"
___ "How Firm a Foundation"
___ *"It's Me, It's Me, O Lord" ("Standing in the Need of Prayer")
___ *"Lift Every Voice and Sing"
___ *"Lord, Keep Us Steadfast in Your Word"
___ *"My Prayer Rises to Heaven"
___ *"Near to the Heart of God"
___ *"O Jesus, I Have Promised"
___ "Prayer Is the Soul's Sincere Desire"
___ "We'll Understand It Better By and By"
___ *"With God as Our Friend"

Reading the Scripture

___ See the first suggestion under "Drama and Movement" below.

___ Another way to read the lesson would be to have someone dressed like Jesus come to the front of the sanctuary and kneel in prayer. Turn the lights down low. Let the person speak Jesus' words from memory.

___ Have a person read the gospel lesson from the lectern, but have another person introduce the reading with these words:

> *This morning's gospel lesson comes from what is known as Jesus' high priestly prayer. Listen to what Jesus says about us to God, hear what he asks God to do for us, and take heart in what you hear.*

Responses to the Word

___ Invite the worshipers to be in intercessory prayer for each other. Just as Christ prayed for them, let them pray for each other.

___ Use the prayer printed above after the sermon.

___ Many denominational books of worship have prayers and litanies for the church. Use one of these for the worshipers to pray for themselves and the church, just as Christ first prayed for them.

___ Invite the worshipers to join in the affirmation of faith printed above.

___ After a sermon on following Christ's truth in a hostile world, have the congregation sing some of the hymns and songs listed above that proclaim the assurance of God's protection of the church.

Drama and Movement

___ After the congregation gathers, turn the sanctuary lights down low. Let an unseen reader speak the words of the gospel lesson over the public address system. The effect should be something like listening in on Jesus praying. There are several ways to follow a beginning like this, but one would be to form the entire service around the words of Jesus' prayer. Verses 6-8 could be read again to introduce the proclamation part of the worship service. Verses 9-12 might lead into a time of thanksgiving and communion. Then the sending forth part of the worship service could be introduced with verses 13-19. The worship planners can determine how much they want to base the different acts of worship on the words of Jesus' prayer.

___ Gather a group of adults who enjoy history. Ask them to research and prepare a report on how the world has hated those who belong to Christ. This report could be presented in the style of a news broadcast that looks back over the entire Christian experience. Be careful that this not get too heavy with the blood and guts of centuries of Christian persecution. Careful writing, even salted with a little humor, can make the presentation more palatable to contemporary Christians. After all, the purpose is not to make the worshipers paranoid, but just to provide a springboard for understanding Jesus' meaning in verses 14-15. Shining some light on how God has protected believers from the evil one over the centuries will help soften the tendency toward paranoia, too. History provides ample evidence of God's protection, but it is more difficult to uncover because humans prefer to concentrate on the evil rather than the good, even when recording history.

Visuals

___ Have an artist in the congregation prepare a mural, sculpture or banner that shows Jesus praying the prayer that composes this gospel lesson.

___ Ask an artistic person in the congregation to make a banner with the words "...so that they may have my joy made complete in themselves." The banner should be bright, joyful, and even a bit playful. The banner could be made using just the words, or the artist may add figures and other graphics as they need to help the worshipers appreciate the words.

Anthems and Special Music

Lord, Sanctify Me Wholly — J. Pasquet — SATB w/keyboard — HTF
Thus Spake Jesus — M. Head — low or high solo w/organ — BH

Organ and Other Keyboard Music

Christians, While On Earth Abiding (Werde Munter) — found in *Nine Chorale Preludes* — J. Pasquet
     — AF
How Firm A Foundation (Foundation) — found in the *Diane Bish Organ Book*, vol. 4 — D. Bish —
     FBM
Lift Every Voice and Sing (Lift Every Voice and Sing) — D. Busarow — found in *Concordia Hymn
     Prelude Series*, vol. 30 — CPH

PENTECOST SUNDAY

Revised
Common: John 15:26-27; 16:4b-15
Episcopal: John 20:19-23* or
John 7:37-39a+ or
John 14:8-17#
Lutheran: John 7:37-39a+

Gail Throckmorton Warner

Note: We bow in thankful joy that Jesus did not leave us alone in the world, waiting for the end time. Jesus sends the Advocate to stand beside us and testify to the truthfulness of what Jesus taught us to believe.

* See the Second Sunday of Easter and Pentecost Day in *Worship Workbook For The Gospels, Cycle A* for more resources on this text.
\+ See Pentecost Day in *Worship Workbook For The Gospels, Cycle A* for more resources on this text.
\# See the Fifth Sunday of Easter in *Worship Workbook For The Gospels, Cycle A* for more resources on this text.

Printed Resources

___ Greeting

Ldr: The Advocate comes,
from the Father to us.
Jesus sends this holy friend.
Cng: **Gentle Murmur, Rushing Wind, New Flame eager with might,**
come to your church assembled.
Ldr: The Spirit of Truth comes,
from the Father
to testify on Jesus' behalf.
Cng: **Holy Gift, Miraculous Sign, Life-Blood filling the vine,**
come to your church assembled.
Ldr: The Holy Spirit of God comes
to open our trembling lips
and energize our tongues with truth.

Cng: **Voice of Prayer, Loving Power, Healer of every divide,**
     come to your church assembled.
(Have the congregation join in singing the hymn "Like the Murmur of the Dove's Song.")

___ Prayer

Holy Paraclete, Spirit of God,
   forget the wind and flames and other such powerful stuff.
   There are days to march into battle, but not today.
Today we need you as Holy Comforter,
   wrapping us in gentle folds of caring,
   warming us in deep piles of love.
Be our Godly Counselor,
   patiently listening to our moans,
   sorting through all our confusion.
Let us lean on you, Cosmic Helper.
   Until Christ returns, hold our hands
   and help us get through, one day at a time.
Stand beside us, Faithful Advocate.
   Take our part in the world's hostile court.
   Tell us once more that Jesus' love saves.
We'll march with you again tomorrow, Paraclete Friend,
   but today we just need you to hold us
   and reassure us that God's love conquers all. Amen.

___ Commissioning and Blessing

Men and women, children of God,
   the Advocate is among us.
We can stand firm in our faith,
   because the Advocate will prove
   that our trust in Jesus is not in vain.
We can stand firm,
   because the Advocate will convict
   the world of its sin.
We can stand firm,
   because the Advocate leads us into all truth
   about the future judgment of this world.
Rejoice and be true,
   because everything that is God's is in Jesus' hands,
   and everything that Jesus has is declared to us
   by the Advocate that Jesus sends among us. **Amen.**

Hymns and Choruses

(The asterisk [*] indicates hymns or choruses that are addressed to God and can be used as prayers.)

___ *"Come Down, O Love Divine"
___ *"Come, Gracious Spirit, Heavenly Dove"
___ *"Come, Holy Ghost, God and Lord"
___ *"Come, Holy Ghost, Our Hearts Inspire"
___ *"Come, Holy Ghost, Our Souls Inspire"
___ *"Come, Holy Spirit"
___ *"Come, Oh, Come, O Quickening Spirit"
___ *"Creator Spirit, by Whose Aid"
___ *"Daw-Kee, Aim Daw-Tsi-Taw" ("Great Spirit, Now I Pray")
___ *"Holy Spirit, Thou Art Welcome"
___ *"Holy Spirit, Truth Divine"
___ "In His Presence"
___ *"O Come and Dwell in Me"
___ "O Day Full of Grace"
___ *"O For a Heart to Praise My God"
___ *"O Holy Spirit, Enter In"
___ *"O Spirit of the Living God"
___ *"O Thou Who Camest from Above"
___ *"Spirit of Faith, Come Down"
___ *"Spirit of God"
___ *"Spirit of God, Descend upon My Heart"
___ *"Spirit of the Living God"
___ *"Spirit Song"

Reading the Scripture

___ Intersperse the reading of the gospel lesson with the congregation responding by singing the hymn, "Holy Spirit, Come, Confirm Us." Alternate the verses of the lesson with the stanzas of the hymn as follows:
> Verses 26-27
> Stanza 1
> Verses 4b-7
> Stanza 2
> Verses 8-11
> Stanza 3
> Verses 12-15
> Stanza 4

___ Introduce the reading of the gospel lesson with these words.

Our lesson from the Gospel of John tells us what Jesus said to prepare the disciples for his leaving them. Put yourself in their place as you listen to the reading today. Remember that these hearers had been with Jesus through his three years of ministry. They had seen his life threatened and knew he was in serious danger of being killed. Jesus had talked of dying and being raised again. Listen carefully to John's gospel as we hear how Jesus will help his followers, even after he leaves them.

Responses to the Word

___ Use the prayer printed above after the sermon as a way for the worshipers to relate to the Holy Spirit as a comforter, counselor, advocate and helper.

___ Have the worshipers join in an affirmation of their faith in Jesus Christ, as a way to reaffirm their convictions about Jesus Christ.

___ Have the pastor, or a respected lay person, lead the worshipers in praying for the Holy Spirit to guide the congregation in "all the truth" and "declare ... the things that are to come." This might be in regards to some specific new direction that the congregation is considering or in terms of seeking a vision for the future mission of the congregation.

Drama and Movement

___ Recruit some liturgical dancers to provide an interpretation of the meaning of verses 8-11. There is a lot packed in these few verses, and dancers can take them apart and expand upon them to help the worshipers understand the meaning. For example, sin is not believing in Christ after all that he has done. Have a dancer use his or her body to remind worshipers of what Christ has done, while the other dancers reveal the sin of disbelieving. To help this, the dancers showing disbelief might be contrasted with others who show by their actions that they believe. The same thing could be done by a mime group if dancers are not available.

Visuals

___ Challenge an artist in the congregation to come up with a banner or mural that depicts Jesus leaving his followers and the Holy Spirit going to them. The challenge lies not in depicting Jesus and his followers, but in how to reveal the invisible Spirit. Many artists have used light or a descending dove to accomplish this. Let your artist decide for himself or herself how this can be done for your congregation.

___ Verse 8 says that the Holy Spirit "will prove the world wrong about sin and righteousness and judgment." To illustrate this have a person prepare three flower arrangements. One would be made of red flowers (sin), one of white flowers (righteousness), and one of dark-colored flowers (judgment). The white arrangement could be much larger and more showy, or all three arrangements could be the same size. A sentence in the worship bulletin would clue in the congregation to the symbolism.

Anthems and Special Music

(John 15:26-27; 16:4b-15)
Come, Thou Holy Paraclete — F. Jackson — SATB w/organ — PA
Every Time I Feel the Spirit — D. Adelmann — AATTBB unaccompanied — PA
Gracious Spirit, Heed Our Pleading — W. Niwagila/E. Hovland — SATB w/opt. percussion — from
     With One Voice — AF

Peace I Leave With You — J. Roberts — low or high solo w/organ — GS
The Spirit of Truth — K. Nystedt — SAB w/organ — CPH

(John 20:19-23)
See Easter 2 and Pentecost Day in *Worship Workbook For The Gospels*, *Cycle A*
See Easter 2 in *Worship Workbook For The Gospels*, *Cycle B*
Dona Nobis Pacem — Traditional — 3-part canon — from *With One Voice* — AF
This is the Day — A. M. Bush — Unison w/keyboard — from *Songs of Rejoicing* — SPC
We Walk by Faith and Not by Sight — S. McFarland — Unison w/keyboard — from *With One Voice* — AF

(John 7:37-39a)
See Pentecost Day in *Worship Workbook For The Gospels*, *Cycle A*
Shall We Gather at the River — R. Lowry — SATB unaccompanied — from *With One Voice* — AF

(John 14:8-17)
See the Fifth Sunday of Easter in *Worship Workbook For The Gospels*, *Cycle A*

Organ and Other Keyboard Music

Come Down, O Love Divine (Down Ampney) — Variations on *Down Ampney* — J. Bender — AF
Come, Gracious Spirit, Heavenly Dove (Wareham) — found in *Ten Hymn Preludes*, set II — H. Willan — CFP
Come, Holy Ghost, Our Souls Inspire (Veni Creator) — Chorale and Variations on *Veni Creator* — M. Duruflé— DUR
Come, Holy Ghost, Our Souls Inspire (Veni Creator) — Partita on *Veni, Creator Spiritus* — M. B. Bennett — AF

TRINITY
SUNDAY

Revised
 Common: John 3:1-17*
Episcopal: John 3:1-16*
Lutheran: John 3:1-17*

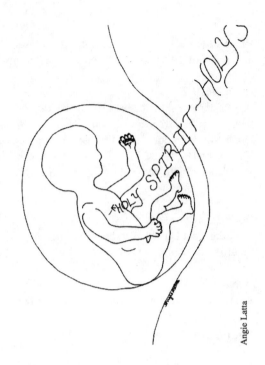

Angie Latta

Note: We bow in reverent worship before the God whose love is known in creating the world, in sending Jesus to bring eternity, and in sending the Spirit to bring new life.

---

* This passage is also covered on the Second Sunday of Lent in *Worship Workbook For The Gospels, Cycle A*.

Printed Resources

___ Greeting

Ldr: Turn on the lights!
　　Throw the doors wide open!
　　Shout and sing!
Cng: **For we want the whole world to know that we believe**
　　in the love of God,
　　in the salvation of Jesus Christ,
　　and in the new birth through the Holy Spirit!
Ldr: We do not come here under the cover of night.
Cng: **We come in the full light of day,**
　　because we believe in the eternal life offered to us by God!
Ldr: We come to give thanks,
　　and to celebrate the love that God gives,
　　even though it is so undeserved.
Cng: **Receive our worship, God of everlasting love.**
　　May our praise be pleasant in your ears,
　　and fall tenderly upon your heart.

_____ Prayer

Holy God, Loving God,
though our minds cannot understand,
let our hearts find hope and life
in the birth that comes from above.
You give this new birth where you choose.
We sense when it happens,
but cannot grasp the mysteries of how it happens.
We can only rejoice and live out the new reality.
As this Spirit-birth opens your kingdom's gates,
we bow before you in thankful awe and joyful wonder.
Our undeserving flesh dances in the eternity
bestowed upon us by the love and grace of Jesus Christ.
Amen.

_____ Commissioning and Blessing

"God so loved the world that he gave his only Son."
    You are loved. You are redeemed. You are called to faith.
Believe in God's love, and in the salvation of Jesus Christ,
    so that God may bestow upon you the gift of eternal life. **Amen.**

Hymns and Choruses

(The asterisk [*] indicates hymns or choruses that are addressed to God and can be used as prayers.)

_____ "All Who Believe and Are Baptized"
_____ *"Dearest Jesus, We Are Here"
_____ "Freely, Freely"
_____ "Hallelujah! What a Savior"
_____ "How Great Thou Art"
_____ *"Lift High the Cross"
_____ "Morning Glory, Starlit Sky"
_____ "My Tribute"
_____ "O How He Loves You and Me"
_____ "O Love, How Deep"
_____ *"There Is a Redeemer"
_____ "Think About His Love"
_____ "This Is a Day of New Beginnings"
_____ *"This Is the Spirit's Entry Now"
_____ "To God Be the Glory"
_____ "We Know That Christ Is Raised"
_____ "What Wondrous Love Is This"
_____ *"Wide Open Are Your Hands"

Reading the Scripture

___ Recruit three readers for this lesson. Have one read the narration, the second read Jesus' words and the third read the words of Nicodemus.

___ Recruit a soloist and accompianist to sing and play the hymn "This Is a Day of New Beginnings." Have the soloist sing the first two verses of this Brian Wren hymn. Then have another person begin reading the gospel lesson. The accompanist can continue playing the hymn softly as the lesson is read. After reading verse 6, the soloist interrupts and sings the first and third stanza of the hymn. Then the reader continues to the end of the lesson. Then the soloist concludes by singing the first, fourth and fifth stanzas of the hymn. The congregation might be invited to join in singing these last three stanzas.

Responses to the Word

___ Offer the sacrament of baptism for unbaptized worshipers, and the reaffirmation of baptism for the majority who are already baptized.

___ Invite people to come forward to the communion rail to pray for new birth from above. Then, as they pray, have the pastor and some of the elders (or pillars) of the church lay their hands on the heads of the praying worshipers. The pastor can say, "What is born of the Spirit is spirit. (Name) , receive the Holy Spirit of God from Jesus Christ, the Son of God." The practice of laying on hands reaches back to the Apostles and helps people visualize what God is doing invisibly.

___ If the second suggestion under "Reading the Scripture" is used, then a sermon on how God makes all things new might follow the singing. The preacher can emphasize the newness found in the "birth from above." If they have not already sung the hymn as part of the reading, the congregation could join in singing the hymn "This Is a Day of New Beginnings." This would flow naturally into a celebration of holy communion, where worshipers celebrate a new relationship with our Lord.

Drama and Movement

___ The gospel lesson can be staged by two actors dressed as Jesus and Nicodemus. Attempt to have them dress in authentic costumes, rather than the typical bathrobes used by too many congregations. This important exchange deserves our best efforts. The sanctuary lights should be brought down low, too, because this encounter is cloaked by the dark of night. Of course, the actors should deliver their lines from memory, too. This adds another touch of authenticity.

___ A liturgical dancer could dance a solo that gives expression to a soul being born from above. Let the dancer play with the images in the gospel lesson to be expressed in the dance. Consider what type of music could be woven into the dancer's movements to enhance the piece. What musical instrument should be played, and does anyone in the congregation know someone who could play such an instrument?

Visuals

___ Have a congregational artist create a banner depicting "born from above." This person can do this with a shadowy (spiritual) hand reaching down from the top of the banner. The hand cradles an adult figure drawn into the fetal position.

___ Does the congregation have someone who can do cartoons? If so, ask this person to draw a cartoon that illustrates the irony of Nicodemus saying, "Rabbi, we know that you are a teacher who has come from God..." while at the same time, he is afraid to let anyone see him talking to Jesus. If he truly knows that Jesus is from God, then why is Nicodemus sneaking around under the cover of night in order to talk to a teacher from God? A cartoon illustrating this irony could be used for a worship bulletin cover, a banner, or even in literature promoting attendance at this particular worship service where this irony will be addressed in more detail, especially in terms of how so many of us are still doing this today.

Anthems and Special Music

See Second Sunday of Lent in *Worship Workbook For The Gospels*, *Cycle A* and Fourth Sunday of
     Lent, Cycle B
Baptized in Water — Gaelic tune/B. W. Bisbee — SATB w/keyboard, from *With One Voice* — AF
Comfortable Words — L. Betteridge — SATB w/organ — PA
For God So Loved the World — R. Edwards — Unison w/keyboard — from *Songs of Rejoicing* —
     SPC
Great God of All the Universe — J. Pinson — Unison w/keyboard — from *Songs of Rejoicing* —
     SPC
Truly, Truly I Say Unto You — G. Krapf — Unison w/organ — CPH
Unless One is Born Anew — J. Bender — Unison w/organ — CPH

Organ and Other Keyboard Music

All Who Believe and Are Baptized (Es ist das heil) — found in *Orgelwerke II: Chorale Preludes* —
     D. Buxtehude — CFP
Dearest Jesus, We Are Here (Liebster Jesu) — found in *Improvisations on Classic Chorales* — P.
     Manz — MSM
Lift High the Cross (Crucifer) — Partita on *Crucifer* — C. Callahan — CPH

---

1. Fred B. Craddock, John H. Hayes, Carl R. Holladay, Gene M. Tucker, *Preaching the New Common Lectionary: Year B, Lent, Holy Week, Easter* (Abingdon Press: Nashville, 1984), p. 23.

2. *The United Methodist Book of Worship* (Nashville, Tennessee: The United Methodist Publishing House, 1992), pp. 581-584.

PROPER ONE

Episcopal: Mark 1:40-45*

PROPER TWO

Episcopal: Mark 2:1-12*

PROPER THREE

Episcopal: Mark 2:18-22*

*These three gospel lessons are duplicated on the sixth, seventh and eighth Sundays after Epiphany. See those days for resource material.

MAY 29-JUNE 4
PROPER 4
PENTECOST 2

Revised
 Common: Mark 2:23—3:6
Episcopal: Mark 2:23-28
Lutheran: Mark 2:23—3:6

Note: Some mature Chris-
tians have hearts so full of
love and obedience to God
that they understand God's
intentions in giving us the
law. Christ was like this, and
thus able to obey the spirit of
God's law. This is much more
desirable than just obeying
the letter of the law.

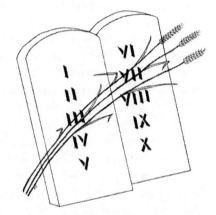

God made the Sabbath for us.

Printed Resources

___ Greeting

(Put Ld2 and Ld3 together at a microphone that allows them to appear in opposition to Ld1.
For example, put them at one side of the chancel and Ld1 at the other side.)

Ld1: This is Sunday, the day of the Lord's resurrection!
Cng: **Let us rejoice and be glad in it!**
Ld2: Yes, this is Sunday, the Christians' sabbath.
       So, don't nag us with stories of hungry people.
Ld3: And don't pester us with offerings for food pantries;
       this is our sabbath and we want to rest.
Ld1: Have you never read what David did
       when he and his companions were hungry?
Cng: **David went into the house of God.**
       He ate the bread of the Presence,
       and he gave some to his companions.
Ld2: "Remember the sabbath day, and keep it holy,"
       says the third of the ten commandments.
Ld3: Actually, that's the fourth commandment, not the third,
       but it means that we should be resting,
       not running around doing good everywhere.

191

Ld1: Do you mean that you would refuse care
      to those who need healing today?
Cng: **Don't you remember that Jesus healed on the sabbath?**
Ld1: O God, tell us again our sacred stories.
Cng: **Melt our hard hearts with your deeds of love.**
Ld1: This is Sunday, the day of the Lord's resurrection!
Cng: **Let us rejoice and be glad in it!**

___ Prayer of Confession and Assurance of Pardon

God who wants the best for your children,
   why do we pervert your caring and love
   into an uncaring and loveless list of rules?
Too often we blind ourselves to human need.
   We spout rules to spare us from caring,
   or to use like clubs to accuse and entrap.
You gave us the law because you loved us.
   You meant your sabbath law to provide one day in seven
   for refreshing and renewing our minds, bodies and souls.
When we use your good gift to prevent the meeting of human need,
   we prove ourselves to be sinful and rebellious children.
   Forgive our sin, and transform our hearts to match yours.
And God who wants the best for your children,
   why do we pervert your holy scriptures
   to give us permission for becoming workaholics?
The sabbath law is for our own good.
   Our minds need time away from work,
   our bodies need rest, and our souls need refreshing.
You gave us the sabbath so that we would have time
   to worship you, and to play with our families and friends.
   This holy rest is your seventh day blessing upon us.
When we work seven days a week, we destroy your good gift.
   We rob you of our worship, and cheat our families and friends.
   We prove ourselves to be sinful and rebellious children.
God who wants the best for your children,
   forgive our rebellion and take away our sin.
   Give us good hearts that produce faithful lives.
(Continue in silent prayer.)
The God who wants the best for all of us
   does not operate from a list of rules and regulations.
   If God did that, there would be no hope for anyone.
Instead, God operates from a love-filled heart.
   Every decision, every judgment, God tempers with love.
   Therefore, our sins are forgiven and hope is restored.

Children of the God who wants the best for all of us,
    your sins are forgiven, and my sins are forgiven.
    Now let us turn to the way of Christ, and sin no more.
Amen.

____ Commissioning and Blessing

God gives you this sabbath to rest,
    body, mind and soul.
May it be a good sabbath for you.
Yet, even as you rest,
    do not close yourself to the needs of others.
Rest is no blessing,
    when it hurts a brother or sister. **Amen.**

Hymns and Choruses

(The asterisk [*] indicates hymns or choruses that are addressed to God and can be used as prayers.)

____ "Be Still and Know"
____ *"Blessed Jesus, at Thy Word"
____ *"Heal Me, Hands of Jesus"
____ *"In Moments Like These"
____ "Lord of the Dance"
____ "No Other Name"
____ *"O Christ, the Healer"
____ *"Open My Eyes, That I May See"
____ "Rise, Shine, You People"
____ "The Gift of Love"
____ "There's a Wideness In God's Mercy"
____ *"Thy Loving Kindness"
____ *"Your Hand, O Lord, in Days of Old"

Reading the Scripture

____ If the Revised Common lectionary is being followed, recruit two of the congregation's favorite storytellers. Have the first tell the story contained in 2:23-28, and the second story-teller can recount the story in 3:1-6. Both storytellers should have the text memorized.

____ See the first suggestion under "Drama and Movement."

Responses to the Word

____ Use the prayer of confession and assurance of pardon printed above as a response to the proclamation of this lesson.

____ Guide the worshipers' silent prayers with the words printed below.

- Take time now to reflect silently on the goodness of God who gives us the sabbath for our rest.
(Silence.)
- Remember and give thanks for God's love and grace that put human need above the strict observance of the sabbath.
(Silence.)
- Listen to the Holy Spirit as God reminds you of times when you put laws and rules above the needs of those around you.
(Silence.)
- Now recommit yourselves to becoming more like Jesus, who shows us the heart of God and calls us to make loving others second only to loving God.
(Silence.)

____ After a sermon on how Christ lifts from us the burdens that others impose on us, have the congregation sing "How Sweet the Name of Jesus Sounds."

Drama and Movement

____ Recruit three or four liturgical dancers or mimes to interpret the gospel lesson.

____ Ask two children's Sunday school classes to act out the two conflict stories in the gospel lesson.

Visuals

____ Ask the congregation's banner makers to make two banners. One should picture stalks of wheat and "the bread of the Presence." The second banner should show a man with a "withered hand." If words are desired, one banner could read "The sabbath," and the second banner, "is for humankind."

____ Wheat and a loaf of bread could be worked into a floral arrangement for use in the sanctuary.

____ Ask one of the artistic people in the congregation to prepare a worship bulletin cover. It could be a creative arrangement with caligraphy to print the words, "The sabbath was made for humankind." Small people figures could be shown dancing around the letters of the words.

Anthems and Special Music

The Gift of Love — H. Hopson — SATB, opt.solo w/keyboard — AG

Organic and Other Keyboard Music

The Gift of Love (O Waly Waly) — found in *Wood Works on International Folk Tunes* — D. Wood — SMP

There's a Wideness in God's Mercy (Lord, Revive Us) — W. Pelz — found in *Concordia Hymn Prelude Series*, vol. 31 — CPH

JUNE 5-11
PROPER 5
PENTECOST 3

Revised
 Common: Mark 3:20-35
Episcopal: Mark 3:20-35
Lutheran: Mark 3:20-35

Note: Those whom Christ calls family are the ones who do the will of God. Let it be so with us.

Gail Throckmorton Warner

Printed Resources

___ Greeting

Ld1: Jesus said, "If a kingdom is divided against itself,
that kingdom cannot stand."

Cng: **Almighty God,**
we call upon you to teach us to stand together,
giving us one heart and mind.

Ld2: Jesus said, "No one can enter a strong man's house
and plunder his property
without first tying up the strong man."

Cng: **Almighty God,**
we call upon you to bind Satan's influence
and to retrieve all that he has stolen from us.

Ld1: Jesus said, "Whoever blasphemes against the Holy Spirit
can never have forgiveness."

Cng: **Almighty God,**
we call upon you to open our eyes and ears
so that we can recognize your Spirit working among us.

Ld2: Jesus said, "Whoever does the will of God
is my brother and sister and mother."

Cng: **Almighty God,**
we call upon you to reveal your will,
so that we can worship you with our obedience.

Ld1: Some say that Jesus has lost his mind,
but we believe that Jesus reveals the mind of God.

Ld2: In Jesus Christ, God has answered all our prayers.

Cng: **Almighty God,**

our hearts overflow with thanksgiving,
and our worship is our humble offering to you.

___ Prayer

Holy God, Jesus was never divided,
but we seem to be constantly divided
with ourselves, with each other and with you.
We want to do your will,
but we spoil our obedience
by chasing after our own selfish whims.
Cast out our unclean spirits,
and pull us together with your Holy Spirit,
so we may be recognized as members of your holy family,
and brothers and sisters to Jesus Christ, our Savior. Amen.

___ Affirmation of Faith

We declare ourselves disciples of Jesus Christ,
who is not divided
but is one with God our Creator.
We maintain that Jesus is full of God's power,
and that power is the Holy Spirit.
God's Spirit is visible in Jesus Christ.
We maintain that Jesus fulfilled God's will on earth,
and that by doing the same we will be recognized
as the family of God in the Spirit of God.
We are convinced that the strong love of Jesus Christ
has saved us from Satan's grasp,
and opened to us the eternal kingdom of God.
We are convinced there is no other savior,
no greater power,
and no one more worthy of devotion and obedience.
Jesus Christ is our love, our life and our hope forever.

___ Commissioning and Blessing

Jesus is stronger than Satan,
and as such has bound Satan
and plunders Satan's house
of all those souls
that Satan stole from God.
Brothers and sisters,
we are safe in the love of Jesus Christ.
Go and tell the world
what our Savior has accomplished. **Amen.**

197

___ Commissioning and Blessing

Jesus said, "Here are my mother and my brothers!
    Whoever does the will of God
    is my brother and sister and mother."
Since we are part of the family of Christ,
    be careful to do the will of God,
    this week and always. Amen.

Hymns and Choruses

(The asterisk [*] indicates hymns or choruses that are addressed to God and can be used as prayers.)

___ "All Hail the Power of Jesus' Name"
___ "Christ Is the World's Light"
___ "For This Purpose"
___ *"Here Comes Jesus"
___ *"Jesus Es Mi Rey Soberano" ("O Jesus, My King and My Sovereign")
___ *"May We Your Precepts, Lord, Fulfill"
___ "No Other Name"
___ "O Blest the House"
___ *"O Christ the Healer, We Have Come"
___ "O Magnify the Lord"
___ "Of the Father's Love Begotten"
___ *"Open My Eyes, That I May See"
___ "The Strong Name of Jesus"

Reading the Scripture

___ Use a choir or a Sunday school class to help with this reading. A narrator and a person to read Jesus' words are needed, too. Use the pattern below for reading the lesson. A choir might even enjoy singing or chanting their parts. If they do this, Christ should sing or chant his part too.

Verses 20-21a	Narrator
Verse 21b	Sopranos and altos
Verse 22a	Narrator
Verse 22b	Tenors and basses
Verse 23a	Narrator
Verses 23b-30	Christ
Verses 31-32a	Altos and tenors
Verse 33a	Narrator
Verse 33b	Christ
Verse 34a	Narrator
Verses 34b-35	Christ

___ Children could be asked to memorize the several one-sentence parables that are contained in this lesson. One person could read the lesson, with different children each reciting the parable they had learned.

Responses to the Word

___ Use the greeting printed above as a prayer-litany following a sermon upon the four parables of Jesus mentioned in the greeting.

___ Use a traditional prayer of confession and assurance of pardon to provide the worshipers a chance to be cleansed of their failures to do God's will, and to be reassured that they are still acceptable as part of God's family. The prayer printed above could be used for this too, but be sure to add an assurance of pardon if it is to be used for a prayer of confession.

___ Invite the worshipers to join in the affirmation of faith printed above.

Drama and Movement

___ Invite the "clowns" in your congregation to put on real greasepaint and do some Christian clowning for the sake of the congregation. Ask these clowns to work up short skits to expand upon and illustrate the several one-sentence parables contained in this gospel lesson. After each skit, read the parable being illustrated by the clowns.

___ Gather a small group of young adults to mime people doing, and failing to do, the will of God. Those who do the will of God receive a sash with the words, "Kin to Christ." Those who do not do God's will receive no sash.

Visuals

___ Recruit volunteers to cut out black paper to form silhouettes picturing Christ coming out a window of a house. Inside the house is Satan, bound and gagged. Ahead of Christ are many little people figures (souls) that are escaping Satan's house with the help of Christ. Tape the black paper silhouettes to a wall in the sanctuary to provide a visual illustration of the gospel lesson.

___ Ask the church youth group to ring the sanctuary with Christ's brothers, sisters, mothers and fathers. To do this, they can trace around their own bodies onto large sheets of paper. Include the youth counselors, other adults and small children in this paper tracing so that people of all sizes can be represented. If the human models strike poses that make them look like they are dancing, then the paper figures will look like they are dancing around God's family on Sunday morning. Having all the paper figures holding hands would add another nice touch to this visual.

___ Use the building blocks from the childrens' nursery, or borrow some from children in the congregation, to make a large pile of blocks in the front of the sanctuary. Arrange this pile to look like a kingdom that has been torn down. Put a note in the worship bulletin to explain that the blocks represent Satan's kingdom that Jesus has torn apart.

Anthems and Special Music

To Do God's Will — Jean Berger — SATB — AF

Organ and Other Keyboard Music

Christ is the World's Light (Christe Sanctorum) — found in *Music for Worship: Easy Trios* — D. Johnson — AF

Of the Father's Love Begotten (Divinum Mysterium) — found in *Six Preludes for Organ* — L. Groom — HWG

Oh, Blest the House (Wo Gott zum Haus) — J. C. Bach — found in *The Parish Organist* — CPH

JUNE 12-18
PROPER 6
PENTECOST 4

Revised
  Common: Mark 4:26-34
Episcopal: Mark 4:26-34
Lutheran: Mark 4:26-34

---

*Note: It is a wondrous thing
to have the kingdom of God
growing all around us. Isn't
it odd that we so seldom notice or celebrate it?*

GARDEN SEEDS

31"It is like a mustard seed, which is the smallest seed you plant in the ground. 32 Yet when planted it grows and becomes the largest of all garden plants with such big branches that the birds of the air can perch in its shade." — Mark 4:31-32

Angie Latta

Printed Resources

___ Greeting

(The congregation's response is the refrain from "The Battle Hymn of the Republic.")
Ld1: Brothers and sisters,
        the seeds of God's coming kingdom have been planted.
Ld2: The seeds sprout and grow,
        though we seldom know how.
Cng: (Singing)
        Glory, glory hallelujah! Glory, glory hallelujah!
        Glory, glory hallelujah! His truth is marching on.
Ld1: With what can we compare the kingdom of God?
Ld2: It is like the smallest of all seeds when sown,
        yet it grows into the greatest of all shrubs.
Cng: (Singing)
        Glory, glory hallelujah! Glory, glory hallelujah!
        Glory, glory hallelujah! His truth is marching on.
(This could be followed by the congregation singing the full text of the hymn.)

___ Prayer

God who sent Jesus to seed our world with your kingdom,
    we rejoice!
That our insignificant testimonies to the gospel help with the planting
    makes our hearts glad.
The almost-invisible growing secretly to a tremendous end
    fills us with delight.

God who works out great secrets right under our noses,
   we praise you.
Until your kingdom blooms full and its branches shelter us,
   we shout our "Amen!"

___ Affirmation of Faith

We affirm
   that God created
the world and all in it
   as part of a grand design,
and that the world and each of us
   has a purpose we are to fulfill.
We maintain Christ is central to God's design,
   and was sent to plant the seeds of a kingdom
that even now is growing, almost invisibly, among us
   and gives new life and hope eternal to all believers.
We trust that the small things we do and say each day
   contribute to the eternal kingdom growing in our world,
and that God's Spirit multiplies each of our small contributions
   to bring immeasurable blessings and good to fulfill God's purpose.

___ Commissioning and Blessing

Jesus still teaches the world
   with parables, stories and other bits of truth,
   as the world is able to hear.
But for you, and the other disciples,
   Jesus explains everything
   so we may know his grace
   and live every day trusting in his love.
Let it be so for you today and always. **Amen.**

Hymns and Choruses

(The asterisk [*] indicates hymns or choruses that are addressed to God and can be used as prayers.)

___ "Arise, Shine Out, Your Light Has Come"
___ "Come, Christians, Join to Sing"
___ "Come Sunday"
___ "Come, Ye Thankful People, Come"
___ *"I Love Thy Kingdom, Lord"
___ "I Want to Be Ready"
___ *"May God Bestow on Us His Grace"
___ "Rejoice the Lord Is King"

___ *"Shine, Jesus, Shine"
___ "Sois la Semilla" ("You Are the Seed")
___ "The Kingdom of God"
___ "Through the Night of Doubt and Sorrow"
___ " 'Thy Kingdom Come!' on Bended Knee"

Reading the Scripture

___ "With many such parables he spoke the word to them." Thus Mark tells us about one of Jesus' favorite teaching methods. Mark also loves to share Jesus' parables in groups. So why shouldn't modern congregations also enjoy the benefit of such teaching? Recruit two or three, or more, good storytellers. Ask them to tell a number of Jesus' parables, one after another. Some congregational singing could be interspersed with the parables. Hymns or songs that refer to the parables could be used, or the worshipers could sing hymns such as "Tell Me the Stories of Jesus."

___ Ask two people to read the gospel lesson. The first should read verses 26-29, the second verses 30-32, and the first concludes with verses 33-34.

Responses to the Word

___ Several weeks ahead of this service announce that worshipers need to prepare for a Kingdom Party. Explain that each worshiper needs to prepare for the service by observing at least one sign of the kingdom of God growing in their family, church, community, nation or world. Worshipers can write down this observation (if they do not feel comfortable speaking in front of the whole congregation) for someone to read in worship, or they can share their observation orally with the congregation. Each Sunday leading up to the day of the Kingdom Party someone should share two or three examples of what kind of signs are to be reported. These could be as simple as a lost wallet returned with cash intact, or an argument prevented by one party extending a bit of grace to the other. They could also be front page news like an entire community joining together to help a neighbor in trouble, or the success of peace talks between two warring nations. Follow the worship service with a congregational meal. If there are too many signs of the kingdom to allow reporting them all in the worship service, then allow more reports to be shared at the congregational meal. But in any case, celebrate what God is doing to transform the world and build a future for the children of God.

___ Both of these parables point to growth and change as being part of the kingdom's coming. Challenge worshipers to take up a devotional life that will allow them individually, and corporately as a church, to grow and change. This might be a time to call the congregation to participate in a major Bible study, or to observe morning and evening prayer in the their homes, or to just take time each day to develop a devotional life by themselves or with their families. All of these activities allow God room to plant new seeds of faith in the people's hearts, as well as to grow and develop the characteristics of a mature Christian.

Drama and Movement

___ Ask an adult who enjoys hamming it up in front of an audience to prepare a skit that illustrates modern kingdom parables of things that begin very small and grow astoundingly large. This person might assume the roll of an absent-minded professor trying to teach his or her students (the congregation). Illustrations that might be used could be a slide of a newborn baby followed by a slide of a huge football or basketball player. Another illustration could be how some people can make a moutain out of a molehill. A slide could show two people arguing over something small. The following slide could show the mushroom cloud of an atomic blast. Just be careful that in the fun of crazy illustrations the point about the kingdom of God growing huge from very small beginnings is not lost.

___ Most congregations include children who are studying some form of dance or ballet. Ask these children to dance the lesson as it is read. An adult will have to help with the choreography. Perhaps the children's dance teacher can do this, or one of the children's mothers. Then as "the seed sprouts and grows" the children can help the congregation see this. The tiny mustard seed that grows large branches and shades birds' nests is made visible by the congregation's children.

Visuals

___ Both of the parables in the gospel lesson have the same emphasis of something very small growing into something very large. Both also hint at the mystery of the growth happening without people knowing what is making it happen. Let your congregation's artists play with illustrating this truth. Perhaps a mural, a large banner, or a series of banners could be very small at the back of the sanctuary and grow in size as it, or they, approach the front of the sanctuary. A person could be sowing seeds at the narrow end of a mural, and behind the person the wheat can be portrayed in several stages of growth, with full heads of ripe wheat at the large end of the mural. The same could be done with mustard seeds at the narrow end, and full-size mustard plants with birds nesting in their branches at the large end. The mustard and wheat could be combined in one mural or banner, or the mustard could be displayed on one side of the sanctuary and the wheat on the other.

___ Contact a wheat farmer and ask for a sheath of wheat with full heads of grain on the stalks. Work this into a display with a few colorful flowers. Balance this with a display of wild mustard that some farmers can provide from their fields, or grow some mustard plants from seed. Flowers can be worked into the mustard, but remember that wild mustard has yellow flowers of its own. A craft store might have a small bird and nest that could be worked into the mustard arrangement for an extra touch of fun.

Anthems and Special Music

For the Fruit of All Creation — W. Rowan — Unison w/keyboard — from *Songs of Rejoicing* — SPC
Song of the Mustard Seed — H. Hopson — Unison w/keyboard — GIA
The Kingdom of God — A. Lovelace — Unison w/keyboard — from *Songs of Rejoicing* — SPC

Organ and Other Keyboard Music

Come, Ye Thankful People, Come (St. George's, Windsor) — found in *A Triptych of Praise and Thanksgiving* — F. Speller — JFB

I Love thy Kingdom, Lord (St. Thomas) — found in *Nine Hymn-Tune Preludes* — A. D. Bassett — LMP

Through the Night of Doubt and Sorrow (Ebenezer) — found in *Ten Hymn Preludes*, set II — H. Willan — CFP

JUNE 19-25
PROPER 7
PENTECOST 5

Revised
 Common: Mark 4:35-41
Episcopal: Mark 4:35-41 (5:1-20)
Lutheran: Mark 4:35-41

**Peace!
Be Still!**

*Note: One of the reasons that
we worship God is that we
continue to be amazed as we
watch God bring peace to our
overwhelming troubles, even
when our faith has failed us
and we have accused God of
not caring.*

Printed Resources

___ Greeting

Ldr: When the storms of life are raging,
       when the world is tossing me,
       like a ship upon the sea...
Cng: **There's one who rulest wind and water
       standing by thee.**
Ldr: In the midst of tribulation,
       when the host of hell assail,
       and my strength begins to fail...
Cng: **There's one who never lost a battle
       standing by thee.**
Ldr: In the midst of persecution,
       when my foes in war array,
       undertake to stop my way...
Cng: **There's one who saved Paul and Silas
       standing by thee.**
(Sing the hymn "Stand By Me")

___ Prayer

Lord,
    there's quite a number of us gathered here today

206

whose minds are full of troubles big and small.
It's like we're in a big storm.
    The winds are blowing us way off course,
    and the waves are nearly beating us to pieces.
We know that our faith should be stronger,
    but fear has overcome us,
    and we can do nothing more than turn to you.
You're our only hope, Lord,
    and we know that we can count on you.
So, please, Lord,
    stand up in this rocking boat,
    and say those wonderful words once again,
    "Peace. Be still."
All our troubles will lay down in quiet defeat,
    if you will just say the words, Lord.
    And, Lord,
    thanks for being here with us.
Amen.

___ Affirmation of Faith According to Mark's Gospel

I affirm God as my Creator,
    who sent Jesus Christ, the Son of God,
    who is filled by the Holy Spirit of God,
    and is sent to bring good news of salvation.
I am confident that Jesus makes the lepers clean,
    forgives those paralyzed by sin,
    makes stormy seas peaceful and quiet,
    removes the spirits of madness,
    heals those with uncontrollable disease,
    raises the dead back into life,
    feeds the hungry multitudes,
    walks on the waters of chaos,
    extends his ministry to outsiders,
    makes the deaf hear, the mute speak,
    and restores sight to the blind.
I trust in Jesus Christ, the Son of God,
    whose transfigured glory outshines Elijah and Moses,
    and whose prayers cast out the worst spirits of uncleanness.
    Jesus turns the world upside-down with his truth,
    and throws the robbers out of God's house of prayer.
    Jesus is not trapped in the foolish thinking of the world,
    but sees beyond to things that are yet to come.
I trust in Jesus who communes with his disciples,
    and sacrifices his life to save ours.

I have faith that Jesus conquers death, eternally,
   and leads us away from all the tombs that would entrap us.
I anchor all my hope in the awesome power of Jesus Christ,
   who leads us into the kingdom of the Almighty God
   and whose Spirit supplies the faith needed for the journey.

___ Commissioning and Blessing

"Peace! Be still!" Jesus said to the wind and waves,
   and the wind ceased and the sea calmed.
Our Savior speaks with the same power
   to the troubles in your lives.
So, do not be afraid. Keep the faith.
   You are greatly loved by one
   whom even the wind and sea obey. **Amen.**

Hymns and Choruses

(The asterisk [*] indicates hymns or choruses that are addressed to God and can be used as prayers.)

___ *"A Shield about Me"
___ "Be Still, My Soul"
___ "Beams of Heaven as I Go"
___ "Children of the Heavenly Father"
___ *"Eternal Father, Strong to Save"
___ "Faith, While Trees Are Still in Blossom"
___ "Give to the Winds Thy Fears"
___ "God Is My Refuge"
___ "God Will Make a Way"
___ "Have No Fear, Little Flock"
___ "How Firm a Foundation"
___ "In His Presence"
___ *"Jesus, Lover of My Soul"
___ *"Jesus, Savior, Pilot Me"
___ *"Lonely the Boat"
___ *"Stand By Me"
___ "There's Within My Heart a Melody"
___ "Who Trusts in God, a Strong Abode"

Reading the Scripture

___ Invite one of the teenagers in the congregation to memorize this gospel lesson and to tell it to the congregation as a story.

___ Use the first suggestion under "Drama and Movement" below. Follow the children's drama by reading the gospel lesson. When the reader gets to the point where Jesus speaks in verses 39 and 40, let the child who was instructed to say these words repeat them as part of the reading.

Responses to the Word

___ Invite the worshipers to join in the affirmation of faith printed above.

___ After a sermon on how Jesus calms the storms in our lives, invite the worshipers to come forward and gather around the communion rail for prayer. Let them pray in silence for a while, and then give a prayer that sums up the petitions of the people gathered there.

Drama and Movement

___ Do a children's message with drama. Have the children gather in a make-believe boat in the front of the sanctuary. The person doing the children's message can get in the boat with them. Designate one child to be Jesus, and ask this child to sleep in the stern. The rest of the children make sounds like the wind blowing, and they rock back and forth as their make-believe boat tosses on the waves. A couple children could be asked to help by bailing water out of the boat. Imagine the boat to be sinking, and ask the children to lighten the boat by throwing unnecessary things overboard (no brothers or sisters though). Finally, talk to the children about waking Jesus. Have one of the children do this. Jesus stands up, and shouts, "Peace! Be still!" to the wind and waves. (Jesus could have been chosen earlier and instructed in his part.) Everybody stops rocking and they stop making wind sounds. Then Jesus turns to the children and says, "Why are you afraid? Have you still no faith?" Talk to the children about how amazing it is that Jesus can make the wind stop and the waves lie down.

___ Gather a group of adults to compose and present two or three short parables that echo this story of the storm on the lake. They can either act out these parables, or just tell them like Jesus did. For example, tell a story about a mother rushing to the hospital with her unconscious child. She fears the worst as the nurses rush the child through closed doors. She paces the floor and prays, but hours go by. The mother begins to accuse God of not answering her prayers, of not caring. Finally, a doctor comes out and tells the mother that her child has regained consciousness and that the mother can take the child home in a couple hours. Her fears relieved, the mother drops exhausted into a waiting room chair. Now she can relax. She picks up a magazine. The lead article is titled, "Why So Much Fear? Is There Faith No More?" The mother sits amazed as it begins to dawn upon her that God has granted her a miracle.

Visuals

___ Ask one of the artists in the congregation to sketch a design where the words "Peace! Be still!" are written in such a way that the outline of the letters form the shape of a boat. Then surround this boat shape with huge towering waves. Use this design for the worship bulletin cover or a banner.

___ Ask someone in the congregation to draw the silhouette of a boat tossing on the waves. (Check Sunday school literature for a picture to use as a model.) You may want to include people and a sleeping Jesus in the silhouette, too. Put this silhouette on a large piece of cardboard, paint it all black, and then cut it out. Prop this up somewhere in the sanctuary where it will be visible to the congregation. Set bouquets of blue flowers around the boat shape. (Instead of painting the whole silhouette black, some people might be able to paint the boat and people in more lifelike colors.)

___ If your congregation has paraments with the boat symbol on them, then this would be a good Sunday to use these paraments.

Anthems and Special Music

In the Storm — F. DeVries — Unison w/keyboard — from *Songs of Rejoicing* — SPC

Organ and Other Keyboard Music

Children of the Heavenly Father (Tryggare kan ingen vara) — Lois McClusky — AF
Eternal Father, Strong to Save (Melita) — Variations on the Navy Hymn — M. Joseph — HWG
Jesus, Savior, Pilot Me (Pilot) — J. Ferguson — found in the *Concordia Hymn Prelude Series*, vol. 35 — CPH

JUNE 26-JULY 2
PROPER 8
PENTECOST 6

Revised
 Common: Mark 5:21-43
Episcopal: Mark 5:22-24, 35b-43
Lutheran: Mark 5:21-43

Note: So many people come to Jesus on their hands and knees, begging for mercy. These same people, after being with Jesus, stand erect, full of new hope. Everyone who comes to this divine healer can experience their lives transformed like this. So why do we wait?

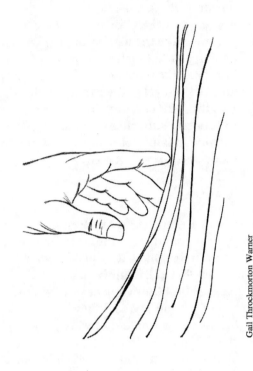

Gail Throckmorton Warner

Printed Resources

___ Greeting

Ldr: "My little daughter is at the point of death,"
 Jairus said to Jesus.
 "Come and lay your hands on her,
 so that she may be made well and live."
Cng: **Jesus, come and lay your hands on us,**
 so that we may be made well and live.
Ldr: "If I but touch his clothes,
 I will be made well,"
 the hemorrhaging woman said to herself.
Cng: **Just let us touch the hem of your garment, Lord,**
 and we will be made well.
Ldr: Jesus healed the woman of her disease,
 and Jesus lifted Jairus' daughter from death.
Cng: **Then there is hope for us.**
 Come, Lord Jesus, come.

____ Prayer

Merciful Healer,
   we come like Jairus,
   begging your help for one we love.
   We come like the hemorrhaging woman,
   hoping just to touch your garment.
   We come like mourners hovering over a twelve-year-old girl,
   unbelieving, yet still wishing death's defeat.
Give us the faith of a desperate father.
   Like a long-suffering woman,
   trusting in hope, let us reach out and know your power,
   today and forever. Amen.

____ Prayer

Keeper of Resurrection Mysteries,
   you command, "Let the children come,"
   and you delight as they play at your feet.
And when they fall deathly sick,
   every child hears your healing words.
   "Get up," you say, and they get up,
   just as you got up out of your grave.
Lord of life and death,
   help us to trust your love of children,
   for those who "get up" and live on here;
   and for those who "get up" and live on there,
   to play eternally at your feet. Amen.

____ Commissioning and Blessing

Jesus told the woman who had hemorrhaged for twelve years,
   "Daughter, your faith has made you well; go in peace."
Now, in the name of Jesus Christ I say to you,
   may your faith make you well too,
   and may the peace of God go with you always. **Amen.**

____ Commissioning and Blessing

When Jesus brought Jairus' daughter back to life,
   he strictly ordered them that no one should know.
   That was before Jesus had completed his work.
Now that Jesus has died and has come back to life,
   you are under new orders, to tell everyone
   about the Savior who lifts people from death.
Go, in the name of Jesus Christ,
   and share the good news with everyone you meet,
   and the Spirit of Christ go with you always. **Amen.**

Hymns and Choruses

(The asterisk [*] indicates hymns or choruses that are addressed to God and can be used as prayers.)

___ *"Abba Father"
___ "Be Still and Know"
___ "Children of the Heavenly Father"
___ "Come, Ye Disconsolate"
___ "God Loved the World"
___ "He Is Jehovah"
___ *"Heal Us, Emmanuel, Hear Our Prayer"
___ *"I Am the God That Healeth Thee"
___ *"Jesus' Hands Were Kind Hands"
___ "Let Us Plead for Faith Alone"
___ *"My Life Is in You, Lord"
___ *"O Christ, the Healer"
___ *"O God, Whose Will Is Life and Good"
___ "When Jesus the Healer Passed Through Galilee"
___ "Woman in the Night"
___ *"Your Hand, O Lord, in Days of Old"

Reading the Scripture

___ Recruit two readers for this gospel lesson. Have a man read verses 21-24a, a woman read verses 24b-34, and the man conclude by reading verses 35-43.

___ Divide the gospel lesson between two readers, as suggested above. But ask them to tell the stories from memory, rather than just reading them. Ask them to use their best storytelling technique.

Responses to the Word

___ Offer the worshipers a healing service. Use the four traditional acts of healing: (1) prayer, (2) anointing with oil, (3) laying on of hands, and (4) holy communion. Services for healing can be found in *The Book of Common Prayer, Book of Worship United Church of Christ* and *The United Methodist Book of Worship*. If healing services have never been offered to the congregation, then take some time to explain what will be done as part of the service. It is also important to lay a good biblical and theological foundation for the worshipers to understand God's healing work. With these preparations accomplished, invite the worshipers to come forward to the communion rail to receive healing for themselves or to pray for the healing of another.

___ Have the worshipers join in affirming their faith that Jesus is no common man, but the Son of the living God, with power over life and death.

___ Gather the doctors, nurses and other medical personnel in your community. Honor them for participating in God's healing ministries. Consecrate them and pray for them. Use the hymn "O God, Whose Will Is Life and Good."

Drama and Movement

___ Ask a group of youth or adults to dramatize the gospel lesson. They can either silently do this as the lesson is read, or the actors could speak the words of the people in the story with the narration being provided by a reader. Or by adding a bit of dialogue the actors could recount the entire lesson.

___ Four dancers could interpret this lesson as it is read. One could take the role of Jesus, a second dancer the role of Jairus, the third the role of the woman with the hemorrhage, and the fourth (a child?) the role of Jairus' daughter.

Visuals

___ Touch is an important part of this gospel lesson. Ask an artist in the congregation to consider ways that Jesus' touch or the touching of Jesus can be illustrated for the congregation. One possibility would be taking slide photographs of people touching one another, and projecting these during the worship service.

___ Recruit a person (or persons) to make two banners. The first should depict Jesus taking the hand of Jairus' daughter, and the second should depict the woman with the hemorrhage touching the hem of Jesus' cloak.

Anthems and Special Music

(Mark 5:21-24a, 35-43)
Draw Us in the Spirit's Tether — H. Friedell — SATB w/organ — HWG
Draw Us in the Spirit's Tether — H. Friedell — SATB w/ keyboard — from *Hymnal Supplement 1991* — GIA
There Was Jesus by the Water — R. Edwards — Unison w/keyboard — from *Songs of Rejoicing* — SPC

(Mark 5:24b-34)
O Christ the Healer, We Have Come — R. Gieseke — SAB w/organ — CPH
The Healing of the Woman in the Throng — T. W. Hart — high solo w/keyboard — GS

Organ and Other Keyboard Music

Children of the Heavenly Father (Trygarre kan ingen vara) — found in *Worship Service Music for the Organist* — A. Jordan — BP

JULY 3-9
PROPER 9
PENTECOST 7

Revised
 Common: Mark 6:1-13
Episcopal: Mark 6:1-6
Lutheran: Mark 6:1-13

staff and sandals \'staf-an(d)-'san-dᵊls\ n-conj-n(pl): only items taken by Jesus's twelve chosen disciples

Note: Jesus puts people in the position of believing or not believing in him. The wonder is that no one is forced to believe. Yet those of us who have come to believe recognize the great loss suffered by those who choose not to believe.

Angie Latta

Printed Resources

___ Greeting

Ld1: The Gerasene demoniac recognized Jesus as the Son of God,
       and the unclean spirits in him were cast out.
Ld2: Jairus believed in Jesus' power to save his daughter,
       and Jesus lifted her from death.
Ld1: The woman with chronic hemorrhaging had faith in Jesus,
       and she was healed of her disease.
Ld2: But the people of Jesus' hometown would not believe,
       and he could do no deeds of power there,
       except for healing a few sick people.
Cng: **Lord of life,**
       cast out the spirits that make us doubt you,
       lift us from the death of unbelief,
       fill us with the faith that trusts you,
       and work your deeds of power among us.

___ Prayer for Missionaries

God, whose desire is to save your children from every evil,
   Jesus called the twelve and sent them out two by two.
Now, in Jesus' name, we send missionaries throughout the world.
   Give these modern ambassadors

215

authority over today's unclean spirits.
Let them be faithful in calling our world to repentance.
Let them cast out the demons that corrupt our society,
and heal those full of disease and sickness.
Especially we lift up to you
the names of the missionaries supported by this congregation.
Pour out your blessing and authority upon
(name the missionaries supported by your congregation).
Keep us faithful in meeting their material needs,
so that these ambassadors of Christ may focus
on making the name of Jesus familiar around the world. Amen.

___ Prayer of Confession and Assurance of Pardon

Almighty God, who uses the ordinary to do the extraordinary,
we look at Jesus' family and the people of his hometown
and we fault them for not believing in Jesus.
"They heard his astounding teaching,
and they saw the powerful deeds he performed," we say.
"Then why did they not believe?"
But we forget
how often professionals and other experienced helpers
can help everyone but members of their own family.
Forgive us, Holy God,
for faulting those who are so very much like us.
Forgive us for turning away the help you send to us,
just because the one you send is too familiar and ordinary.
Forgive us, Merciful God,
and give us the humility and faith to receive
all those whom you send to us.
(Continue in silent prayer.)
Brothers and sisters, fellow sinners,
    despite the general disbelief,
    there were some in Nazareth whom Jesus healed of disease.
And Jesus' mother, when she stood at the foot of the cross,
    did not reject Jesus' appointment of a disciple to help her.
And Jesus' brother, James, not only came to believe,
    but became a leader of the early Church.
So, we are not beyond hope,
    because God holds us in everlasting love,
    offers us the forgiveness of our sin,
    and continues to send ordinary people
    to provide extraordinary help in our times of need.

___ Commissioning and Blessing

The people of Jesus' hometown were astounded by his teaching,
   but they did not believe and took offense at him.
You have heard Jesus' disciples repeating his teaching today.
May God bless you with believing hearts,
   and fill you with wonder and praise,
      as you see our Savior work great deeds of power among us. **Amen.**

Hymns and Choruses

(The asterisk [*] indicates hymns or choruses that are addressed to God and can be used as prayers.)

___ "Christ for the World We Sing"
___ *"Lord, Speak to Us, that We May Speak"
___ *"Lord, You Give the Great Commission"
___ *"O Christ, Our Light, O Radiance True"
___ *"Open My Eyes, That I May See"
___ "Open Your Ears, O Faithful People"
___ "Rise, Shine, You People!"
___ "Sing of Mary, Pure and Lowly"
___ "Sois la Semilla" ("You Are the Seed")
___ "Song for the Nations"
___ *"Spirit of God, Descend upon My Heart"
___ "Spread, Oh, Spread, Almighty Word"
___ " 'Tis So Sweet to Trust in Jesus"
___ *"Thy Word Is a Lamp unto My Feet"
___ "We've a Story to Tell to the Nations"
___ "When Jesus the Healer Passed Through Galilee"
___ "Ye Servants of God"
___ *"Your Kingdom Come, O Father"

Reading the Scripture

___ Recruit two people to read the gospel lesson. The first should read verses 1-6a, and the second should read verses 6b-13.

___ This is a good lesson for a storyteller to recount. Ask one of the storytellers in the congregation to tell these two stories from memory.

Responses to the Word

___ Have the worshipers pray for the work of Christian missionaries using the prayer above. Name the missionaries whose work the congregation has supported in the last year. Issue an invitation to hear from members of the congregation who believe they are being called by God to go into mission work.

217

____ Invite the worshipers to pray the prayer of confession printed above.

____ Invite the worshipers to join in an affirmation of faith, stating their belief in Jesus as the Christ, the Son of God.

Drama and Movement

____ Recruit three people to present a clown interpretation of verses 6b-13. One clown can act as the Jesus figure, who is preparing two of his disciples to be sent out in mission. The two have their bags packed, but "Jesus" insists on seeing what they are taking. He begins to unpack the suitcases. The clowns can use their imagination as to what kinds of "bread" they have packed. Anything from ice cream to candy bars might be unloaded. There might even be a snack that "Jesus" passes out to the entire congregation. Then "Jesus" asks for the clowns' wallets, and empties the wallets before returning them to the two clowns. "Jesus" continues to push for other money. The two produce several wads of bills, a huge pile of credit cards, a piggy bank and a hammer, and whatever other kinds of money their imagination can supply. Then "Jesus" gives them each a pair of shoes, which are funny-looking of course, and a staff. Then "Jesus" notices that one of the clowns has several layers of extra clothing. A production follows in removing all the extra clothes that the clowns have on, and does not stop until "Jesus" notices that the next layer is bare skin. Finally, "Jesus" produces a feather duster for both clowns, and shows them how to remove the dust from their shoes when a place does not welcome their message. Then "Jesus" sends off the two clowns, waving a goodbye that is part sad and part happy. If the clowns are talking clowns, they might be heard outside the sanctuary casting out a demon or healing a person of disease.

Visuals

____ Have someone use paper and wooden spindles to make scrolls. Use these scrolls and bouquets of flowers to decorate the sanctuary.

____ Ask someone to draw a family tree of Jesus, and use it for a worship bulletin cover.

____ Ask someone who likes to make arrangements to prepare a floral arrangement to emphasize a pair of sandals and a walking staff that decorate the sanctuary in a central location. Then, at the back or side of the sanctuary or some other location that makes it appear the objects are discarded, place a whole loaf of bread, some large coins, a bag, and a tunic-like outfit of clothing. A note in the worship bulletin might explain the arrangement.

Anthems and Special Music

Lord, You Give the Great Commission — J. Wilson — SATB unaccompanied — HP

Organ and Other Keyboard Music

Lord, You Give the Great Commission (Abbot's Leigh) — Abbot's Leigh — A. Lovelace — HP

Spirit of God, Descend Upon My Heart (Morecambe) — found in *Interpretations*, Book XII — D. Cherwien — AMSI

Ye Servants of God (Lyons) — found in *Three Hymns of Praise*, set 4 — R. Hobby — MSM

JULY 10-16
PROPER 10
PENTECOST 8

Revised
  Common: Mark 6:14-29
Episcopal: Mark 6:7-13*
Lutheran: Mark 6:14-29

*Note: Those who bow only
before the throne of their own
self-interest suffer the same
limited vision as do the
mentally insane, who likewise
can see nothing but them-
selves.*

Herodias had a grudge.

* See the previous chapter (Proper 8) for material related to this text.

Printed Resources

___ Greeting

Ld1: When people first began hearing about Jesus,
      some thought he was John the baptizer
      raised from the dead.
Ld2: But others said he was Elijah.
Ld1: And still others thought he was one of the prophets of old.
Ld2: Who do you say Jesus is?
Cng: **Jesus is the Son of God,
      and our Savior.**
(Follow this with the worshipers singing a hymn such as "We Believe in One True God" or
"I Know Whom I Have Believed.")

___ Litany on Power

Ldr: When King Herod heard of Jesus
      he feared it was the beheaded John,
      raised from the dead.
Cng: **Herod's self-centeredness and guilt
      led him into this mistake.**
Ldr: And Luke tells us that when Herod finally met Jesus
      he expected entertainment from Jesus working some sign.

Herod was blind
to the most powerful person he would ever meet,
one who would be raised from the dead.

Cng: **Tyrants seldom understand real power.**

Ldr: Tyrants, big and small,
believe power is being able to sacrifice others
to maintain their own honor and position.

Cng: **But Christ shows us real power**
when he sacrifices himself for others.

Ldr: Power is not about silencing one's critics,
nor getting revenge against those you hate,
as Herodias plotted against John the Baptist.

Cng: **John the Baptist found real power**
in being righteous and holy,
and thus free to speak the truth.

Ldr: Human power is full of temptations
for using it without concern for others,
and in disregard of truth and justice.

Cng: **Godly power is full of love and mercy,**
and is used for the sake of others
to extend the righteousness of God.

Ldr: May God give us the heart of Christ,
that all our words and deeds
reflect his power for love.

Cng: **May it be so with all of us. Amen.**

___ Commissioning and Blessing

Ldr: There are many like John the Baptist
who have given everything to proclaim God's truth
in a world that wants to hear anything but the truth.
Now I send you out into that same world,
in the name of God and our Holy Savior, Jesus Christ,
to say, and do, and be God's truth,
in your homes, schools, businesses, and everywhere
that truth lies forgotten and justice is denied.

Cng: **We go.**
May the Spirit of God and Christ go with us.

Ldr: Amen.

Cng: **Amen.**

Hymns and Choruses

(The asterisk [*] indicates hymns or choruses that are addressed to God and can be used as prayers.)

___ "Am I a Soldier of the Cross"
___ "Be Still, My Soul"
___ *"Before Thy Throne, O God, We Kneel"
___ *"Christ the Victorious"
___ "Faith of Our Fathers"
___ *"God, You Have Given Us Power to Sound"
___ *"I Want a Principle Within"
___ "Jesus Calls Us"
___ *"Lord, I Want to Be a Christian"
___ *"Make Me a Captive, Lord"
___ *"O Crucified Redeemer"
___ *"O God of Earth and Altar"
___ *"O God of Every Nation"
___ *"O Young and Fearless Prophet"
___ "Sing with All the Saints in Glory"
___ *"Thy Kingdom Come, O God"
___ "We'll Understand It Better By and By"
___ "What Does the Lord Require"

Reading the Scripture

___ This reading begins at an awkward place. Introduce it with these words:

> *When Jesus sent the twelve out in teams to proclaim that all should repent, and they successfully cast out demons and healed many of sickness, news began spreading about Jesus. The days of the old covenant were coming to an end, and God was about to do something new. Jesus would soon clash with those caught up in the violence of the old ways, but not soon enough to spare the life of the last of the old prophets. Listen to what happened when news of Jesus began to spread.* (Begin reading the gospel lesson.)

___ Divide the reading between two people as printed below:

Ld1: King Herod heard of it, for Jesus' name had become known.
Ld2: Some were saying, "John the Baptizer has been raised from the dead; and for this reason these powers are at work in him."
Ld1: But others said, "It is a prophet, like one of the prophets of old."
Ld2: But when Herod heard of it, he said,
Ld1: "John, whom I beheaded, has been raised."
Ld2: For Herod himself had sent men who arrested John, bound him, and put him in prison
Ld1: on account of Herodias, his brother Philip's wife,
Ld2: because Herod had married her.
Ld1: For John had been telling Herod,
Ld2: "It is not lawful for you to have your brother's wife."
Ld1: And Herodias had a grudge against him, and wanted to kill him.
Ld2: But she could not,

Ld1: for Herod feared John, knowing that he was a righteous and holy man,
Ld2: and he protected him.
Ld1: But an opportunity came when Herod on his birthday gave a banquet for his courtiers and officers and for the leaders of Galilee.
Ld2: When his daughter Herodias came in and danced,
Ld1: she pleased Herod and his guests;
Ld2: and the king said to the girl,
Ld1: "Ask me for whatever you wish, and I will give it."
Ld2: And he solemnly swore to her,
Ld1: "Whatever you ask me, I will give you, even half of my kingdom."
Ld2: She went out and said to her mother, "What should I ask for?"
Ld1: She replied, "The head of John the Baptizer."
Ld2: Immediately she rushed back to the king and requested, "I want you to give me at once the head of John the Baptist on a platter."
Ld1: The king was deeply grieved;
Ld2: yet out of regard for his oaths and for the guests, he did not want to refuse her.
Ld1: Immediately the king sent a soldier of the guard with orders to bring John's head.
Ld2: He went and beheaded him in the prison, brought his head on a platter,
Ld1: and gave it to the girl.
Ld2: Then the girl gave it to her mother.
Ld1: When his disciples heard about it, they came and took his body, and laid it in a tomb.

Responses to the Word

___ Have the congregation join in the litany on power printed above.

___ Use the second suggestion under "Drama and Movement" printed below, and then invite the congregation to sing the hymn "Lord, I Want to Be a Christian."

Drama and Movement

___ Recruit a group of "wanna-be thespians" from the congregation. Ask them to act out this scripture for the congregation.

___ Give the reading of this lesson the kind of drama that is found in it. Turn off the lights in the sanctuary, and put a spotlight on the reader. Have an accompanist softly play serious, dark music to highlight the reading. When the reading is finished, switch the spotlight to another person, who begins to recite a more contemporary story of a powerful person who sacrificed others for his or her own selfish ends. Then switch the spotlight to another and another as the stories of misused power continue. Finally, switch the spotlight onto the pastor who begins to contrast Christ's use of power with Herod's and those in the stories. Bring the sanctuary lights up slowly to emphasize the brightness of the truth revealed in Jesus.

Visuals

___ It may be too gruesome for some to use, but a dancing girl's veil and an executioner's ax would make an appropriate symbol for this gospel lesson.

___ Recruit an artist to sketch Herodias (also called the daughter of Herodias in Matthew or Salome in Josephus' writings) dancing before Herod. Her mother might be added in the background, as though she were already plotting John's death.

___ Have a photographer in the congregation find a copy of one of the famous paintings of the scene in this lesson, such as Caravaggio's "Salome." (Check art books in the local library.) The photographer then should photograph the painting and make it into one or more slides that could be projected in the sanctuary during the scripture reading or sermon.

___ Ask someone in the congregation to provide a floral arrangement of bright red flowers to represent John the Baptist and all the other martyred prophets who died for proclaiming God's truth. A sword might protrude from the arrangement, or the sword-like leaves of the houseplant called mother-in-law's tongue might be used.

Anthems and Special Music

Faith of Ours — N. Goemanne — SATB, congregation w/organ and opt. trumpet — GIA

Organ and Other Keyboard Music

Faith of Our Fathers (St. Catherine) — C. McKinley — found in *A Collection of Thanksgiving Music* — compiled by J. Holler — HWG
O God of Earth and Altar (King's Lynn) — found in *Preludes on Ten Hymntunes* — D. Schack — AF
O God of Every Nation (Tuolumne) — found in *A New Song* — G. Krapf — SMP

JULY 17-23
PROPER 11
PENTECOST 9

Revised
 Common: Mark 6:30-34, 53-56
Episcopal: Mark 6:30-44
Lutheran: Mark 6:30-34, 53-56

Sheep Without a Shepherd

Gail Throckmorton Warner

Note: In the first days, people come to Jesus for rest, to hear his teaching, and to be healed. We still do this today, because Jesus is still the greatest of all teachers and healers.

Printed Resources

___ Greeting

Ldr: Jesus said to his disciples,
"Come away to a deserted place all by yourselves
and rest awhile."
Cng: **Jesus, we also need your rest.**
Ldr: Jesus saw the crowds were like sheep without a shepherd,
so he began to teach them many things.
Cng: **Jesus, be our shepherd and teach us.**
Ldr: Wherever Jesus went people brought the sick to him,
and if the sick even touched the fringe of his cloak
they were healed.
Cng: **Jesus, brush us with your cloak's fringe,
and heal our sickness too.**

___ Greeting

(Use the hymn "Serenity" as the congregation's response below. This hymn can be found in *The United Methodist Hymnal.*)

Ldr: The twelve apostles gathered around Jesus,
just like we are now.
"Come away by yourselves," he said to them,
"and rest awhile."

Cng: (Sing "Serenity")
Ldr: Jesus had sent the apostles out with his authority,
and their ministry was much like ours.
And as we know, there was so much coming and going
they had no leisure even to eat.
So Jesus took them to a deserted place by themselves,
just as he has brought us to this place of quiet peace.
Cng: (Sing "Serenity")
(Ask a flutist [from a nearby high school band?] to play a quiet piece while the worshipers
rest and enjoy Christ's healing peace. Prayer would provide a good transition into the rest
of the worship experience.)

___ Litany on Christ's Compassion

Ldr: Crowds were a part of Jesus' life,
and crowds held all kinds of people:
Lft: **Believers and unbelievers,**
and those who did not know what they believed;
Rgt: **Some were curious, others desperate,**
and still others treacherous.
Ldr: Crowds arrived, with all their demands,
when Jesus and the disciples tried to rest.
Lft: **Yet Jesus had compassion upon them.**
Rgt: **They were like sheep without a shepherd,**
and he began to teach them.
Ldr: Always Jesus had compassion on these people.
All: (Sing the chorus "Lead Me, Lord.")
Ldr: "The hour is late," the disciples told Jesus,
and they asked him to send away the crowd
so they could buy themselves something to eat.
Lft: **But Jesus told his disciples to feed the crowd.**
Rgt: **"Are we to buy bread for all of them?" they asked Jesus.**
Ldr: Jesus asked how many loaves the disciples had,
and they answered, "Five, and two fish."
Then Jesus took, blessed and broke the loaves.
He fed more than five thousand people.
All: (Sing the chorus "Lead Me, Lord.")
Ldr: Wherever Jesus went people recognized him.
Lft: **They brought the sick to him wherever he was,**
and they begged Jesus
to let them touch even the fringe of his cloak.
Rgt: **And all who touched it were healed.**
Ldr: Always Jesus had compassion upon the crowds.
All: (Sing the chorus "Lead Me, Lord.")

____ Commissioning and Blessing

You have enjoyed sabbath rest in this place,
  where we have gathered around the risen Christ.
Now go back to the villages, cities and farms
  where many still need a shepherd,
  and still need the healing Jesus offers.
Jesus' Spirit and power are upon you.
  Know that even as you shepherd and heal others,
  Jesus will shepherd and heal you.
Receive this blessing in the name of our living God,
  Our Sabbath, our Shepherd, and our Strength. **Amen.**

Hymns and Choruses

(The asterisk [*] indicates hymns or choruses that are addressed to God and can be used as prayers.)

____ *"Blessed Jesus, at Thy Word"
____ *"Come, My Way, My Truth, My Life"
____ *"Fill My Cup, Lord"
____ *"Heal Me, Hands of Jesus"
____ *"Heal Us, Emmanuel, Hear Our Prayer"
____ "I Heard the Voice of Jesus Say"
____ *"O Christ, the Healer"
____ *"Savior, Like a Shepherd Lead Us"
____ "Serenity"
____ *"The King of Love My Shepherd Is"
____ *"The Lord's My Shepherd, I'll Not Want"
____ *"Thy Loving Kindness"
____ *"Thy Word Is a Lamp"
____ "Turn Your Eyes upon Jesus"
____ "We Would See Jesus"
____ "When Jesus the Healer Passed Through Galilee"

Reading the Scripture

____ Since the two passages chosen for the Revised Common Lectionary reading do not flow together well, use these introductions to the readings to smooth the gap between the texts. Recruit two people for this reading. One should read these introductions, and the other the gospel passages.

"Jesus' ministry around the Sea of Galilee included many trips on the sea itself. Today's lessons recount what happened when Jesus came ashore in two different locations. The first landing is in a 'deserted place.' Listen to the gospel of Jesus Christ."
(Read verses 30-34.)

"The second landing we read about today is in the village of Gennesaret. Listen to the gospel of Jesus Christ."
(Read verses 53-56.)

___ Break the reading between verses 30-34 and verses 53-56. Have the worshipers sing the chorus "His Name Is Wonderful" between the readings and at the conclusion of the readings. The Episcopal lesson can also be broken at verse 34, with the worshipers singing in between and at the ending of the reading. The more traditional hymn "When Morning Gilds the Skies" can be used instead of the chorus suggested above. The worshipers can sing the first two stanzas between the readings, and the last two at the conclusion of the readings.

Responses to the Word

___ Provide contemporary disciples a leisurely time to eat. Celebrate holy communion with them, just as we hear in the verses that follow this gospel lesson that Jesus fed the five thousand.

___ This may be a time to offer healing to those in need. Be ready to pray, anoint with oil and lay hands on those who are sick.

___ Pick up the theme of "coming away to rest" that is suggested in the second greeting printed above. Carry this theme through the entire worship service. Keep the music soft and restful. Do not have the worshipers stand as much as usual. Have the worship leaders speak in relaxed, soft tones. Let the worship leaders carry more of the service, and reduce the number of responses from the worshipers. Provide more special music than usual, but keep it soft and restful too. Every congregation needs to rest once in awhile. And if some people fall asleep, then you will have done for the modern disciples what Jesus wanted to do for the first disciples.

Drama and Movement

___ Ask a group of adults to prepare a dramatic presentation based upon the high drama in Mark's sixth chapter. Pick up on the idea of what it must have been like to be one of Jesus' first disciples. Beginning in verse 6b, Jesus calls the disciples and then sends them out in ministry! Carry no bread, no bag, no money, he told them! And while they are carrying out this ministry, word is spread that King Herod has murdered John the Baptist. When the disciples finally get to return to Jesus, he plans to take them to a deserted place to eat and rest. But the crowds follow them, and they end up helping Jesus feed over five thousand people. (Cooks in your church can identify with this.) Then Jesus makes his disciples take a boat across the Sea of Galilee, probably still trying to give them some rest. But there was no rest as the disciples strained at the oars against an opposing wind. Jesus goes to them, walking on the water. The disciples are frightened because they believe Jesus must be a ghost. When he gets into the boat the wind stops. The poor disciples are totally confused and do not understand how the wind stopped or how they managed to feed so many with so little bread. Their hearts are hardened. But there is no time to reflect, because as soon as

228

they land people begin bringing every sick person in the area to Jesus for healing. It was not easy being a disciple of Christ then, and it still is not easy today.

___ A solo dancer could portray Jesus and make the words of this lesson visible to the worshipers.

Visuals

___ Ask the congregation's textile artists to prepare two very large panoramic banners. One can show numerous sheep gathering around a new shepherd. Add the words, "They were like sheep without a shepherd, and he began to teach them." The second banner can show people bringing the sick on mats and begging Jesus to let them just touch the fringe of his cloak. Add the words, "They brought their sick and those who touched even the fringe of his cloak were healed."

___ No great artists would be needed to prepare a long, narrow banner to hang across the front of the sanctuary. Use stencils and markers to add these words, "Come away to a deserted place all by yourselves and rest a while." (To center the words on the banner put the "a" in "all" at the center of the banner. Add the other letters as you move toward either end of the banner.)

___ Ask someone to sketch a Currier and Ives-type scene of people hurrying from villages, cities, and fields to get close to Jesus. Such scenes are full of wonder for children of all ages. The many little details that capture one moment in so many different lives is what makes such sketches so much fun, and pack so much meaning. This could be done as a large sketch that could be reduced down by a copier for the worship bulletin covers. Doing such a sketch on a computer with a color printer would allow for the production of bulletin covers in color, although this latter process would not be nearly as fast as on a copier.

Anthems and Special Music

Let Us Talents and Tongues Employ — Jamaican Folk/D. Potter — Unison w/keyboard — from *With One Voice* — AF

Praise the One Who Breaks the Darkness — R. Edwards — Unison w/keyboard — from *Songs of Rejoicing* — SPC

There's a Wideness in God's Mercy — C. Hampton — Unison w/keyboard — from *Hymnal Supplement 1991* — GIA

Organ and Other Keyboard Music

Come, My Way, My Truth, My Life (The Call) — C. H. Heaton — found in the *Concordia Hymn Prelude Series,* vol. 39 — CPH

JULY 24-30
PROPER 12
PENTECOST 10

Revised
 Common: John 6:1-21
Episcopal: Mark 6:45-52
Lutheran: John 6:1-21

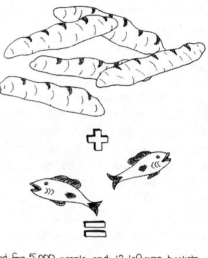

Note: If the miracles are only signs pointing to Christ, how much greater he must be than these astounding miracles. Truly, the one before whom we bow is beyond human comprehension.

Food for 5,000 people and 12 leftover baskets.

Angie Latta

Printed Resources

___ Greeting

Ldr: With just five barley loaves and two fish,
       Jesus fed the crowd of five thousand people.
Cng: **O God, feeding five thousand was nothing.**
       Every day Jesus feeds millions
       with the living bread of his body.
Ldr: After the five thousand ate,
       the disciples gathered up more fragments
       than there were loaves in the beginning.
Cng: **O God, every little gift from us,**
       Jesus multiplies and magnifies
       to meet a world of need, with great abundance.

___ Greeting

(The tune for the congregation's response below is the hymn "Stand By Me.")
Ld1: In the darkness,
       when the strong winds blow and the seas become rough,
       terror stalks through our hearts.
Ld2: That is when Jesus comes walking across the tossing seas.

Cng: (Singing)
  When the storms of life are raging, stand by me;
  when the storms of life are raging, stand by me.
  When the world is tossing me, like a ship upon the sea,
  thou who rulest wind and water, stand by me.
Ld1: At our darkest hour,
  when our strength has failed and exhaustion overwhelms us,
  the deeps under the waves seem to offer our only chance for rest.
Ld2: That is when Jesus comes walking across the tossing seas.
Cng: (Singing)
  When the storms of life are raging, stand by me;
  when the storms of life are raging, stand by me.
  When the world is tossing me, like a ship upon the sea,
  thou who rulest wind and water, stand by me.

___ Litany

Ldr: Jesus fed five thousand
  with just five barley loaves and two fish.
  But when those he fed wanted to make him their king,
  he withdrew to a mountain by himself.
Cng: **Jesus is not a bread king.**
Ldr: Jesus feeds us in times of want.
  But when we ask him for a luxury car,
  Jesus withdraws to the mountain by himself.
  There he prays for our empty souls.
Cng: **Jesus is not a bread king.**
Ldr: Jesus hears our prayers for hungry children.
  But when we will not share with them our bread,
  Jesus withdraws to the mountain by himself,
  so that he does not curse our hard hearts.
Cng: **Jesus is not a bread king.**
Ldr: Millions of Christians pray, "What are we among so many?"
  and Jesus remembers what he did with just twelve.
  Jesus withdraws to the mountain by himself,
  to pray that we may learn faith.
Cng: **Jesus is a heart king.**
Ldr: When we feed upon Jesus' self-giving love,
  and let it nourish our hearts,
  Jesus takes us to the mountain with him,
  where we may be directed by God's will.
Cng: **Jesus is a heart king.**
  And when we make him king in our hearts,
  all who hunger will be satisfied,
  with plenty left over.

For Jesus is a heart king,
who wants to reign in our hearts forever.

___ Commissioning and Blessing

In the name of the Creator, Savior and Holy Presence,
    may the compassion of Christ satisfy your hunger,
    may the power of Christ come to you in stormy times,
    may the living bread of Christ nourish your soul,
    and may you have the humility to eat your fill. **Amen.**

Hymns and Choruses

(The asterisk [*] indicates hymns or choruses that are addressed to God and can be used as prayers.)

___ "Come, Let Us Eat"
___ "Eat This Bread"
___ *"Eternal Father, Strong to Save"
___ *"Fill My Cup"
___ "How Firm a Foundation"
___ *"I Come, O Savior, to Your Table"
___ *"Jesus, Lover of My Soul"
___ *"Jesus, Savior, Pilot Me"
___ *"Lonely the Boat"
___ *"O Food to Pilgrims Given"
___ *"O Jesus, Blessed Lord"
___ *"O Living Bread from Heaven"
___ *"Stand By Me"
___ *"Take Our Bread"
___ *"There's Within My Heart a Melody"
___ *"We Remember You"
___ *"We Who Once Were Dead"
___ *"You Satisfy the Hungry Heart"

Reading the Scripture

___ This would be a good text for a storyteller to relate.

___ To emphasize the presence of two stories in the lesson contained in the Revised Common Lectionary, recruit two readers. Have the first read verses 1-14, and the second read verses 15-21.

Responses to the Word

___ How can you not celebrate holy communion?

232

____ An affirmation of faith would be an appropriate response to these signs.

____ Celebrate Jesus' power over the raging storms in our lives by singing several of the hymns that were inspired by Jesus' walking on the water and calming the storm.

Drama and Movement

____ A dialogue sermon on this text could bring out some of the drama inherent in John's gospel. Such a sermon could point out how the story of feeding five thousand, the walking on water, and Peter's confession (John 6:69) seem to have been linked together before the writing of any of the gospels. Another element to be lifted up from the feeding story is the meaning that John points to in it. It is obvious that Jesus will not be a bread king providing for the crowd's needs. But the story is about more than just Jesus' compassion and ability to work miracles. When the rest of chapter six is read, John makes sure that we hear the eucharistic tones in the feeding of the five thousand. The bread Jesus is going to give is his body.[1] Where does this dramatic truth touch the life of a widow sitting in the pew, a teenager struggling with temptation, a mother juggling job and family, or a man whose career is in jeopardy? There is a lot of challenge here that a good dialogue sermon could address.

____ Soften the sanctuary lighting if possible. Let the organist play the prelude as usual, but then let silence follow the prelude. Let the silence be long enough that the congregation is brought to attention by the silence. Then have a small group of people, dressed in Middle Eastern costumes from the first century, enter and make their way to the chancel. This group represents Jesus and his disciples. By their gestures, they can be seen to be discussing how to feed the crowd that has gathered. One of the disciples points to a boy having five barley loaves and two fish. At Jesus' silent direction, the disciples go to a boy in the congregation (recruited before the service), and receive the gift of loaves and fish. Then Jesus takes the loaves, silently gives a prayer of thanks, breaks the loaves, and the disciples distribute them to everyone in the congregation. The disciples, working in silence, should be generous in the size of portions, and offer seconds and thirds. When all have eaten all they want, twelve baskets of bread (hidden before the service) appear to be gathered up from the leftovers. These are placed on or around the altar table. The pastor then steps forward and reads the gospel lesson. Then worship leaders use the first greeting printed above to lead the worshipers on into the service. After worshiping the congregation can be asked to take the leftovers to shut-ins and others not in attendance at the service.

Visuals

____ Many of the visuals prepared for this lesson can be used for five Sundays, because all five of the next Sundays are built on lessons from the sixth chapter of John. Perhaps one new visual could be added each week.

____ Ask the youth group to paint and cut out several ships from flattened pieces of cardboard. Hang these ships at angles on the sanctuary walls so that they look as if they are being tossed by some wild waves.

233

___ Search out a wood carver to carve five loaves of bread and two fish to be displayed in the church's sanctuary. If there are no woodcarvers, try someone who works in ceramics or some other medium that can be sculpted. The finished products may need to be bigger than life to be seen in large sanctuaries. Displaying them will be another challenge. Consider using a burlap sack (or other rough fabric), and making the loaves and fish look like they have just spilled out of it. Depending upon the medium used for sculpting, live green plants might be used to add warmth and visual interest to the display.

___ Have the children in the congregation draw one (or both) of the scenes of Jesus feeding the five thousand or Jesus walking on water. Provide their finished art with colored paper frames and hang their masterpieces around the sanctuary.

Anthems and Special Music

(John 6:1-15)
Be Not Afraid — Bertrand/Brown — med. solo w/piano — BM

Organ and Other Keyboard Music

I Come, O Savior, to Your Table (Ich sterbe taglich) — M. Sedio — MSM
O Living Bread From Heaven (Aurelia) — found in *Grace Notes* — M. Albrecht — AF
We Who Once Were Dead (Midden in de dood) — found in *Nine Hymn Improvisations* — P. Manz
    — MSM

JULY 31-AUGUST 6
PROPER 13
PENTECOST 11

Revised
 Common: John 6:24-35
Episcopal: John 6:24-35
Lutheran: John 6:24-35

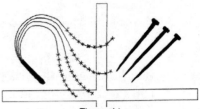

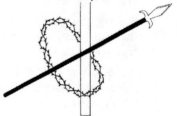

They said,
"What sign are you
going to give us then, so
that we may see it and
believe you?"

*Note: We bow in humble
belief because the sign Jesus
gives is his life on the cross.
With this bread, our souls will
never be hungry again.*

Printed Resources

___ Greeting

Ldr: Jesus said, "Do not work for the food that perishes,
 but for the food that endures for eternal life."
Cng: **Jesus, teach us the difference.**
Ldr: "I am the bread of life," Jesus said.
 "Whoever comes to me will never be hungry,
 and whoever believes in me will never be thirsty."
Cng: **Jesus, give us this bread always.**

___ Prayer

Father who gives true bread from heaven,
    we have no use for the manna Moses gathered,
    nor for the miraculous loaves Jesus used to feed five thousand.
There is only one bread we want, only one bread we need,
    and that bread is called Jesus Christ.
Give us this bread of life always,
    for without him we wither with starvation.
    But with Christ all hunger is gone.
In these earthly bodies we crave that heavenly taste
    of the eucharist of Jesus' sacrifice.
This food endures forever,
    and gives life to the world you created.
For Jesus Christ, we give you thanks and praise,
    now and for all eternity. Amen.

____ Affirmation of Faith

Ldr: Jesus said, "This is the work of God,
      that you believe in him whom he has sent."
All: **I believe that God sent the manna from heaven**
      that Moses and the Israelites ate,
      and I believe that God has sent Jesus Christ,
      the true bread from heaven,
      that gives life to the world.
      Whoever believes in Christ will never be hungry,
      and will never be thirsty,
      but will eat of the food
      that endures for eternal life.
      Upon Jesus Christ, God the Father has set his seal,
      and to Jesus Christ I trust my immortal life.
      I declare myself a follower of Christ, a Christian.
      By Christ I will live,
      by Christ I will die,
      and by Christ I will live again.

____ Commissioning and Blessing

Hunger. Thirst. Death. They have nothing to do with us!
   For we have tasted the bread of life!
Feed on this true bread from heaven today, tomorrow and forever,
   and you will learn the meaning of eternity. **Amen.**

Hymns and Choruses

(The asterisk [*] indicates hymns or choruses that are addressed to God and can be used as prayers.)

____ *"Become to Us the Living Bread"
____ *"Bread of Heaven on Thee We Feed"
____ *"Bread of the World, in Mercy Broken"
____ *"Break Thou the Bread of Life"
____ "Come, Let Us Eat"
____ "Come, Sinners, to the Gospel Feast"
____ *"Deck Thyself, My Soul, with Gladness"
____ *"Fill My Cup, Lord"
____ *"Here, O My Lord, I See Thee"
____ *"I Am the Bread of Life"
____ "Let Us Break Bread Together"
____ *"O Food to Pilgrims Given"
____ "When Jesus Died to Save Us"

Reading the Scripture

____ Use the refrain from the hymn "You Satisfy the Hungry Heart" as a response to the gospel lesson. Have someone read verses 24-27. Then have the worshipers sing the refrain. The reader continues with verses 28-32, and the worshipers sing the refrain again. The reader concludes with verses 33-35, and the worshipers sing the refrain one more time.

____ Ask someone who knows how to lead chanting to lead the choir in chanting this lesson. Have someone read verses 24-25a. Then have the choir chant the words of the crowd. The person who is most familiar with chanting can chant Jesus' words. Make the dialogue flow more easily by omitting the words like "Jesus answered them (verse 26)," "Then they said to him (verse 28)" and so on.

Responses to the Word

____ After preaching on the gospel lesson, lead the worshipers in the affirmation of faith printed above.

____ If the congregation is to celebrate holy communion, have one or two people arrive early to bake bread in the church kitchen. The delicious scent will add much to the service of worship, and the taste of fresh-baked bread will add much to the worshipers' delight in Jesus Christ, the bread of life.

____ The pastor can lead the worshipers in a prayer. Some may want to accept Christ as their Savior for the first time, and others may want to reaffirm or renew their belief. The worshipers could be invited to come forward to the communion rail, but it is not really necessary. They can pray just as fervently in their pews.

Drama and Movement

____ For people new to the family of Christ and for those not yet biblically literate, have a group present a short reenactment depicting God giving manna to the Israelites (Exodus 16). Do this before reading the gospel lesson so that people understand the reference to this event in the lesson.

____ Two liturgical dancers could add a visual interpretation of this gospel lesson as it is read. One would take the part of the crowd, and the other the part of Jesus. Obviously, if more dancers are available they could also participate as part of the crowd.

Visuals

____ Challenge the best artist in the congregation to provide a sketch of Jesus' face. Frame this sketch with the words, "I am the bread of life. Whoever comes to me will never be hungry, and whoever believes in me will never be thirsty." Use this for a worship bulletin cover. A very large sketch could be hung in the sanctuary.

___ An alternative to the above idea is to use a portrait of Christ that is commercially available. Frame this portrait with the words suggested above. Hang this portrait in a classroom when it is no longer needed in the sanctuary.

___ Have several people in the congregation bring homemade loaves of various types of bread. Display these in a glorious pile in the front of the sanctuary. Use cut flowers in the display to add visual appeal. After the service take the loaves to a nearby nursing home for the residents to enjoy.

Anthems and Special Music

Bread of the World — L. Bourgeois — SATB w/keyboard — from *Hymnal Supplement 1991* — GIA
Eat This Bread — J. Berthier — SATB w/opt. keyboard and treble instruments — GIA
I Am the Bread of Life — E. Englert — SATB w/keyboard and treble instruments — WL
I Am the Bread of Life — J. Schiavone — 2-part w/keyboard — GIA
I Am the Bread of Life — S. Toolan — SATB w/keyboard — from *Hymnal Supplement 1991* — GIA
I Am the Bread of Life — H. Willan — Unison w/keyboard — CPH

Organ and Other Keyboard Music

Come, Let Us Eat (A Va De) — fround in *6 Hymn Preludes* — J. Eggert — CPH
Deck Thyself, My Soul, with Gladness (Schmucke dich) — found in *11 Chorale Preludes* — J. Brahms — KAL
Let Us Break Bread Together (Let Us Break Bread) — found in *Communion Music for Manuals* — C. Callahan — MSM

AUGUST 7-13
PROPER 14
PENTECOST 12

Revised
 Common: John 6:35, 41-51
Episcopal: John 6:37-51
Lutheran: John 6:35, 41-51

Note: Those whom God draws to Jesus Christ cannot help but bow down in thanksgiving, praise and service as they feast on the bread of life.

Gail Throckmorton Warner

Printed Resources

___ Greeting

Ldr: "It is written in the prophets,
    'And they shall all be taught by God.' "
Cng: **God of life, we come to be taught by you.**
Ldr: Jesus said,
    "Everyone who has heard and learned from the Father
    comes to me."
Cng: **We come. Feed us, Living Bread from heaven.**

___ Greeting

Jesus said, "No one can come to me
    unless drawn by the Father who sent me."
Brothers and sisters, in the name of Jesus Christ,
    I pray that it is our Father who has drawn you here today;
    because all those drawn to Christ
    will be raised up on the last day.
(The worshipers respond by singing the hymn "I Know Whom I Have Believed.")

___ Prayer

God of salvation and life,
    the Israelites murmured against Moses because of hunger.
    You gave them manna from heaven to eat,

239

and they complained because they had no meat.
In the same way,
    the Jews murmured against Jesus' claim to be from heaven.
    "We know his father and mother," they said.
    "How can he be the bread that came down from heaven?"
God save us from murmuring!
    Our complaints mark our rebellion against you.
    Murmuring shows all the world that you have not chosen us,
    that we have not been drawn to your ways.
Silence our mouths from voicing complaints.
    Close our ears to the murmuring of others.
    Draw us to the living bread that came down from heaven,
    and let Christ's flesh nourish our hearts.
God of salvation and life,
    let us live forever on the bread you give.
    Use our faith to draw others to the bread of life,
    and on the last day raise us up to be with you always. **Amen.**

___ Commissioning and Blessing

Jesus said, "I am the living bread that came down from heaven.
    Whoever eats of this bread will live forever;
 and the bread that I will give for the life of the world
    is my flesh."
Brothers and sisters, we have tasted this living bread.
    Now may we learn to live by this bread alone. **Amen.**

Hymns and Choruses

(The asterisk [*] indicates hymns or choruses that are addressed to God and can be used as prayers.)

___ *"Become to Us the Living Bread"
___ *"Bread of Heaven, On Thee We Feed"
___ "Eat This Bread"
___ *"Father, We Thank Thee Who Hast Planted"
___ *"Hallelujah, My Father"
___ *"Humbly I Adore Thee, Verity Unseen"
___ "I Am the Bread of Life"
___ *"I Call on Thee, Lord Jesus Christ"
___ *"Lamp of Our Feet, Whereby We Trace"
___ "Let the Hungry Come to Me"
___ "Let Us Break Bread Together"
___ *"O Bread of Life from Heaven"
___ *"O Christ, the Word Incarnate"

___ *"O Food to Pilgrims Given"
___ *"O Living Bread from Heaven"
___ *"Shepherd of Souls, Refresh and Bless"
___ *"You Satisfy the Hungry Heart"

Reading the Scripture

___ Have the worshipers sing the hymn "Break Thou the Bread of Life" as a prayer for illumination preceding the gospel lesson. The worshipers can repeat the short hymn after the reading as a response to the lesson and a bridge to the sermon.

___ Recruit four readers for this lesson. One can read the narration, and one can read Jesus' words. The other two can read the questions posed by the Jews. They can speak the questions to one another in a quiet, secretive way if these two can be grouped at a microphone away from the other two readers.

Responses to the Word

___ For congregations that celebrate holy communion weekly this is no challenge. But for a congregation that celebrates communion only quarterly or monthly, it would be a real challenge to celebrate this sacrament each of the five weeks that the sixth chapter of John is being read. Who knows, such an experiment might take the congregation back to the weekly communion practiced in the early church and practiced by a majority of Christians in the world.

___ One response to this lesson is a commitment by the worshipers to reading and studying the Word of God, the life-giving bread come down from heaven. Jesus not only speaks the Word, but Jesus is the Word.[2] Ask worshipers to stand in order to indicate their commitment to reading and studying the Word. Have the ushers pass out free contemporary translations of the Bible to any who want them. (There is always someone in the congregation willing to underwrite the cost of such a project.) If a commitment to group Bible study is preferred over individual study, then ask the worshipers to form into small study groups that will commit to meeting in one another's homes. Materials to guide their study might be offered to the groups, or just appoint someone to lead them through the text of the Bible itself. Home study groups have another benefit. They can reach out to unchurched neighbors and begin feeding others on the bread from heaven.

Drama and Movement

___ With this gospel lesson, congregations following a lectionary are halfway through John's sixth chapter. This might be a good time for a group to present a reenactment of the events in this sixth chapter. A major dramatic presentation could provide a much needed boost of interest during the summertime, as well as provide a good context for the worshipers to remember John's sixth chapter a long time. A minimum of props would be needed, and this chapter contains a lot of dialogue. A narrator could provide some of the descriptive material. People would be needed to play the roles of Jesus, the disciples and the crowd. Costuming would add much to the reenactment.

241

_____ Recruit a group of adults to plan and produce a contemporary skit about a husband and wife. The husband complains about what the Christian faith expects him to believe. He can accept that Jesus was a good man who taught a good way to live, but claims such as Jesus coming down from heaven are too hard to believe. His wife, on the other hand, is drawn unquestioningly to Jesus Christ. What seems to be naivete to him is deep faith to her. The pastor can use such a skit as a springboard for the sermon.

Visuals

_____ If the sculpted loaves and fishes, suggested for Proper 12, are still available, then the loaves could be used for this lesson, too. Use long pieces of white cotton or linen to flow over the altar table, and form a background for the sculpted bread. Add a rough wooden cross to the arrangement to remind worshipers that the bread Christ gives is his flesh. If sculpted loaves are not available, then real loaves of bread can be used. Real loaves could be used in the celebration of holy communion.

_____ Ask one of the congregation's textile artists to prepare a banner showing an open Bible and the words, "I am the living bread that came down from heaven."

Anthems and Special Music

Be Not Afraid — Bertrand/Brown — med. solo w/piano — BM
Bread of Life — F. Mendelssohn — Solo voice w/keyboard — found in _Lift Up Your Voice_ — COB
Eat This Bread — J. Berthier — SATB w/keyboard — from _Hymnal Supplement 1991_ — GIA
Ego sum panis vivus (Bread of the Living) — W. Byrd — SATB w/opt. keyboard — BBL
Ego sum panis vivus (Bread of the Living) — G. P. Palestrina — SATB unaccompanied — GIA
Halleluya — South African — SATB unaccompanied — from _Hymnal Supplement 1991_ — GIA
I Am the Living Bread — B. Harwood — SATB w/organ — OUP
I Received the Living God — R. Proulx — SATB w/keyboard — from _Hymnal Supplement 1991_ — GIA
The Living Bread — J. S. Bach/J. Roff — Unison or 2-part mixed w/organ — WL
This is Indeed the Prophet — J. Bender — 2 part w/keyboard — CPH

Organ and Other Keyboard Music

I Call On Thee, Lord Jesus Christ (Ich ruf zu dir) — found in _Organ Works_, vol. 1 — J. S. Bach — BAR
O Bread of Life from Heaven (O Welt, ich muss dich lassen) — R. Haan — Found in _Hymn Preludes for Holy Communion_, set 2 — CPH

AUGUST 14-20
PROPER 15
PENTECOST 13

Revised
 Common: John 6:51-58
Episcopal: John 6:53-59
Lutheran: John 6:51-58

"Whoever eats my flesh and drinks my blood has eternal life, and I will raise him up at the last day." – John 6:54

Angie Latta

Note: John is very plain.
Unless we eat and drink Jesus
Christ, we will not live
forever.

Printed Resources

___ Greeting

(The Choir sings the chorus, "Eat This Bread," that comes out of the Taize Community.)

Chr: (Sings the chorus.)
Cng: **You, Lord, are our living bread,**
 giving your own flesh for the life of the world.
Chr: (Sings the chorus.)
Cng: **You are our true food, our true drink.**
 Abide in us, and let us abide in you.
Chr: (Sings the chorus.)
Cng: **Feast of life, feast from heaven,**
 feed us till we want no more.
(This could be followed with the hymn "O the Depth of Love Divine.")

___ Great Thanksgiving Prayer

Ldr: The Lord be with you.
Cng: **And also with you.**
Ldr: Lift up your hearts.
Cng: **We lift them up to the Lord.**
Ldr: Let us give thanks to the Lord our God.
Cng: **It is right to give our thanks and praise.**
Ldr: It is right, and a good and joyful thing,
 always and everywhere to give thanks to you,
 Creator of heaven and earth.
 You led the Israelites out of slavery in Egypt,

243

and fed them manna from heaven when they were hungry.
You taught them not to live by bread alone,
but by every word that comes out of your mouth.
And so, with your people on earth
and all the company of heaven,
we praise your name and join their unending hymn.

Cng: **Holy, holy, holy Lord, God of power and might,**
heaven and earth are full of your glory,
Hosanna in the highest.
Blessed is he who comes in the name of the Lord.
Hosanna in the highest.

Ldr: Blessed indeed is the one you send.
For when we did not follow you,
when we forgot how to eat from your hand,
and when we ignored your teachings,
you sent living bread from heaven.
This bread of life, Jesus Christ our Savior,
leads us out of slavery to sin and death,
feeds us so that we are never hungry,
and establishes your truth in our hearts.
For those who receive him,
who eat his flesh and drink his blood,
you give eternal life and raise them up on the last day.
On the night in which he gave himself up for us,
he took bread, gave thanks to you, broke the bread,
gave it to his disciples, and said:
"Take, eat; this is my body which is given for you.
Do this in remembrance of me."
When the supper was over, he took the cup,
gave thanks to you, gave it to his disciples, and said:
"Drink from this, all of you;
this is my blood of the new covenant,
poured out for you and for many
for the forgiveness of sins.
Do this, as often as you drink it,
in remembrance of me."
And so,
in remembrance of these your mighty acts in Jesus Christ,
we offer ourselves in praise and thanksgiving
as a holy and living sacrifice,
in union with Christ's offering for us,
as we proclaim the mystery of faith.

Cng: **Christ has died; Christ is risen; Christ will come again.**

Ldr: Once again send your Spirit down from heaven
to make these gifts of bread and wine
to be the flesh and blood of Jesus Christ.

And as we eat his flesh and drink his blood,
let us become his living body in this world.
Then send us out in ministry to all the world,
until we are raised up on the last day,
to feast at your heavenly banquet for all eternity.
Through your Son Jesus Christ,
with the Holy Spirit in your holy church,
all honor and glory is yours, almighty Father,
now and forever.

Cng: **Amen.**

___ Commissioning and Blessing

You have eaten the flesh of Christ,
    and you have drunk of his blood.
Now Jesus Christ abides in you,
    and you abide in Christ.
May you always be full of Christ,
    so that on the last day,
    you may also be raised up
    to live forever
    with the Father, Son and Holy Spirit. **Amen.**

Hymns and Choruses

(The asterisk [*] indicates hymns or choruses that are addressed to God and can be used as prayers.)

___ *"Become to Us the Living Bread"
___ *"Bread of Heaven on Thee We Feed"
___ *"Bread of the World, in Mercy Broken"
___ *"Break Thou the Bread of Life"
___ "Come, Let Us Eat"
___ "Come, Sinners, to the Gospel Feast"
___ *"Fill My Cup, Lord"
___ *"For the Bread Which You Have Broken"
___ *"Here, O My Lord, I See Thee"
___ *"I Am the Bread of Life"
___ "Let All Mortal Flesh Keep Silence"
___ "Let Us Break Bread Together"
___ "Now the Silence"
___ *"O Food to Pilgrims Given"
___ "O the Depth of Love Divine"

Reading the Scripture

____ Have the congregation read the lesson responsively as printed below.

Lft: **"I am the living bread that came down from heaven.**
Rgt: **Whoever eats of this bread will live forever;**
Lft: **and the bread that I will give for the life of the world is my flesh."**
Rgt: **The Jews then disputed among themselves saying,**
Lft: **"How can this man give us his flesh to eat?"**
Rgt: **So Jesus said to them,**
Lft: **"Very truly, I tell you, unless you eat the flesh of the Son of Man and drink his blood, you have no life in you.**
Rgt: **Those who eat my flesh and drink my blood have eternal life, and I will raise them up on the last day;**
Lft: **for my flesh is true food and my blood is true drink.**
Rgt: **Those who eat my flesh and drink my blood abide in me, and I in them.**
Lft: **Just as the living Father sent me,**
Rgt: **and I live because of the Father,**
Lft: **so whoever eats me will live because of me.**
Rgt: **This is the bread that came down from heaven,**
Lft: **not like that which your ancestors ate, and they died.**
Rgt: **But the one who eats this bread will live forever."**

Responses to the Word

____ Celebrate holy communion so that the worshipers may eat and drink Christ's flesh and blood.

____ Invite the unbelievers and uncommitted in the congregation to make their first commitment. Invite those who have wandered away from their first commitment to recommit themselves. This is a way to call upon these people to eat and drink Jesus Christ. Those who accept this invitation can join in a prayer led by the pastor. Another way to do this would be to combine an altar call with the reception of holy communion. Just announce that to receive communion is to receive Christ. This is what is happening anyway. Using altar call language just makes this connection clearer to some people.

Drama and Movement

____ There are medleys of songs. Why not a medley of meals? Remember and celebrate some of the many meals that Jesus ate with his disciples. Start with the feeding of five thousand in this sixth chapter of John. Jesus' last supper has to be included, of course. Also include his communion with the disciples on the road to Emmaus (Luke 24:13-35), and the communion at the Sea of Galilee (John 21:1-14). The book of Acts tells us how the church continued to experience Christ as they broke bread together (Acts 2:37-47, 20:7-12, and 27:33-38). There may also be some very memorable communions in the more recent history of the congregation that might be included in such a medley. The gospels tell us of many meals that Jesus ate with his disciples. Not all of them are clearly defined as being eucharistic in nature, but it could be argued that any meal where Christ is present is a communion meal.

___ Christianity's holy communion is unique among the world's religions. Stage a conversation between a Jew, a Muslim and a Christian around the topic of Christians eating the flesh and drinking the blood of their Savior. Better yet, do not just stage this. Invite people who really are Jewish and Muslim to have this conversation as part of the worship service. Do not expect the three to be able to reconcile the differences around these issues, but they will certainly bring issues into focus that people who grew up Christian have never much considered. Preachers could preach themselves blue in the face trying to get their congregations to hear the scandal of Jesus' words, while one conversation with a Jew and a Muslim would ensure that everyone heard the scandal.

Visuals

___ One of the traditional images that comes to mind for this gospel lesson is Christ on the cross with the blood flowing from his side being caught in a chalice. There are also images with the Lamb of God shown with blood flowing from his side and being gathered in a chalice. If such imagery is used on some of the church's paraments, then this would be an especially good day to use these paraments. Or some seamstresses could make a set of paraments using these images. It would be very simple to order the symbols from a place like C.M. Almy & Son (10 Glenville St., Box 2628, Greenwich, CT 06836-2628). These symbols are easy to sew onto parament sets.

___ Since the gospel lesson is very graphic, then why not make the visuals very graphic too? Place a small restaurant-style table in the front of the sanctuary. Put two chairs at the table. Cover the table with a white table cloth. Set the table with elegant china, crystal and silver. Add some lighted candles, cloth napkins, and a vase of cut flowers. The only foods that should be visible on the table are a big loaf of bread and a bottle of wine (or a crystal pitcher of grape juice). The crystal goblets can be filled with wine (or grape juice), too. An alternative to the table for two would be even more graphic. Set the church's altar table as described above, and put chairs around it. Be sure that the congregation can handle this powerful visual. This is very graphic, just like the gospel lesson. Congregations that could handle this well might even enjoy receiving holy communion by coming and filling the chairs around the altar table.

Anthems and Special Music

Ad Regias Agni Dapes — G. A. Bernabei — SATB unaccompanied — PA
Ave Verum Corpus — R. Giles — SAB unaccompanied — PA
Eat This Bread — J. Berthier — SATB w/keyboard — from *Hymnal Supplement 1991* — GIA
Halleluya — South African — SATB unaccompanied — from *Hymnal Supplement 1991* — GIA
I Call to My God for Help — R. Gieseke — SAB unaccompanied — CPH
Jesus, My Breath, My Life, My Lord — R. Hopp — SATB w/keyboard — from *Songs of Rejoicing* — SPC
O Salutaris Hostia — M. Sitton — SATB unaccompanied — PA
The Eyes of All — G. Schroth — SATB w/organ — JFB

Three Motets — A. MacMillan — SSATB w/organ ad. lib. — PA
Verily, Verily I Say Unto You — T. Tallis — SATB — from *Anthems for Choirs I* — OUP

Organ and Other Keyboard Music

Here, O My Lord, I See Thee Face to Face (Farley Castle) — found in *Deck Thyself with Gladness* —
    D. N. Johnson — AF
Let All Mortal Flesh Keep Silence (Picardy) — Al Travis — MSM

AUGUST 21-27
PROPER 16
PENTECOST 14

Revised
  Common: John 6:56-69
Episcopal: John 6:60-69
Lutheran: John 6:56-69

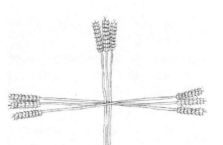

"This is the bread that came down from heaven, not like that which your ancestors ate, and they died. But the one who eats this bread will live forever."

Note: "The words that I have spoken to you are spirit and life," Jesus says. How can we do anything but give our absolute total attention to every word from our Savior?

Printed Resources

___ Greeting

Ld1: Jesus said, "Those who eat my flesh and drink my blood abide in me, and I in them."
Ld2: Because he said this, many of his disciples turned back and no longer went about with him.
Ld1: "Do you wish to go away also?" Jesus asks.
Cng: **Lord, to whom can we go?**
     You have the words of eternal life.
Ld2: "It is the spirit that gives life;
     the flesh is useless," Jesus said.
Ld1: And he told his disciples,
     "The words that I have spoken to you are spirit and life."
Cng: **We have come to believe and know**
     that you are the Holy One of God.

___ Prayer

God who sends life,
    Jesus' teaching is difficult.
It is hard to accept that Jesus is different from Moses.
    Jesus does not give proofs to silence our doubts,
    refuses to allow us to make him king,
    comes from heaven defying human reason,
    and shocks us with demands

to eat his flesh and drink his blood.
But most difficult of all,
Jesus teaches that eternal life is a gift.
Jesus wants us to surrender all our means of control.
We cannot buy life.
We cannot choose, or prove, or earn,
or even understand the gift you give.
We can only receive.
God, we are caught,
because we truly believe that Jesus is the Holy One,
and has the words of eternal life.
O God, give us strength, courage and faith
so that we may receive the gift you send in Jesus. Amen.

___ Affirmation of Faith

We acknowledge and trust the one and only Living God,
who sent manna from heaven
to sustain the Israelites,
and who sent Jesus Christ
as our living bread.
We put all our hope in Jesus Christ, the Holy One of God,
who gives his flesh for the life of the world.
Jesus' words are spirit and life,
his flesh is true food,
and his blood is true drink.
We are confident that as we hear and obey Jesus' words,
and commune with him in the eucharist,
the Spirit of Christ abides in us
and we abide in Christ.
Then on the last day, we will be raised up
to live eternally with the one Living God. Amen.

___ Commissioning and Blessing

The teaching of Jesus is difficult.
Many hear it and turn away from following.
But you are still here,
because you believe Jesus is the Holy One of God,
who has the words of eternal life.
And because you believe,
the life Christ offers is in you.
May you continue in faithfulness,
and be raised up on the last day. **Amen.**

Hymns and Choruses

(The asterisk [*] indicates hymns or choruses that are addressed to God and can be used as prayers.)

___ *"Around You, O Lord Jesus"
___ *"Become to Us the Living Bread"
___ *"Break Thou the Bread of Life"
___ *"Bread of Heaven on Thee We Feed"
___ *"Come, Thou Fount of Every Blessing"
___ *"Here, O My Lord, I See Thee"
___ "Holy Is He"
___ "Holy Is the Lord"
___ *"Holy Is Your Name"
___ *"Humbly I Adore Thee, Verity Unseen"
___ *"I Am the Bread of Life"
___ "I Know Whom I Have Believed"
___ *"Lamp of Our Feet, Whereby We Trace"
___ *"O Depth of Love Divine"
___ *"O Saving Victim, Opening Wide"
___ *"Spirit of Faith, Come Down"
___ "We Believe in One True God"
___ "When Jesus Died to Save Us"
___ *"Worthy, You Are Worthy"

Reading the Scripture

___ Recruit three people for reading this lesson. One should read Jesus' words, one the narration, and one the words of the disciples and of Peter.

___ Ask the choir to intersperse the chorus "Eat This Bread" (from Taize, France) with the reading of the lesson. Break the lesson as follows:
   Verses 56-58
   Chorus
   Verses 59-63
   Chorus
   Verses 64-69
   Chorus

Responses to the Word

___ Have the worshipers join in affirming their faith using the affirmation printed above.

___ Have the worshipers pray the prayer printed above.

___ Enjoy a holy communion with the emphasis upon surrendering all human control simply to receive the heavenly gift that God offers in Jesus Christ. This emphasis can be made in the sermon, the hymns and prayers, and even the words with which the worshipers are invited to receive the sacrament.

Drama and Movement

___ Three dancers could work together to interpret this lesson as it is read.

___ Ask the youth group to put on the white-face make-up of mimes. They can take the roles of Christ, the disciples who stop following Jesus, and the disciples who stay with him (including even the "devil").

Visuals

___ Ask the seamstresses in the congregation to make a banner with three figures on it. The central figure is that of Christ. The one on the left has its back turned to Christ, representing those who "turned back and no longer went about with him." The figure on the right faces Jesus and has bowed down at Jesus' feet. This figure represents those who join with Peter in believing Jesus to be the Holy One of God.

___ Ask one of the young computer buffs in the congregation to run off two banners on computer paper. The first should read, "Jesus, we have come to believe and know," and the second banner should read, "that you are the Holy One of God." Put these two banners on the wall across the front of the sanctuary. If the sanctuary has a cross hung high up on the wall, the banners could be angled up toward the cross, in the shape of an upside-down "V".

Anthems and Special Music

Eat This Bread — J. Berthier — SATB w/keyboard — from *Hymnal Supplement 1991* — GIA
Lord, To Whom Shall We Go — W. Mudde — SATB unaccompanied — AF

Organ and Other Keyboard Music

Around You, O Lord Jesus (O Jesu, an de dina) — D. Busarow — found in *Concordia Hymn Prelude Series*, vol. 34 — CPH
Come, Thou Fount of Every Blessing (Nettleton) — G. Hancock — found in *The Bristol Collection of Contemporary Hymn Tune Preludes for Organ*, vol. 1 — HF
Humbly I Adore Thee, Verity Unseen (Adore te devote) — A. Hutchings — found in *Seasonal Preludes for Organ* — NOV

---

1. Fred B. Craddock, John H. Hayes, Carl R. Holladay, and Gene M. Tucker, *Preaching the New Common Lectionary: Year B, After Pentecost* (Nashville: Abingdon Press, 1985), pp. 109-110.

2. Fred B. Craddock, John H. Hayes, Carl R. Holladay, Gene M. Tucker, *Preaching the New Common Lectionary: Year B, After Pentecost* (Nashville: Abingdon Press, 1985), pp. 127-129.

AUGUST 28-SEPTEMBER 3
PROPER 17
PENTECOST 15

Revised
  Common: Mark 7:1-8, 14-15, 21-23
Episcopal: Mark 7:1-8, 14-15, 21-23
Lutheran: Mark 7:1-8, 14-15, 21-23

Whatever goes in from outside

cannot
defile.

Note: May God spare us from fulfilling the prophecy, "This people honors me with their lips, but their hearts are far from me; in vain do they worship me."

Printed Resources

___ Greeting

(Use the hymn "O For a Heart to Praise My God" for the worshipers' response below.)
Ldr: Jesus quoted the prophet Isaiah saying,
      "This people honors me with their lips,
      but their hearts are far from me;
      in vain do they worship me."
Cng: **God, save us from giving mere lip-service!**
Ldr: Children of God, Jesus said,
      "It is from within, from the human heart,
      that evil intentions come."
Cng: (Sing "O For a Heart to Praise My God.")

___ Prayer[1]

God of truth,
    cut through the camouflage of our religious trappings.
    Measure our inner life with the standard of Christ.
    Compare our motivations with Jesus' self-giving love.
    Test our secret thoughts with the light of Christ's truth.
Then give us clean hearts,
    and hold us close to you forever. Amen.

___ Prayer of Confession and Assurance of Pardon (From Psalm 51)

Have mercy on me, O God,
   according to your steadfast love.
 For I know my transgressions,
   and my sin is ever before me.
 Indeed, I was born guilty,
   a sinner when my mother conceived me.
You desire truth in the inward being;
   therefore teach me wisdom in my secret heart.
Create in me a clean heart, O God,
   and put a new and right spirit within me.
Do not cast me away from your presence,
   and do not take your holy spirit from me.
   Restore to me the joy of your salvation.
(Continue in silent prayer.)
The sacrifice acceptable to God is a broken spirit;
   a broken and contrite heart God will not despise.
Fellow sinners, rejoice;
   for God has purged and washed you with forgiveness.
With clean hearts and right spirits,
   open your lips and declare your praise to God.
(The "Gloria Patri" or another song of praise should follow this prayer.)

___ Commissioning and Blessing

Know this one thing.
   Christ died for you
   while your hearts were still far from God;
   and while your evil intentions continued to defile you,
   Christ resurrected new hope for you.
Now may God bless you with clean hearts,
   from which only good intentions can come. **Amen.**

Hymns and Choruses

(The asterisk [*] indicates hymns or choruses that are addressed to God and can be used as prayers.)

___ *"All That I Need"
___ *"Change My Heart, O God"
___ *"Come Down, O Love Divine"
___ *"Come, Holy Ghost, Our Hearts Inspire"
___ *"Holy Spirit, Truth Divine"
___ *"I Want a Principle Within"
___ *"In My Life, Lord, Be Glorified"

___ *"Jesus, Thine All-Victorious Love"
___ *"Lift Up Your Heads, Ye Mighty Gates"
___ *"Lord, I Want to Be a Christian"
___ *"O Come and Dwell in Me"
___ "O For a Heart to Praise My God"
___ *"O Spirit of the Living God"
___ *"O Thou Who Camest from Above"
___ *"Open My Eyes, That I May See"
___ "Seek the Lord"
___ *"Spirit of God, Descend upon My Heart"
___ *"With All My Heart"

Reading the Scripture

___ Recruit three readers for this lesson. Divide the reading as outlined below:

    Reader 1 - verses 1-2
    Reader 2 - verses 3-4
    Reader 1 - verse 5a
    Reader 3 - verses 5b-6a
    Reader 2 - verses 6b-7
    Reader 3 - verse 8
    Reader 1 - verse 14a
    Reader 3 - verses 14b-15 and 21-23

Responses to the Word

___ Have the worshipers sing the hymn "O For a Heart to Praise My God."

___ Lead the worshipers in praying the prayer of confession printed above.

___ Insert paper hearts in each worshiper's bulletin. After the sermon, ask the worshipers to write on the paper hearts all the evils that come from their own hearts. After this act of confession, let the worshipers come forward and put their hearts in a paper shredder. (This could be borrowed from a nearby bank or law office.) Then give the people new hearts, and let them write good intentions on these hearts that they then get to take home with them.

Drama and Movement

___ A group of clowns could take the role of fussy Pharisees, fretting over minor things while neglecting what is truly important. As such they could be "Exhibit A" for the preacher trying to explain to the congregation about what Jesus meant in pointing his followers to look deep inside themselves, rather than just focusing on externals.

___ Recruit a family group (they do not have to be actually related to one another, just willing to act as if they are) to act out a modern illustration of the gospel lesson. Mom calls the family to the supper table. The television is on, and can be heard throughout the family's conversation. Mom is engrossed in the talk show guests arguing over one of the typical low-life sexual perversions that seem to fill these programs with emptiness. Junior, his big sister (and other family members?) come to the table ready to eat. Mom notices Junior's dirty hands. She loses her temper, and begins ranting about how many times she has told him to wash his hands before coming to the table. When Junior skulks out to wash his hands, big Sis accuses Mom of being a hypocrite. She points out the filth that her mother is watching on television is worse than Junior's dirty hands. Mom makes the typical excuses and rationalizations for the program being on while she was fixing supper. Dad arrives just in time to hear big Sis remind Mom of the string of perversions that have been on the television talk show the last five nights while the family ate supper. Dad quiets big Sis, and reminds her of her duty to honor her mother. Junior returns, and points out Dad's dirty hands. Before Mom can scold Dad, Dad cautions her to be nice to him because he just managed to buy tickets for the show that Mom and two of her friends have been dying to attend. The show is a popular male stripper act. When big Sis hears this, she stomps out of the room, saying that she is going to find somewhere clean to eat her supper. Dad looks around, can't see any dirt, and wonders what his daughter is talking about.

Visuals

___ Ask the church's youth group to prepare two banners. Both banners show a large heart with words flowing out of them. The first heart has jagged lightning bolt-type lines blasting out of the heart in all directions. Each jagged line carries a word describing the evils that Jesus names in verses 21 and 22. From the other heart flows a smooth stream of lines that spread across the bottom of the banner. Words that are opposites to the ones printed on the other banner are carried in this stream. No other words are necessary, but if the banners are hung together, a sign can be hung over them asking, "Which heart would you want in your body?"

___ See if you can find someone in the congregation who can draw cartoons. Ask him to draw a cartoon of a mother bird holding a big, disgusting bug over the open mouths of her fledglings. Add the words, "Whatever goes in from outside cannot defile."

Anthems and Special Music

Come Down, O Love Divine — K.Riehle — SATB unaccompanied — OUP

Organ and Other Keyboard Music

Come Down, O Love Divine (Down Ampney) — found in *Six Organ Preludes* — C. Alwes — AF
Come, Holy Ghost, Our Souls Inspire (Veni Creator) — found in *Ten Chorale Improvisations for the Church Year* — M. Bedford — HF
Lift Up Your Heads, Ye Mighty Gates (Truro) — found in *Music for Service with Truro* — P. Whear — LMP

SEPTEMBER 4-10
PROPER 18
PENTECOST 16

Revised
  Common: Mark 7:24-37
Episcopal: Mark 7:31-37
Lutheran: Mark 7:24-37

*Note: What if Jesus never
crossed the boundaries of his
day? Think of the billions of
people who would not be part
of God's family today. Then
praise God, who sent Jesus
across those boundaries!*

Printed Resources

___ Greeting

Ldr: Jesus cannot hide.
Cng: **People followed him to Tyre,**
      where he cast the demon out of a woman's daughter.
Ldr: Everywhere Jesus goes, people follow.
Cng: **People found him in the region of the Decapolis,**
      where he healed a deaf man with a speech impediment.
Ldr: And we are still following Jesus.
Cng: **We have found Jesus in this place,**
      and here we find the healing we need.
Ldr: We are here, Jesus, because of you.
Cng: **Blessed Jesus, Holy Healer, Gift of God,**
      we are here because you are life.

___ Greeting

Ld1: Jesus went into the region of Tyre.
Cng: **They were Gentiles like us, Lord.**
Ld2: There he healed the daughter of a Syrophoenician woman.
Cng: **She was not one of your chosen ones, Lord.**
Ld1: Then Jesus went into the region of the Decapolis.
Cng: **They too were Gentiles like us, Lord.**
Ld2: There Jesus healed a deaf man with a speech impediment.

Cng: **Jesus, you do a new thing, extending God's grace to all,**
   Jew and Gentile, rich and poor,
   East and West, South and North.
(Have the congregation join in singing the hymn "In Christ There Is No East or West.")

___ Prayer

God of truth and light,
   teach us to lose arguments as graciously as Jesus.
When the quick-witted Syrophoenician woman
   turned Jesus' logic to her daughter's defense,
   Jesus recognized the truth of her words
   and granted the healing of her daughter.
Jesus did not stonewall the truth,
   he didn't bluster or stammer,
   he didn't nurse injured pride,
   and he didn't walk away in anger.
God, let us be more like Jesus.
   Help us recognize the truth when we hear it,
   even in the heat of an argument.
   Then give us the strength to act accordingly.
Like Jesus, let us do the right thing,
   so that others can see your power shaping us
   and be drawn to your eternal truth and life. Amen.

___ Prayer

O God,
why do we have to have one church for Blacks,
   another for Whites, another for Hispanics,
   another for Natives, and another for Asians?
And why do we have to have one church for professionals,
   and another for bluecollar workers,
   and another for people on welfare?
This is not the way Jesus taught.
   He crossed all the boundaries in his day.
   Send him to lead us across today's boundaries.
Gather all your children, O God,
   into one glorious congregation
   that points the way for the rest of our world. Amen.

___ Commissioning and Blessing

If you are going to follow Jesus this week,
   you will have to go into some foreign lands,
   because Jesus has already gone there ahead of us.

And when you go,
    may you be blessed with all the miracles you need,
    in the name of God, our Creator, Savior and Guide. **Amen.**

Hymns and Choruses

(The asterisk [*] indicates hymns or choruses that are addressed to God and can be used as prayers.)

___ "Bind Us Together"
___ "Come, Ye Disconsolate"
___ *"Dear Lord, for All in Pain"
___ *"Heal Us, Emmanuel, Hear Our Prayer"
___ *"Help Us Accept Each Other"
___ *"Here, O Lord, Your Servants Gather"
___ "I Love You with the Love of the Lord"
___ *"In Adam We Have All Been One"
___ "In Christ There Is No East or West"
___ *"Jesus, Lord, We Look to Thee"
___ "Jesus Our Friend and Brother"
___ *"Make Us One"
___ *"O Christ, the Healer"
___ "O Church of God, United"
___ *"O For a Thousand Tongues to Sing"
___ *"O Son of God, in Galilee"
___ "Rise, Shine, You People"
___ "The Church's One Foundation"
___ "What a Friend We Have in Jesus"
___ *"When Jesus the Healer Passed Through Galilee"
___ *"Your Hand, O Lord, in Days of Old"

Reading the Scripture

___ Recruit three readers, at least one of whom should be a woman. One reader should read the narrative, and one should read Christ's words. A woman should read the words of the Syrophoenician woman, and also the words of the crowd in verse 37.

___ Since there are two different stories in this gospel lesson, divide the reading between two different people. Use a woman to read verses 24-30, and a man to read verses 31-37.

Responses to the Word

___ Invite the worshipers to join in one of the two prayers printed above.

___ Prior to the service, meet with the church's mission committee to consider a new mission to "foreigners" or to people whom most of the congregation holds in disdain. Then during the service introduce this new mission and challenge the worshipers to follow Christ's lead to reach out to these people. The congregation may still consider these people unclean, but it is obvious that this is not how Christ considers such people. Invite the worshipers to adopt this new mission by taking a vote, by offering their money, or by signing up to go and work with these people.

___ Invite the worshipers to participate in a ritual for healing. Such rituals traditionally include: prayer, anointing with oil, laying on of hands, and holy communion. Model rituals can be found in *The Book of Common Prayer* (Kingsport, Tennessee: The Church Hymnal Corporation and Seabury Press, 1977), pp. 453-457; *Book of Worship, United Church of Christ* (New York: United Church of Christ Office for Church Life and Leadership, 1986), pp. 306-320; and *The United Methodist Book of Worship* (Nashville, Tennessee: The United Methodist Publishing House, 1992), pp. 613-623.

Drama and Movement

___ Have some of the children in the congregation act out the two scenes in the gospel lesson.

___ Liturgical dancers could provide a visual interpretation of the gospel lesson as it is read.

___ Ask an adult Sunday school class to discuss how Jesus went into foreign lands and ministered to the people there. Then ask them to consider where the foreign lands are today, and how the church should be ministering in those places. (Remember, some of these foreign places may be in the church's own neighborhood.) Then ask the class to prepare and produce a skit that will challenge the congregation to begin a ministry in one of these foreign places.

Visuals

___ Ask the best artist in the congregation to paint two paper banners. Using large sheets of paper, the artist should paint one scene of the Syrophoenician woman begging Jesus to heal her daughter. The second scene should show Jesus healing the deaf man with a speech impediment.

___ Since geography plays such an important part of understanding this gospel lesson, have someone draw a map of the areas involved. Use it as a bulletin cover. (Many maps are copyrighted, so it is not wise to just take one out of a book and lay it on the copy machine.)

Anthems and Special Music

God Hath Done All Things Well — M. Franck — SATB w/organ — CPH
He Hath Done All Things Well — J. Bender — SATB w/organ — CPH
O Christ the Healer, We Have Come — R. Gieseke — SAB w/organ — CPH

Organic and Other Keyboard Music

The Church's One Foundation (Aurelia) — P. Bunjes — found in *The Parish Organist*, part 1 —
    CPH
Christ is Made the Sure Foundation (Westminster Abbey) — K. Lee Scott — MSM
Come, Ye Disconsolate (Consolator) — found in *Twenty Hymn Preludes* — P. Stearns — TP

SEPTEMBER 11-17
PROPER 19
PENTECOST 17

Revised
 Common: Mark 8:27-38*
Episcopal: Mark 8:27-38* or
                   9:14-29
Lutheran: Mark 8:27-38*

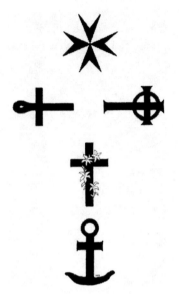

Note: We bow down easily before a Savior who is blessing and helping us, but it is much more difficult to submit to a Savior who wants us to take up a cross.

* More material relating to Mark 8:31-38 can be found on the Second Sunday of Lent in this book.

Printed Resources

___ Greeting

(Ld1 and Ld5 should be at microphones in the front of the sanctuary. Ld2, Ld3 and Ld4 should be sitting in the pews, and just shout out their response from there.)
Ld1: Jesus asked his disciples, "Who do people say that I am?"
Ld2: John the Baptist!
Ld3: Elijah!
Ld4: One of the prophets!
Ld1: Then Jesus asked, "Who do you say that I am?"
Ld5: "You are the Messiah."
Ld1: Then Jesus began to teach them about the Son of Man.
Cng: **Teach us, Messiah. Teach us.**

___ Prayer

(The choir sings stanzas of the hymn "Am I a Soldier of the Cross" as a response to the congregation's prayer.)
Cng: **Lord, it is frightening to hear Christ's call.**
        "Deny yourself." "Take up your cross."
        "Lose your life, and you will save it."

We came to Jesus because of love,
and peace, and blessing.
Chr: (Sing stanzas 1, 2, and 3.)
Cng: **God, we will follow Jesus.**
We are not ashamed of his name.
We are not babes to be carried.
We will follow. Our hearts are ready.
Jesus gave everything for us, can we do less?
Chr: (Sing stanzas 4, 5, and 6. The congregation can join in if they wish.)

___ Affirmation of Faith

I am convinced that Jesus is the Messiah,
that he had to undergo great suffering,
be rejected by the elders, chief priests and scribes,
and be killed.
Then after three days he rose again.
And I acknowledge that if I want to follow him,
I must deny myself and take up my cross;
because those who lose their life for Christ's sake,
and for the sake of the gospel,
will save it.
I am not ashamed of what I believe,
and I am not ashamed that Jesus Christ is my Savior.

___ Commissioning and Blessing

Ldr: Can you follow someone whom important people reject?
A lot of people do not want anything to do with Jesus,
and some of them will make your life very difficult
if you continue to follow the one we call Christ.
Cng: **Jesus, we willingly take up this cross.**
Ldr: If you follow Christ, you will lose you life.
Cng: **We give our lives for the one who gave his life for us.**
Ldr: And Jesus will lift up your life, and give it back to you,
and you will never die again.
Cng: **Amen and amen!**

Hymns and Choruses

(The asterisk [*] indicates hymns or choruses that are addressed to God and can be used as prayers.)

___ *"Am I a Soldier of the Cross"
___ *"Are Ye Able"
___ "Come, Follow Me, the Savior Spoke"

___ *"Father, I Adore You"
___ "He Is Lord"
___ "I Am Crucified with Christ"
___ *"I Extol You"
___ "I Know Whom I Have Believed"
___ *"Jesus Is My Lord"
___ *"Jesus, Lord to Me"
___ "Let Us Ever Walk with Jesus"
___ "Lift High the Cross"
___ "Must Jesus Bear the Cross Alone"
___ "Onward, Christian Soldiers"
___ "Rejoice, Ye Pure in Heart"
___ "Stand Up, Stand Up for Jesus"
___ "Take Up Thy Cross"
___ " 'Take Up Thy Cross,' the Savior Said"
___ "We Believe in One True God"
___ *"We Bow Down"
___ "Where He Leads Me"
___ *"You Are My God"

Reading the Scripture

___ Recruit three readers for this lesson. One should read the narrative, one the words of Jesus, and one the words of Peter and the other disciples.

Responses to the Word

___ Use the second suggestion under "Drama and Movement" as a response of the congregation to a sermon on Peter's affirmation of Christ.

___ Hand out the pocket-size crosses suggested under "Visuals." Suggest that the worshipers use them as reminders of this gospel lesson.

Drama and Movement

___ Use two dancers to interpret the lesson while it is read.

___ Have the congregation sing the chorus "We Bow Down" (or "You Are Lord of Creation") while a solo dancer makes the words visible.

___ Since one of the main ideas in this lesson is following Jesus, why not have a religious parade? Meet at the church building, and then have a parade to a nearby park or a parishioner's home (with a big yard). Have the worshipers put on nametags at the church. Then, partway along the parade route, stop and explain how those who lose their lives for Christ's sake will save it. Have the worshipers throw their nametags in a trash can to emphasize this point. Then, at the park or parishioner's home, give the worshipers new nametags and invite them to celebrate holy communion and enjoy a picnic lunch. The food could be catered by a fast food restaurant or prepared by a few members of the congregation. (Be sure to care for people who have trouble walking by providing special transportation for them. Some parents of small children may need extra help, too.)

Visuals

___ They do it for parade floats, why not do it for our Lord? Make an arch over the altar table with chicken wire and lightweight lumber. Decorate the arch with flowers. Use one color of flower to fill in the background and another color to spell out "You are the Messiah." If you do not have a ready source for a lot of flowers (like a field of wildflowers), or a lot of cash to buy them, use colored tissue paper instead. Twist it, and stuff it into the holes in the wire. Use two colors, one for the background and a contrasting color to spell out the words.

___ There are several sources for small metal or wood crosses that can be purchased at low prices. Check the advertising in the religious magazines that come to the church for these sources. Purchase these to be given to the worshipers to carry in their pockets or purses as a reminder of Jesus' call to take up the cross and follow him. (There may also be a member of the congregation who would love to spend a few days in his or her workshop making such crosses.)

Anthems and Special Music

(Mark 8:27-38)
Above the Voices of the World Around Me — A. Fedak — Unison w/keyboard — from *Songs of Rejoicing* — SPC
Thou Art Jesus, Savior and Lord — Schütz/Coggin — SATB — AF
Weary of All Trumpeting — H. Distler — Unison hymn w/keyboard — found in *Hymnal Supplement 1991* — GIA
What Fabled Names from Judah's Past — C. Doran — Unison hymn w/keyboard — found in *New Hymns for the Lectionary: To Glorify the Maker's Praise* — OUP

(Mark 9:14-29)
Here, Master, in This Quiet Place — W. Rowan — Unison w/keyboard — from *Songs of Rejoicing* — SPC
Above the Voices of the World Around Me — A. Fedak — Unison w/keyboard — from *Songs of Rejoicing* — SPC

Organ and Other Keyboard Music

Rejoice, Ye Pure in Heart (Marion) — found in *Hymn Preludes for the Liturgical Year* — F. Peeters — CFP
Stand Up, Stand Up for Jesus (Webb) — A. Jordan — RME
We Believe in One True God (Ratisbon) — found in *New Every Morning* — R. Warner — SMP

SEPTEMBER 18-24
PROPER 20
PENTECOST 18

Revised
 Common: Mark 9:30-37
Episcopal: Mark 9:30-37
Lutheran: Mark 9:30-37

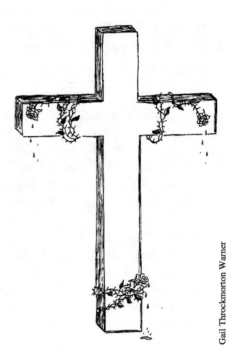

Note: Why does Jesus insist on saying things that we do not want to hear? Does our world really need to be turned upside down? And are we ready to surrender our lives to a Savior who would do this to our world?

Gail Throckmorton Warner

Printed Resources

___ Greeting

(Call a child to the front of the sanctuary. One of the ornery ones with a reputation for upsetting adults would be best. [It would also be a good idea to speak to the child and his or her parents before the service so that their cooperation is gained.] Then say the following words.)

Ld1: Jesus said, "Whoever welcomes one such child in my name
    welcomes me,
    and whoever welcomes me
    welcomes not me but the one who sent me."

Ld2: That all we adults,
    gathered for something as important as worshiping God,
    should take up valuable time because of one child is...
    well, it is the way that Jesus teaches us to behave.

Cng: **Jesus, if this is what you teach,**
    then this is what we will do.

(Have the worshipers sing the song "Jesus Loves the Little Children.")

___ Greeting

Ldr: Jesus taught his disciples, saying,
    "The Son of Man is to be betrayed into human hands,
    and they will kill him,
    and three days after being killed, he will rise again."

Cng: **Lord, we have all heard that before.**
     What we really want to know is
     who has the final decision on the roof.
     Is it the pastor, the women's group or the trustees?
     (Other issues and official groups or individuals can be substituted to fit the context.)
Ldr: Jesus said, "Whoever wants to be first
     must be last of all and servant of all."
Cng: **Lord, teach us how to be servants.**

___ Greeting

Ldr: There were times that Jesus took his disciples aside,
     away from the concerns of the crowds,
     in order to teach them how to be his disciples.
Cng: **Today is one of those times.**
Ldr: Yes, Jesus has brought you here
     so that you can learn to be his disciples.
Cng: **God, grant us ears that hear,**
     hearts that understand,
     and the faith to be a disciple of Jesus Christ.

___ Prayer

Lord, there are days when you talk to us,
     but we do not understand,
     and are afraid to ask you to explain.
And there are days when you question us,
     but we remain silent,
     because we know you will not like our answer.
Lord, help us to trust you,
     and to be honest with you,
     so that we can have a real relationship with you. Amen.

___ Prayer

(Have the choir sing the hymn "Were You There" as the response in this prayer.)
Cng: **Jesus, you said,**
     "The Son of Man is to be betrayed into human hands."
     Lord, we are human.
     Were we there, causing your death?
Chr: (Sing the first stanza.)
Cng: **Lord, it was not just the Jews,**
     the priests, the Pharisees, or the scribes.
     We were there, every single one of us.
     Our hands hammered those nails into your flesh.
Chr: (Sing the second and third stanzas.)

Cng: **Lord, you said,**
    "The Son of Man is to be betrayed into human hands,
    and they will kill him."
    We were there, Lord,
    and knowing that causes us to tremble.
Chr: (Sing the fourth and fifth stanzas.)

___ Commissioning and Blessing

Remember who you are as disciples of Jesus Christ.
    You are servants to all you meet,
    and no one is too inconsequential
    to receive your service in Christ's name.
This is how Jesus wants you to travel through this world,
    and this is how Jesus will bless you. **Amen.**

Hymns and Choruses

(The asterisk [*] indicates hymns or choruses that are addressed to God and can be used as prayers.)

___ *"All Praise to Thee, for Thou, O King Divine"
___ "Ask Ye What Great Thing I Know"
___ "At the Name of Jesus"
___ "Hallelujah! What a Savior"
___ "I Come with Joy"
___ *"Jesu, Jesu"
___ "Jesus Loves the Little Children"
___ *"Jesus, United by Thy Grace"
___ *"Lord, Forever at Thy Side"
___ *"Lord of Glory, You Have Bought Us"
___ *"Lord, Whose Love Through Humble Service"
___ *"My God, Accept My Heart This Day"
___ *"O God of Mercy, God of Light"
___ *"O Master, Let Me Walk with Thee"
___ "The Church of Christ, in Every Age"
___ "Where Charity and Love Prevail"

Reading the Scripture

___ Recruit three upper elementary children to read the gospel lesson. The first should read verses 30-32, the second verses 33-35, and the third verses 36-37.

___ Ask one of the congregation's natural-born storytellers to memorize and tell the story in this gospel lesson. For special effect, have this person pick up a little child from the congregation when he or she gets to the part where Jesus takes a little child into his arms.

Responses to the Word

____ Invite the worshipers to join in a traditional affirmation of faith. Follow this with a time of silent prayer, and then sing the hymn "What Wondrous Love Is This."

____ Challenge the congregation to begin a new outreach ministry to the children living in the neighborhood of the church, or to children in some area where the congregation is involved in mission.

____ Challenge the worshipers to take on one of the dirty jobs at the church that provides no glory, takes a lot of energy or time to accomplish, and no one else wants to do. Put a list of such jobs in the worship bulletin. They could include things like: wash windows, pick up the cigarette butts around the entrances to the church, clean out the church attic or basement, fix the plumbing in the restrooms, clean the cupboards in the church kitchen, tune up the church van, polish the pews, remove the cobwebs up near the ceiling, clean the blades of fans, and on and on it can go.

Drama and Movement

____ Have an adult group present each of Jesus' passion predictions (Mark 8:31-33, 9:30-32, and 10:32-34). Have them also present Jesus' instructions on discipleship, and show how the disciples do not understand Jesus' meaning.

____ Ask the youth group to prepare a puppet presentation that is a modern retelling of the gospel lesson. Have them put this in their own words.

Visuals

____ Set several of the paintings of Jesus with children (usually these can be found in children's Sunday school rooms) in conspicuous places in the sanctuary.

____ This would be a good time to have the children color the worship bulletin covers. Run the bulletins on the church copying machine. Leave the front blank. Give the children crayons and let them decorate the covers as they choose. Let them draw children with Jesus, pictures of their church building, pictures of people worshiping at the church, or whatever they please. (Remember, though, that each child will probably need to color several bulletins.) And do not forget to let the young artists sign their masterpieces, so that the children and adults can enjoy talking about the pictures after the worship service.

____ Attach a red rose to the cross in the sanctuary to draw attention to Christ's prophecy of his being killed. If the cross is especially large then attach three red roses at the points where the nails would have been driven.

Anthems and Special Music

At the Name of Jesus — B. Krogstad — SATB w/orchestra — WM

Organic and Other Keyboard Music

At the Name of Jesus (King's Weston) — found in *Nine Hymn-Tune Preludes* — A. Denniston — LMP

Lord, Whose Love in Humble Service (Beach Spring) — L. Trapp — found in *Laudate* vol. 1 — CPH

O Master, Let Me Walk With You (Maryton) — W. Held — found in *Concordia Hymn Preludes Series* vol. 31 — CPH

SEPTEMBER 25-OCTOBER 1
PROPER 21
PENTECOST 19

Revised
  Common: Mark 9:38-50
Episcopal: Mark 9:38-43, 45, 47-48
Lutheran: Mark 9:38-50

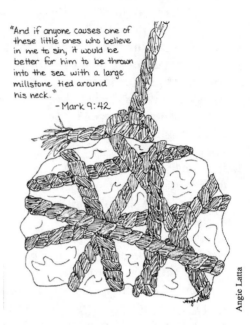

"And if anyone causes one of these little ones who believe in me to sin, it would be better for him to be thrown into the sea with a large millstone tied around his neck."

– Mark 9:42

Angie Latta

Note: There are two sides in this world, those who are for Christ and those who are against Christ. People who do even the smallest thing for Christ's side will be rewarded. And anyone not actively opposing Christ, is for Christ.

Printed Resources

____ Greeting (or use this as a litany)

Ldr: Jesus said, "You are the salt of the earth."
Cng: **Lord, put the taste of Christ's love**
     in our mouths and in our deeds.
Ldr: Jesus said, "For everyone will be salted with fire."
Cng: **Lord, as our love is tested,**
     preserve us with your strength.
Ldr: Jesus said, "If salt has lost it saltiness,
     how can you season it?"
Cng: **Lord, if love does not flavor our actions;**
     then what value are we to anyone?
Ldr: Jesus said, "Have salt in yourselves,
     and be at peace with one another."
Cng: **Lord, let love season our every thought and desire,**
     and use it to bring peace to our fellowship.

____ Prayer of Confession and Assurance of Pardon

God of heaven and earth,
   forgive us for our jealousy.
We see the congregation down the street succeed

where we have failed,
   and we assume that their theology is wrong
   or that maybe they have sold out to the world.
We would demand that they stop using your name,
   because they do not follow us.
Remind us again of Jesus' words,
   "Whoever is not against us is for us."
Like scribes and Pharisees,
   we have drawn a circle to keep others out;
   but Jesus drew a larger circle
   and brought others in.
(Continue in silent prayer.)
Brothers and sisters,
   there are those who would exclude us
   from the fellowship of Christians;
but Jesus called us by name,
   sacrificed his life for our forgiveness,
   and sent us to proclaim the same good news to others.
You are claimed, you are forgiven,
   and you are commissioned with the title "Christian."
Now let the love of Christ guide your hearts,
   and be at peace with one another. **Amen.**

___ Commissioning and Blessing

Not everyone will follow you,
   but if they are not against you,
   then they are for you.
   And if they give you even a cup of cold water,
   then they will not lose their reward.
In the name of our Creator, Savior and Guide,
   may you live in peace with one another. **Amen.**

Hymns and Choruses

(The asterisk [*] indicates hymns or choruses that are addressed to God and can be used as prayers.)

___ *"A Charge to Keep I Have"
___ *"Bind Us Together"
___ *"Dear Lord, Lead Me Day by Day"
___ "He Is Our Peace"
___ *"I Want a Principle Within"
___ "In Christ There Is No East or West"
___ *"Lead Us, O Father, in the Paths of Peace"
___ *"Lord, I Want to Be a Christian"

272

___ *"Make Us One"
___ *"O Love that Casts Out Fear"
___ *"Put Forth, O God, Thy Spirit's Might"
___ *"Reign in Me"
___ "The Church's One Foundation"
___ "Trust and Obey"
___ *"Where Cross the Crowded Ways of Life"

Reading the Scripture

___ This would be a good lesson to divide between the leader and the congregation. Or divide the congregation in half, and let each half alternate reading the lesson. Have people use pew Bibles, or a text that is provided with the worship bulletins, then let the people read every other verse.

___ Recruit four readers for this gospel lesson. Let the first read verses 38-41, the second verse 42, the third verses 43-48, and the fourth verses 49-50.

Responses to the Word

___ Lead the worshipers in the prayer of confession printed above.

___ After a sermon focusing on verses 42-48, lead the worshipers in a silent prayer of confession with these words.
Consider the times you have put a stumbling block in front of one of God's little ones, and confess this terrible sin to God. (Give time for silent prayer.)
Consider what it is in your life that causes you to sin and be condemned to the unquenchable fire. Confess this to God. (Give time for silent prayer.)
Then offer the assurance of pardon with these words.
By the death and resurrection of Jesus Christ you are forgiven and have a fresh opportunity to serve faithfully. Jesus has already broken the millstone around your neck, and has already cut away whatever it is in you that causes you to sin. Give thanks, and cling to Christ for all of your life.

___ Use the fourth suggestion under "Visuals," and give the worshipers small packets of salt after a sermon focusing on verses 49-50. The worshipers might be challenged to indicate their willingness to become more salty Christians by coming forward to receive the small packets of salt. An alternative would be to offer them a pinch of salt to swallow as they come forward to kneel at the communion rail in prayer. (Be careful not to give people so much that the salt chokes them. They only need enough that allows the taste to linger in their mouths.)

Drama and Movement

___ Ask a few clowns in the congregation (the kind with greasepaint on their faces, not the jokers) to prepare a skit on verses 38-41. Clowns could have a lot of fun with the jealousy of the disciples. They become concerned that someone is working miracles in Christ's

273

name but is not following their orders. The person performing the miracles might even be portrayed as a person from another denomination of the Christian church.

___ Mimes could provide an interpretation to accompany the reading of the gospel lesson.

___ Ask two people to develop and deliver a dialogue between a believer and an unbeliever. The believer could initiate the dialogue by inviting the unbeliever to a worship service. The unbeliever could react with something like, "Go to church and worship Jesus the great amputator? Not me!" Then the unbeliever could quote verses 43-48, and rant a bit about how no one is going to cut off his or her hands or feet, or gouge out his or her eyes. The believer could respond with surprise that the other can quote scripture. Then the believer can offer to help the other person in understanding what it is that they just quoted. The believer could explain that Christians take sin very seriously, and would rather suffer almost any consequence than lose their relationship with God. The Christian faith is not something to be switched on and off at the convenience of the believers. Christians are determined, the believer can point out, to undergo any kind of suffering rather than risk offending God.

Visuals

___ Set up a small table near the sanctuary entrance with a pitcher of ice water and glasses of ice water. In smaller sanctuaries, this could be displayed in the front of the sanctuary. Be sure to protect the table from the water that condenses on the outside of the pitcher and glasses.

___ Do you have access to a millstone? If it is very big, then you probably cannot move it. Perhaps a millstone made from papier mâché would work just as well. In any case, it would be a lot lighter to carry into the sanctuary. Set the millstone in the front of the sanctuary. It could even be leaning against something. Put some flowers next to the millstone to draw the worshipers' eyes to it.

___ Ask an artistic youth in the congregation to prepare a Picasso-like banner of hands, feet, eyes and the flames of hell. Perhaps the "worm" that never dies could even be worked in. This banner could be made from a single piece of fabric and the youth could use fabric paint to produce the work of art.

___ Pass out small packets of salt to the worshipers. Ask them to take them home and use them as reminders that they are to be the salt for the world. The packets could be put together like the little packets of rice handed out at weddings.

Anthems and Special Music

Where Cross the Crowded Ways of Life — C. F. Mueller — SATB unaccompanied — GS

Organ and Other Keyboard Music

Where Cross the Crowded Ways of Life (Germany) — found in *Worship Service Music for the Organist* — A. Jordan — BP

OCTOBER 2-8
PROPER 22
PENTECOST 20

Revised
 Common: Mark 10:2-16
Episcopal: Mark 10:2-9
Lutheran: Mark 10:2-16

Note: Since God seems biased toward unifying people, then it would seem that those who worship God would want to put less emphasis on protecting their individuality and more on preserving their unity.

Printed Resources

___ Greeting

Ldr: Brothers and sisters,
     we are created in God's image.
Cng: **Male and female, you created us, O God.**
Ldr: As men and women, O God,
     we lift up one voice to praise you, our Creator.
Cng: **What God has joined together,**
     let no one separate.

___ Greeting

Ldr: Jesus said, "Let the little children come to me...
     for it is to such as these that the kingdom belongs."
Cng: **Make our hearts, Eternal Father,**
     like those of little chilren.
Ldr: And Jesus said, "Truly I tell you,
     whoever does not receive the kingdom of God
     as a little child will never enter it."
Cng: **Truly, Eternal Father,**
     make our hearts like those of little children.

___ Prayer

God who created us male and female,
    you build a kingdom where two can become one;
    where no one is too small or too broken;
    where your love lasts when our love fails;
    where we can find shelter from our enemy, death;
    where we can trust you as our heavenly parent,
    for every breath, every heartbeat, every second of life;
    and where we are gathered in like little children,
    to be held safe and secure from all harm.
Before you we bow, and to you we cling.
    May your name be honored on earth,
    as it is in heaven. Amen.

___ Litany on Christian Marriage (from Genesis 1:26-31 and 2:18-25; Jeremiah 33:10-11; John 15:9-17; Ephesians 5:21-33; Song of Solomon 8:6-7; 1 Corinthians 13; and Mark 10:9)

Lft: **In God's own image, God created humankind.**
Rgt: **Male and female God created them.**
Lft: **Bone of bone and flesh of flesh, the two become one.**
Rgt: **Both were naked and they were not ashamed.**
Lft: **And the voice of mirth, the voice of gladness,**
    the voice of the bridegroom and the voice of the bride,
    the voices of those who sing lifted their joy to God.
Rgt: **Give thanks to the Lord of hosts,**
    for the Lord is good,
    for God's steadfast love endures forever!
Lft: **"This is my commandment," Jesus said,**
    "that you love one another as I have loved you."
Rgt: **"No one has greater love than this,**
    to lay down one's life for one's friends."
Lft: **Wives, be subject to your husbands**
    as you are to the Lord.
Rgt: **Husbands, love your wives,**
    just as Christ loved the church
    and gave himself up for her.
Lft: **Love is strong as death,**
    passion fierce as the grave.
Rgt: **Many waters cannot quench love,**
    neither can floods drown it.
Lft: **Love is patient.**
Rgt: **Love is kind.**
Lft: **Love is not envious, or boastful, or arrogant, or rude.**
Rgt: **Love does not insist on its own way.**

Lft: **Love is not irritable or resentful.**
Rgt: **Love does not rejoice in wrongdoing,**
       but rejoices in the truth.
Lft: **Love bears all things.**
Rgt: **Love believes all things.**
Lft: **Love hopes all things.**
Rgt: **Love endures all things.**
Lft: **Love never ends.**
Rgt: **Faith, hope and love abide,**
       and the greatest of these is love.
Lft: **What God has joined together let no one separate.**

___ Commissioning and Blessing

There are those who would stop you from going to Jesus.
Know that Christ intervenes on your behalf,
    lays his hands upon you,
    and blesses you eternally. **Amen.**

___ Commissioning and Blessing

Husbands and wives, honor God,
    as you honor and care for each other.
Singles, honor God,
    as you keep your celibacy.
Little children, all, honor God,
    by living joyfully in God's kingdom.
And may God's blessing be forever upon you. **Amen.**

Hymns and Choruses

(The asterisk [*] indicates hymns or choruses that are addressed to God and can be used as prayers.)

___ "As Man and Woman We Were Made"
___ "Children of the Heavenly Father"
___ *"Heavenly Father, Hear Our Prayer"
___ "Jesus Loves Me"
___ "Jesus Loves the Little Children"
___ *"O Perfect Love"
___ *"Our Parent, by Whose Name"
___ "Tell Me the Stories of Jesus"
___ " 'Tis the Gift to Be Simple"
___ "When Love Is Found"
___ *"Your Love, O God, Has Called Us Here"

277

Reading the Scripture

____ Divide the reading of this lesson between two readers and the men and women in the choir as follows:

Verse 2	- Reader 1
Verse 3a	- Reader 2
Verse 3b	- Whole Choir
Verse 4	- Reader 1
Verse 5a	- Reader 2
Verses 5b-8a	- Choir Men
Verses 8b-9	- Choir Women
Verse 10	- Reader 1
Verse 11a	- Reader 2
Verse 11b	- Choir Men
Verse 12	- Choir Women
Verse 13	- Reader 1
Verse 14a	- Reader 2
Verse 14b	- Choir Men
Verse 15	- Choir Women
Verse 16	- Reader 2

Responses to the Word

____ Offer couples an opportunity to renew their marriage vows. Announce this well in advance, because some will want to invite friends and family. Follow the worship service with a reception for the couples.

____ Challenge the congregation to begin a new outreach ministry to the children living in the vicinity around the church. Put an insert in the worship bulletin, and ask the worshipers to mark this to indicate how they will help with this new ministry. The signed inserts could be put in the offering plates, along with their financial gifts.

Drama and Movement

____ Have the children's choir present special music that picks up the theme of Jesus loving the children. If there is no organized children's choir, then ask an adult to gather one together for this Sunday.

____ If your church does not have one, borrow or rent a video projector from a nearby university, video library, school, or business. Choose three or four clips from contemporary movies to illustrate the sermon. With this gospel lesson and the movie clips, the preacher could speak about divorce, or about husbands and wives becoming one. The pastor could even document society's changing attitudes about marriage by choosing films from different decades. (Because movies are protected by copyright, you will need to secure permission to show them in public. The easiest way to accomplish this is to pay a fee of $95 per year to the Motion Picture Licensing Corp., 58 Jeremiah Rd., Sandy Hook, CT 06482 [800-515-8855]. Then you can show as many videos as you want.)

Visuals

___ Ask the Sunday school teachers to prepare a set of paraments and a stole for the pastor. Have them use a light green fabric, cut and hemmed to fit. Then have the children in the Sunday school dip their hands into various colors of paint and make handprints on the paraments and stoles.

___ Ask a group of young adults in the congregation to make two banners. Onto the first they should sew a heart, separated into two halves. Flames, representing conflict, should be sewn between the halves. Then they should add the words, "Many things can tear one into two." Another heart should be sewn onto the the second banner. This heart shows signs of being rejoined into one, with the scars of stitches proclaiming the healing. God's hands, reaching down from the top of the banner, hold the heart tenderly together. A needle with thread might be seen in one of God's hands. Then the words "Only God can make two into one" are added.

Anthems and Special Music

I Am Sure of What I Hope For — A. M. Bush — Unison w/keyboard — from *Songs of Rejoicing* — SPC

Jesus Loves Me — H. Williams — Unison w/keyboard — from *Songs of Rejoicing* — SPC

Let the Children Come Unto Me — J. Bender — med. solo w/keyboard — from *Two Solos for Baptism* — CMP

Let the Children Come — A. M. Bush — Unison w/keyboard — from *Songs of Rejoicing* — SPC

Let the Little Children — S. Baar — Unison w/keyboard, flute or violin — from *Songs of Rejoicing* — SPC

Let the Little Children Come to Me — T. Beck — SATB w/organ — CPH

Let the Little Children Come to Me — M. Bender — Unison w/oboe, flute, or violin and organ — CPH

Little Children Welcome — R. Hopp — Unison w/keyboard — from *Songs of Rejoicing* — SPC

Suffer the Little Children — R. Hausman — med. solo w/piano — from *52 Sacred Songs* — GS

Suffer the Little Children — A. Jordan — Unison w/keyboard — HP

The Kingdom of God — J. Roff — Unison or 2-part w/keyboard — HWG

Three Hymns for Special Occasions — L. Betteridge — SATB w/organ — PA

When Jesus Left His Father's Throne — English Folk/R. Vaughan Williams — SATB w/keyboard — from *Hymnal Supplement 1991* — GIA

Organ and Oter Keyboard Music

As Man and Woman We Were Made (Sussex Carol) — Variations on *Sussex Carol* — R. Haan — CPH

O Perfect Love (Perfect Love) — Three Variations on *O Perfect Love* — J. Linker — HWG

Our Parent, by Whose Name (Rhosymedre) — found in *Three Welsh Hymn Tune Preludes* — R. Vaughan Williams — GAL

OCTOBER 9-15
PROPER 23
PENTECOST 21

Revised
 Common: Mark 10:17-31
Episcopal: Mark 10:17-27 (28-31)
Lutheran: Mark 10:17-31

Note: We bow before the Lord in worship Sunday after Sunday so that we will never forget that the treasure available to us in heaven is greater than any we can gather in this world.

Printed Resources

___ Greeting

Ldr: A man asked Jesus, "What must I do to inherit eternal life?"
And Jesus answered him, "You know the commandments."
Lft: **You shall have no other gods.**
Rgt: **You shall not make for yourself an idol.**
Lft: **You shall not make wrongful use
of the name of the Lord your God.**
Rgt: **Remember the sabbath day and keep it holy.**
Lft: **Honor your father and your mother.**
Rgt: **You shall not murder.**
Lft: **You shall not commit adultery.**
Rgt: **You shall not steal.**
Lft: **You shall not bear false witness against your neighbor.**
Rgt: **You shall not covet anything that belongs to your neighbor.**
Ldr: Jesus looked at the man who asked him this question,
loved him and said, "You lack one thing."
All: **Lord, love us, and tell us if we lack anything.**

___ Prayer

**Holy God, who alone is called good,
we come to you seeking eternal life.**

We come seeking Jesus Christ,
    the true fountain of youth.
Strengthen our resolve, steel our nerve,
    to trust Jesus' every word,
    to follow his every direction,
    to throw ourselves upon the mercy of his grace.
We want to live forever, eternal God.
    We do not want to die.
    Let nothing in this world
    keep us from the treasure
    that Christ is preparing for us in heaven. Amen.

___ Prayer of Confession and Assurance of Pardon

Good and loving God,
    we know the grief of the rich man.
    We too have many possessions.
For us to sell what we own
    and give it to the poor
    would be very difficult.
We see people nearby living in poverty.
    We see people in other nations,
    who can never hope to have a fraction of what we have.
Then we see our own wealth, and it grieves us.
    How can we ever enjoy the treasures of heaven?
    How can we camels squeeze through the needle's eye?
Good and loving God,
    is there no hope for us?
    How can we be saved?
(Pause for silent reflection.)
Jesus looked at his disciples and said,
    "For mortals it is impossible, but not for God;
    for God all things are possible."
Brothers and sisters, disciples of Jesus Christ,
    God has looked at us very carefully,
    and despite all that we lack,
    we still are forgiven,
    we are loved,
    we are God's.
Is there any treasure on earth or in heaven
    that is greater than this?
Cling to this treasure with all your life,
    and the distractions of this world will fall away,
    and the camel will dance in the kingdom of God. **Amen.**

___ Commissioning and Blessing

Brothers and sisters, Jesus said,
 "Many who are first will be last,
 and the last will be first."
Therefore, put yourselves last in this world,
 so that Christ, the alpha and the omega, the first and the last,
 may make you first in the life to come. **Amen.**

___ Commissioning and Blessing

(Lead into this by singing the hymn "Jesus Calls Us.")
Ldr: Jesus calls us, saying, "Christian, follow me."
Cng: **Lord, we are willing to leave everything behind
  to follow you.**
Ldr: Jesus tells us,
  "Truly, there is no one who has left house
  or brothers or sisters, or mother or father,
  or children or fields, for my sake
  and for the sake of the good news,
  who will not receive a hundredfold now in this age
  — houses, brothers and sisters, mothers and children,
  and fields with persecutions
  — and in the age to come eternal life."
Cng: **We give our hearts to thine obedience, Lord Jesus.
  We will serve and love thee best of all.**
Ldr: May your treasure always be found in our triune God.
Cng: **Amen, and amen!**

Hymns and Choruses

(The asterisk [*] indicates hymns or choruses that are addressed to God and can be used as prayers.)

___ "Awake, My Soul, Stretch Every Nerve"
___ *"Before Thy Throne, O God, We Kneel"
___ *"Change My Heart, O God"
___ "Deck Thyself, My Soul, with Gladness"
___ *"Father All Loving, Who Rulest in Majesty"
___ *"Father, I Adore You"
___ *"I'm Loving You More Every Day"
___ *"In My Life, Lord, Be Glorified"
___ "Jesus Calls Us"
___ *"Make Me a Servant"
___ *"O God Who Shaped Creation"
___ "Rise Up, O Men of God"
___ "Rise Up, Ye Saints of God"

___ "Seek Ye First the Kingdom of God"
___ *"Take My Life, and Let It Be Consecrated"
___ *"Take My Life, that I May Be"
___ *"The Greatest Thing"
___ "Trust and Obey"
___ *"We Are an Offering"
___ "When We All Get to Heaven"
___ *"With All My Heart"

Reading the Scripture

___ Divide the reading among three people. Have the first read verses 17-22, the second read verses 23-27, and the third read verses 28-31. Between the first and second readers, have the congregation sing the first verse of "Seek Ye First the Kingdom of God." Then between the second and third readers have the worshipers sing the second verse. When the reading is finished the worshipers can sing both verses again.

___ Another way to divide the lesson among three readers is to assign the narrative to one reader, the words of Christ to a second reader, and the words of the rich man and the disciples to a third reader.

___ A good storyteller could memorize this gospel lesson and tell it from the heart. Modern people listen to stories better than they do to people reading from the Bible. It is a sad commentary on us, but it is true.

Responses to the Word

___ Since this text pushes people to reconsider where their hearts are, what their real priorities are, and what kind of treasure they seek, then this might be a good time to challenge the worshipers concerning their financial support of the church's ministries.

___ Invite the worshipers to pray the prayer of confession printed above.

___ Invite the worshipers to surrender any and all things that they have placed before their love for God and their obedience to Christ. Have them pray silently to surrender these obstacles to complete faithfulness and obedience. Then lead them in accepting Jesus Christ into their hearts as their Lord and Savior. Celebrate this change in their lives by inviting them to reaffirm the covenant that God made with them in their baptism. A good example of how this can be done can be found in *The United Methodist Book of Worship* (Nashville: The United Methodist Publishing House, 1992), pp. 111-114, or *The United Methodist Hymnal* (Nashville: The United Methodist Publishing House,1989), pp. 50-53.

Drama and Movement

___ Ask any Christian clowns in the congregation to prepare a skit on trying to fit a camel through the eye of a needle.

___ Set up a dialogue sermon. Let several people offer excuses and rationalizations for not complying with Jesus' words to "...go, sell what you own, and give the money to the poor...." The pastor can provide the gospel lesson's response to these excuses and rationalizations. For example, one person could argue that wealthy people can use their money to make more money for helping the poor. The pastor could respond that Jesus gave this command not for the benefit of the poor, but so that the wealthy man could have treasure in heaven.

Visuals

___ This might be a good time for one or more artists in the congregation to prepare a large mural to be hung in the sanctuary. On the left side of the mural they can portray a wealthy man (or woman, or couple) in the process of selling everything he owns. An auction would be one way to picture this. On the right side of the mural show the same man working in a facility that is feeding hungry people, giving shots to children, and so on.

___Recruit a flower arranger from the congregation. Ask this person to prepare two vases that are the same size, shape and color. In one vase, this person should prepare a large, full arrangement of beautiful flowers. The second vase should include only one small flower, and nothing else. Then put the two vases on opposite sides of the altar table (if that is where your congregation places flowers to honor God) or on opposite sides of the chancel. The worship bulletin might include a note explaining that the flowers are meant to show the contrast that Jesus saw between the rich man in the gospel lesson and the poor people who lived all around him.

Anthems and Special Music

Camel in the Eye — A. Allen — Unison w/keyboard — found in *Choir Book for Saints and Sinners*
    — AG
Treasure in Heaven — K. K. Davis — Solo w/keyboard — RDR
You Satisfy the Hungry Heart — R. Kreutz — Unison w/keyboard — from *With One Voice* — AF

Organ and Other Keyboard Music

Deck Thyself, My Soul, With Gladness (Schmucke dich) — found in *Deck Thyself, My Soul With Gladness* — D. N. Johnson — AF
Jesus Calls Us O'er the Tumult (Galilee) — found in *Softly and Tenderly*, vol. 1 — D. Wood — SMP

OCTOBER 16-22
PROPER 24
PENTECOST 22

Revised
 Common: Mark 10:35-45
Episcopal: Mark 10:35-45
Lutheran: Mark 10:35-45

Note: Want to become a big shot and have lots of special privileges? Forget Christianity. Christ wants us to be like him. And Christ is a servant to others, and gives his life as a ransom for many.

Gail Throckmorton Warner

Printed Resources

___ Greeting

Ldr: The kingdom of God is not what many would expect.
Lft: **In the world, people who are recognized as leaders lord it over everyone else.**
Rgt: **And people who reach greatness become tyrants over everyone around them.**
Ldr: This is not the way it works among Christ's disciples.
Lft: **For us, whoever wishes to become great must be a servant to everyone else.**
Rgt: **And whoever wishes to be first among us must become a slave to all of us.**
Ldr: Jesus, Servant King of the new world, we come seeking to learn this new way of living.
Lft: **Jesus, fill us with your love.**
Rgt: **Show us how to serve.**
(Have the congregation join in singing the hymn "Jesu, Jesu.")

___ Prayer

Teacher of Truth,
  though the cup you drink is bitter with suffering and death,
  we will drink of it, too.
  Though your baptism drowns you in hell's flames,

285

we will be baptized, too.
Where you go, we will go.
Then, as we join you in death,
  may we be lifted with you into new life.
To sit at your right hand or left, we have no desire,
  merely put us at your feet,
  and our hearts will be full.
Now, Merciful Teacher, grant us the grace needed
  to live as faithfully as we pray. Amen.

___ Commissioning and Blessing

Rulers lording it over others — No!
Great ones acting like tyrants — No!
Servants giving themselves for the needs of others — Yes!
This is the way of Christ,
  and this is the way of Christ's Church.
Let it be your way also,
  and then you will find
  that the Lord of the Church walks beside you.
(The worshipers could respond by singing the round "Gloria, Gloria," or they could sing
one of the many tunes for the "Gloria Patri.")

___ Commissioning and Blessing

We drink from the same cup from which Christ drank,
  we are baptized with the same baptism as Christ,
  we serve others as Christ served and gave himself for many;
  and we will be lifted up with Jesus Christ
  to share in his glory.
Blessed be the name of our Lord,
  and blessed are those who follow in his footsteps. **Amen.**

Hymns and Choruses

(The asterisk [*] indicates hymns or choruses that are addressed to God and can be used as
prayers.)

___ *"All Praise to Thee, for Thou, O King Divine"
___ *"All Who Believe and Are Baptized"
___ "Are Ye Able"
___ *"God of Grace and God of Glory"
___ *"God, Whose Giving Knows No Ending"
___ *"Jesu, Jesu"
___ "Let Us Ever Walk with Jesus"
___ *"Lord, Make Us Servants of Your Peace"

286

___ *"Lord, Whose Love Through Humble Service"
___ *"Make Me a Servant"
___ *"Master, Let Me Walk with You"
___ "Must Jesus Bear the Cross Alone"
___ *"Now Let Us from This Table Rise"
___ *"O God of Youth"
___ *"O Master, Let Me Walk with You"
___ *"Son of God, Eternal Savior"
___ "Take Up Thy Cross"
___ *"Teach Me, My God and King"

Reading the Scripture

___ A good storyteller could bring this story to life for the congregation. Have such a person tell it from memory.

___ One way to help the congregation hear the words of this lesson is to put them into the roles of James and John. Recruit two readers, and put the lesson in the worship bulletin (or on a bulletin insert) as it is divided below.

Ld1: James and John, the sons of Zebedee, came forward to him and said to him,

Cng: **"Teacher, we want you to do for us whatever we ask of you."**

Ld1: And he said to them,

Ld2: "What is it you want me to do for you?"

Cng: **"Grant us to sit, one at your right hand and one at your left, in your glory."**

Ld2: "You do not know what you are asking. Are you able to drink the cup that I drink, or be baptized with the baptism that I am baptized with?"

Cng: **"We are able."**

Ld2: "The cup that I drink you will drink; and with the baptism with which I am baptized, you will be baptized; but to sit at my right hand or at my left is not mine to grant, but it is for those for whom it has been prepared."

Ld1: When the ten heard this, they began to be angry with James and John. So Jesus called them and said to them,

Ld2: "You know that among the Gentiles those whom they recognize as their rulers lord it over them, and their great ones are tyrants over them. But it is not so among you; but whoever wishes to become great among you must be your servant, and whoever wishes to be first among you must be slave of all. For the Son of Man came not to be served but to serve, and to give his life a ransom for many."

Responses to the Word

___ Prepare a worship bulletin insert that lists the various jobs around the church that need servants. These could be things like running the food pantry, washing windows, painting a classroom, typing in the church office, and so on. Such a list could also be expanded to include servants that are needed in the community. These could be things like becoming a volunteer fireman, a hospital volunteer, a hospice worker, running a support group, and so on. After the sermon, offer the worshipers a chance to take on a new servant role by marking something on the bulletin insert that they would do. Then the worshipers could sign their names to the inserts and place them in the offering plates.

___ Let the worshipers reaffirm their baptisms. Go through the traditional baptismal ritual, asking the same questions as when someone is being baptized. Then, instead of baptizing, reaffirm the baptisms that were celebrated earlier in the worshipers' lives. Use a small bowl of water, circle the congregation and toss droplets of water off your fingertips toward the worshipers. As you do this, say the words, "Remember your baptism and be thankful." Follow this with a celebration of holy communion, and the worshipers have a chance to ritualize drinking from the same cup that Christ drank.

___ After a sermon calling the worshipers to faithful living, no matter how difficult the hardships they will face, have them join in praying one of the great prayers of the church that express this theme. Then have them join in singing one of the great hymns of the faith that pick up this theme. See the list printed in the "Hymns and Choruses" section for some hymn suggestions.

___ Invite a missionary to come and relate stories of how people are living out Christ's call to be servants. Then ask the worshipers to support the mission being shared.

Drama and Movement

___ Ask one of the upper elementary Sunday school classes or the junior high class to present a puppet play that will accompany the reading of this gospel lesson. The class may want to elaborate and expand the dialogue, or they could contemporize it into modern language. They could also do the play using a favorite musical style.

___ A group of liturgical dancers could portray Jesus, James and John. Three or four other dancers could portray the other ten disciples, or the choir could be recruited to do this. When the reader reads about the cup from which Jesus drinks, the dancer portraying Jesus could let the congregation see some of Jesus' suffering. When the words are read about Jesus' baptism, the dancer could spread his or her arms to show Jesus on the cross. When Jesus' words about servanthood are read, the Jesus-dancer could provide gestures that indicate acts of service to the other dancers.

Visuals

___ There are lots of ways to use the imagery of the cup and baptismal waters. For example, a large chalice could be used to hold an arrangement of flowers. Blue ribbons flowing out of the arrangement could symbolize the waters of baptism. Red flowers could attest to the fiery nature of the baptism about which Christ is talking in this gospel lesson. Another example would be to construct two large banners. On one, the cup filled with the red of blood is shown with the words "From the same cup." The second banner shows a crashing wave and the words "With the same baptism."

___ Have a video enthusiast visit some nearby mission projects, and then videotape some of the people serving others. Put this together with some moving music, and show it to the congregation following the reading of the scripture lesson. The same could be done with slides and music.

Anthems and Special Music

A Purple Robe — R. Hopp — SATB w/keyboard — from *Songs of Rejoicing* — SPC
By Gracious Powers — J. Hill — Unison hymn w/keyboard — found in *With One Voice* — AF
Jesu, Jesu, Fill Us With Your Love — J. Marshall — SATB w/keyboard — HP

Organ and Other Keyboard Music

God of Grace and God of Glory (CWM Rhondda) — found in *Fourteen Hymn Preludes* — A. Lovelace — AF
God, Whose Giving Knows No Ending (Rustington) — P. Bouman — found in *Concordia Hymn Prelude Series*, vol. 36 — CPH
Son of God, Eternal Savior (In Babilone) — Variations on *In Babilone* — R. Haan — HF

OCTOBER 23-29
PROPER 25
PENTECOST 23

Revised
  Common: Mark 10:46-52
Episcopal: Mark 10:46-52
Lutheran: Mark 10:46-52

Note: There is nothing wrong with people coming to church to ask God for mercy concerning some condition in the person's life. Such action shows that the person believes that God can, and will, provide for the person's need. This is faith.

Printed Resources

___ Greeting

Ldr: Take heart; get up, Jesus is calling you.
Cng: (The people stand up.)
Ldr: Jesus asks, "What do you want me to do for you?"
Cng: **Our teacher, let us see again.**
(Follow with the congregation singing the hymn "Open My Eyes, That I May See")

___ Prayer

Ldr: God of power and might,
      whose nature is always to show mercy,
      we come before you with many needs.
Cng: **When the blind beggar, Bartimaeus, heard Jesus approaching**
      he called out, "Jesus, Son of David, have mercy on me!"
Ldr: Jesus answered him, "Your faith has made you well."
      And Bartimaeus regained his sight, and followed Jesus.
Cng: **Jesus, Son of David, have mercy on us.**
Ldr: There are many people who still need their sight restored.
      Some have never seen a loved one's face,
      some have never understood your good truth, Lord,
      and some have no vision as to what can be.

Cng: **Jesus, Son of David, have mercy on us.**
Ldr: We have leaders who are blind to your ways.
　　 Entire nations stagger and fall over countless obstacles.
Cng: **Jesus, Son of David, have mercy on us.**
Ldr: Our children cannot see the dangers of their actions,
　　 our parents do not fear your wrath,
　　 and we are blinded with selfishness.
Cng: **Jesus, Son of David, have mercy on us.**
Ldr: Even your church is blind to some of the signs you provide.
　　 We often cannot see people's needs, nor recognize justice.
　　 We fall behind because we cannot see ahead.
　　 Our eyes cross with our constant infighting.
Cng: **Jesus, Son of David, have mercy on us. Let us see again.**
(Continue to pray silently.)
Ldr: Take heart, brothers and sisters.
　　 Stand up on your feet. (The worshipers should stand.)
　　 Jesus is calling you.
　　 Your prayers are heard, and your faith has made you well.
　　 Open your eyes. Open your minds. Open your hearts.
　　 And your Savior will show you the way to go from here.
　　 Now keep your eyes on Jesus Christ,
　　 and follow him faithfully wherever he leads you.
Cng: **Jesus, our Teacher, thank you. Amen.**
(The "Amen" could be sung by the congregation.)

___ Commissioning and Blessing

Fellow beggars, we no longer have to sit by the roadside
　　 waiting for help to arrive.
Faith in Jesus Christ has restored our sight.
　　 Now we can follow Christ on the way to the new kingdom.
And as we travel,
　　 may God fill our eyes with many joys and blessings. **Amen.**

Hymns and Choruses

(The asterisk [*] indicates hymns or choruses that are addressed to God and can be used as prayers.)

___ *"Be Thou My Vision"
___ "Carry the Light"
___ *"Heal Us, Emmanuel, Hear Our Prayer"
___ *"I Am the God That Healeth Thee"
___ "I Heard the Voice of Jesus Say"
___ "I Will Celebrate"
___ "Let Us Plead for Faith Alone"

___ *"My Faith Looks Up to Thee"
___ "O For a Thousand Tongues to Sing"
___ *"O God, Whose Will Is Life and Good"
___ *"O Jesus, Joy of Loving Hearts"
___ *"O Son of God, in Galilee"
___ *"Open My Eyes, That I May See"
___ *"Open Our Eyes, Lord"
___ "When Jesus the Healer Passed Through Galilee"
___ *"Word of God, Come Down on Earth"
___ *"Your Hand, O Lord, in Days of Old"

Reading the Scripture

___ Since this is a relatively brief and simple passage, have one of the older children or a youth memorize this. Have the youth practice long enough that the words flow out naturally. The worshipers need to be impressed by the content of the words, not the ability of the young person to memorize.

___ Have a person read this lesson in three parts. In between the parts the worshipers respond to the lesson by singing the hymn "Open My Eyes, That I May See" as outlined below.
    Read verses 46-47
    Sing the first stanza
    Read verses 48-49a
    Sing the second stanza
    Read verses 49b-52
    Sing the third stanza

Responses to the Word

___ If a solo dancer is used to portray Bartimaeus, then let the congregation join in his experience. As worshipers arrive at the church, give them ragged pieces of cloth to wear over their shoulders during the worship service. Then after the scripture has been read and the worshipers have heard the sermon, let the dancer throw off the cloak that marks Bartimaeus as a blind beggar. The dancer can then call on the congregation to throw off their own beggar cloaks (the cloth strips they received upon arrival). The dancer then invites the worshipers to follow Jesus, and as the worshipers fall into line behind the dancer a parade begins (also known as a religious procession). The worshipers, who have now experienced being made well, can joyfully march off around the block, to the church fellowship hall for refreshments, or wherever Christ would have them go!

___ This may be a good time for the congregation to celebrate their healing ministries by including a ritual for healing in the worship service. Let worshipers desiring healing come forward to receive prayer, anointing with oil and the laying on of hands. Holy communion is often connected with healing liturgies, too. Provision may be made for praying for the healing of people who are not in attendance. Such prayer could be followed up by small groups from the congregation going to visit the persons who could not come to the church. They could pray with these persons, anoint them, and offer the laying on of hands for healing. Some instruction would be needed for a group to do this. Perhaps a person from each group could receive some simple instructions about how to offer such ministry to the sick, and this person could serve as the leader of the group.

___ Offer the worshipers a chance to come forward to pray for illumination and vision for some decision or circumstance in their lives. Realize that many people will prefer to do this while remaining seated in the pews. Their prayers will be just as genuine as those who come forward, and God will give them just as much attention. People have different needs at times like this.

___ Some pastors will be contrasting the beggar Bartimaeus who sees and follows Christ with the disciples who still do not see what Christ is doing as he travels to Jerusalem and who will desert him there. If this is the direction of the sermon, then a prayer of confession may be an appropriate response for a church that is once again blind to what Christ is doing in our world.

Drama and Movement

___ A solo dancer could let the congregation see Bartimaeus throw off his ragged cloak, receive his sight, and begin to follow Jesus. The dancer can work with the church's musicians to choose appropriate music.

___ A Sunday school class could act out this gospel lesson. Only three people are needed for the speaking parts (narrator, Jesus, and Bartimaeus), and two or more children could constitute the crowd.

___ Ask the church's youth fellowship to provide a musical rendition of this gospel lesson. They could paraphrase the text and set it to rock, rap, country, jazz, something south of the border, or whatever they prefer. Such a project would be exciting and fun to the young people, and it would impress the witness of this lesson on their minds and the minds of the congregation.

___ Since this lesson is the last episode on Jesus' journey to Jerusalem in Mark's gospel, this might be a good time for a dramatic review of this journey. A group of adults could begin with the transfiguration (Mark 9:2-8) and act out that and the events that followed. The stories that Mark shares about Jesus' journey contain some very deliberate theological work that helps us understand Jesus and his purpose. The dramatic review could end with Jesus' entry into Jerusalem (Mark 11:1-11). The sermon could be used to clarify further some of the theological truths declared in the stories that recount this journey. Congregational prayers and hymns that follow this drama could pick up the themes surrounding the crucifixion and resurrection.

Visuals

___ Dark glasses, a white cane, and a tin cup (for begging) would symbolize a contemporary Bartimaeus. These could be worked into a floral arrangement or used for a banner.

___ Visuals more contemporary to the New Testament would be the ragged cloak left behind by Bartimaeus when Jesus calls him. A chipped clay pot for receiving alms would refer to Bartimaeus' position as a beggar.

Anthems and Special Music

Jesus Said to the Blind Man — C. Alwes — SATB w/organ — AF
Open Our Eyes — K. Lee Scott — SATB w/keyboard — CPH
The Blind Man Stood on the Road and Cried — S. Clary — SATB — WB

Organ and Other Keyboard Music

Be Thou My Vision (Slane) — found in *Three Hymns of Praise*, set 3 — R. Hobby — MSM
My Faith Looks Up to Thee (Olivet) — found in *Twelve Hymn Preludes*, set 2 — S. Bingham — HWG
O Jesus, Joy of Loving Hearts (Walton) — found in *Interpretations*, Book III — D. Cherwien — AMSI

ALL SAINTS' DAY

Revised
  Common: John 11:32-44
Episcopal: Matthew 5:1-12* or
               Luke 6:25-33#
Lutheran: John 11:32-44; Matthew 5:1-12*

I AM THE RESURRECTION AND THE LIFE

Gail Throckmorton Warner

Note: In worship, Christ listens to our complaints about his bad timing and joins us in our grief. Then, according to God's plan, Christ calls our loved ones out of death and sets them free in new life.

* See All Saints' Day in *Worship Workbook For The Gospels, Cycle A* for material on this text.
\# See All Saints' Day in *Worship Workbook For The Gospels, Cycle C* for material on this text.

Printed Resources

___ Greeting

Ldr: Jesus said to Martha,
        "I am the resurrection and the life.
        Those who believe in me, even though they die,
        will live,
        and everyone who lives and believes in me
        will never die.
        Do you believe this?"
Cng: **Lord, I believe that you are the Messiah,**
        the Son of God,
        the one coming into the world.
Ldr: Jesus also said to Martha that if she believed
        she would see the glory of God.
Cng: **Lord, we believe.**
        Let God's glory be seen here today.

___ Prayer

God who creates, nurtures and resurrects,

295

in the midst of life, we have been sealed in death.
When Martha and Mary called Jesus to save Lazarus,
    they did not know that Jesus would have to take Lazarus' place.
When they chided Jesus' tardiness,
    they did not understand the timing necessary to save us all.
When Jesus joined his tears to theirs,
    Martha and Mary did not anticipate Gethsemane's agony.
When Martha said she believed in the resurrection after life,
    she did not know Jesus ends death and begins new life,
    bringing eternity into this world.
Yet, even in their simple faith, Martha and Mary believed Jesus,
    and trusted their brother's lifeless body to Jesus' power.
Now we look back to Lazarus' tomb and know Jesus sets us free,
    as he unbinds us forever from the wrappings of death.
Now the dawning light of your eternal kingdom breaks upon us,
    calling us out of this world's tombs.
Now the glory of Christ shines brightly on our understanding,
    as we see the awful price he paid to save our lives.
Now we dance the thankful joy of Lazarus,
    as we sing our Savior's name outside others' tombs,
    proclaiming life to those still sealed in death. Amen.

___ Commissioning and Blessing

Ldr: "Take away the stone," Jesus demands.
    "Unbind them and let them go," he tells us.
Cng: **Our tasks are clear.**
    So is the mission of our Savior.
Ldr: Yes, Jesus will call the dead back into life.
    God hears Jesus' voice and answers with resurrection.
Cng: **Just as Christ has opened the way for our salvation,**
    we will remove the stones blocking the way for others
    and unbind them from death's rigid grip.
Ldr: May God, who breathed new life into your souls,
    use you to set your neighbors free to live new under God.
    In the name of the Father, Son, and Holy Spirit...
Cng: **Amen!**

___ Commissioning and Blessing

Jesus calls you to new life with God.
You are no longer to be bound to the past,
    but you are set free to live fully for today
    and for the future that is yet to come. **Amen.**

Hymns and Choruses

(The asterisk [*] indicates hymns and choruses that are addressed to God and can be used as prayers.)

___ "All Hail the Power of Jesus' Name"
___ *"Eternal Light, Shine in My Heart"
___ *"Even as We Live Each Day"
___ "How Firm a Foundation"
___ "Hymn of Promise"
___ "I Know Whom I Have Believed"
___ "My Heart Is Longing"
___ "Oh, Sing, My Soul, Your Maker's Praise"
___ "Peace, to Soothe Our Bitter Woes"
___ "Rejoice, the Lord Is King"
___ "Sing with All the Saints in Glory"

Reading the Scripture

___ If the suggestion in "Drama and Movement" below is not used, then divide the reading among several people. Someone to read Mary's, Martha's and Jesus' words would be needed, as well as someone to read the narration. Have the choir read the words of the Jews in verse 36.

___ Ask one of the congregation's storytellers to tell this story from memory.

Responses to the Word

___ Have the congregation sing one or more hymns about the love of Jesus.

___ Have the congregation join in reciting one of the creeds that emphasizes Jesus' power over life and death. Let this response flow right into a hymn that praises this power of Christ.

___ Instruct the worshipers to remain seated as they sing the hymn "Sing with All the Saints in Glory" until the third verse. Tell them that if they believe what they are singing to stand at the third verse, and sing out strongly what they believe. The same could be done with "I Know Whom I Have Believed," except that the people would stand when they begin singing the refrain.

___ Have the congregation join in praying the prayer printed above.

Drama and Movement

___ Many churches stage resurrection dramas at Easter. Why not stage the story of the raising of Lazarus for the celebration of All Saints' Day? To understand the depths of this story, though, it is necessary to portray the whole of chapter 11 in John's gospel. Verses 1-31 lay the foundation for understanding the issues of God's timing that is set in accordance with a plan that is larger than any individual life. Verses 45-57 help us understand that the result of Christ's compassion was that the religious authorities of his day became convinced that they must put him to death. Adding these verses will let the preacher address the fact that Christ sacrificed himself to save us. So, recruit actors and actresses to tell the whole story. If a tomb prop is used at Easter, use the same tomb for this service. Be careful with how Lazarus is bound with cloth. He should look like a buried Hebrew, not an Egytian mummy.

Visuals

——

T
y
pe
the
words
on the
worship
bulletin in the
shape of a teardrop,
like this. Or type the
words in the normal way
and have volunteers cut
the paper in the shape
of teardrop
s.

___ Have someone in the congregation who arranges flowers work with a local florist to prepare an arrangement of flowers like those that are used on caskets. Set this funeral display on the altar table. As the pastor preaches on how Jesus transforms death into life, have the congregational member transform the funeral display into an explosion of color that is shaped into several grand bouquets that celebrate life. At the conclusion of the service, these bouquets that proclaim Jesus' victory over death can be given to worshipers who have lost loved ones in the last year.

Anthems and Special Music

(John 11:32-44)
A Cluster of Canons — W. Billings — Unison canons — PA
The Raising of Lazarus — A. Willaert — SATB w/optional keyboard — RIC

(Matthew 5:1-12)
See All Saints' Day in *Worship Workbook For The Gospels, Cycle A*
Blest Are They — D. Haas — SAB w/keyboard, opt. congregation — GIA
For the Feast of All Saints — G. Near — SATB w/organ — PA

Long Ago and Far Away — R. Hobby — Unison w/keyboard, opt. cantor — MSM
Rejoice in God's Saints — C. H. H. Parry — SATB w/keyboard — from *With One Voice* — AF
The Beatitudes — J. Bender — 2-part w/organ with oboe, viola, cello — CPH
The Beatitudes — P. Christiansen — SATB w/narration — AF
The Beatitudes — S. Panchenko — SSATTB unaccompanied — PA

(Luke 6:25-33)
On Love of One's Enemies — V. Ford — SATB w/keyboard — BP
The Woes — V. Ford — SATB w/keyboard — BP

Organ and Other Keyboard Music

All Hail the Power of Jesus' Name (Miles Lane) — found in *113 Variations on Hymn Tunes* — G. Thalben-Ball — NOV
How Firm a Foundation (Foundation) — found in *American Folk Hymn Suite* — M. Burkhardt — MSM
Sing With All the Saints in Glory (Hymn to Joy) — found in *Praise!* — E. L. Diemer — SMP

OCTOBER 30-NOVEMBER 5
PROPER 26
PENTECOST 24

Revised
  Common: Mark 12:28-34
Episcopal: Mark 12:28-34
Lutheran: Mark 12:28-34

with all your heart

with all your soul

with all your mind

with all your strength

and your neighbor

as yourself.

Gail Throckmorton Warner

*Note: When we bow down
before the One God, and love
God with our whole being, we
are not far from the kingdom
of God.*

Printed Resources

___ Greeting
(The congregational response is the hymn "God of the Sparrow, God of the Whale," available from G.I.A. Publications and in *The United Methodist Hymnal*.)

Ldr: Children of God and disciples of Christ, listen.
        "The Lord our God, the Lord is one;
        you shall love the Lord your God with all your heart
        and with all your soul,
        and with all your mind,
        and with all your strength."
Cng: (Sing verses 1 through 3.)
Ldr: The second greatest commandment is this,
        "You shall love your neighbor as yourself."
Cng: (Sing verses 4 through 6.)

___ Prayer

Let us bow in prayer before the One who has made us,
    who has saved us,
    and who is with us every day.
Take this moment to remember
    the many ways that our God has loved you,
    and give God thanks.
(The people pray silently.)
Remember what Jesus Christ did
    to save you from your sin,

and give God thanks.
(The people pray silently.)
Remember all those times that God's Holy Spirit
    has guided you, comforted you, and strengthened you,
    and give God thanks.
(The people pray silently.)
(Let this prayer flow naturally into the worshipers singing the chorus "Father, I Adore You.")

___ Prayer of Confession and Assurance of Pardon
(This prayer from the church's long tradition is hard to beat.)

Our heavenly Father,
    who by your love has made us,
    and through your love has kept us,
    and in your love would make us perfect:
We humbly confess that we have not loved you
 with all our heart and soul and mind and strength,
    and that we have not loved one another
    as Christ has loved us.
Your life is within our souls,
    but our selfishness has hindered you.
We have not lived by faith.
We have resisted your Spirit.
We have neglected your inspirations.
Forgive what we have been;
    help us to amend what we are;
    and in your Spirit direct what we shall be;
    that you may come into the full glory of your creation,
    in us and in all the people,
through Jesus Christ our Lord. Amen.
(Continue to pray silently.)
Hear the good news.
"God so loved the world that he gave his only Son,
    so that everyone who believes in him may not perish
    but may have eternal life.
Indeed, God did not send the Son into the world
    to condemn the world,
    but in order that the world might be saved through him."
Brothers and sisters,
    in the name of Jesus Christ our sins are forgiven.
Thanks be to God!

___ Commissioning and Blessing

You will discover your life full of joy and peace,
    as you daily grow in loving God,

with heart, soul, mind and strength.
You will discover your greatest blessing,
    as you learn to love your neighbor as yourself.
And our loving God will walk beside you,
    as you draw ever closer to the coming kingdom.

Hymns and Choruses

(The asterisk [*] indicates hymns or choruses that are addressed to God and can be used as prayers.)

____ *"Abba Father"
____ *"All-Consuming Fire"
____ *"Come Down, O Love Divine"
____ *"El Shaddai"
____ *"Father, I Adore You"
____ *"Glorify Thy Name"
____ "God Is Love, and Where True Love Is"
____ "God Is Love, Let Heaven Adore Him"
____ *"Holy Is Your Name"
____ "How Can We Name a Love"
____ *"I Love You, Lord"
____ *"I'm Loving You More Every Day"
____ *"Jesus, Thou Boundless Love to Me"
____ *"Joyful, Joyful, We Adore Thee"
____ *"King of Glory, King of Peace"
____ *"Lord of All Nations, Grant Me Grace"
____ *"Love Divine, All Loves Excelling"
____ *"More Love to Thee"
____ *"O God, I Love Thee"
____ *"O Master, Let Me Walk with Thee"
____ *"O Savior, Precious Savior"
____ *"The Greatest Thing"
____ *"Thee Will I Love, My Strength"
____ "They'll Know We Are Christians by Our Love" ("We Are One in the Spirit")
____ "When Christ Was Lifted from the Earth"
____ "Where Charity and Love Dwell"
____ *"With All My Heart"
____ *"Your Love, O God, Has Called Us Here"

Reading the Scripture

____ If your congregation is fortunate enough to have someone with the skill to do chanting, then ask this person to use his or her skills to chant the beautiful words in this gospel lesson.

___ One of the most vivid human experiences of love is that time when two people are about to be married. Choose such a couple to read the gospel lesson. Their obvious love for each other will add further testimony to the truth that Jesus calls all God's children to joyfully obey.

Responses to the Word

___ Why not hold a love-in? Read the scripture lesson, explain what is about to happen, and then lead the congregation in presenting a concert to God. Use a mixture of choruses and hymns for the congregation to sing their love to God. The ones marked with an asterisk (*) above would all be suitable for such a purpose. Use choirs, soloists, and other special groupings to provide variety and to sing music that would not be possible for the whole congregation. Use instrumentalists to lift up other notes of love to God's ears. Liturgical dancers could add another form of expression to the love songs. Even a small child with just a year of piano lessons can plink out love songs that fall beautifully upon God's ear.

___ Use the prayer of confession printed above to call the worshipers back to the way of Christ.

Drama and Movement

___ Set a challenge before one of the church's adult Sunday school classes. Ask them to use the church library, or a public library, to research the lives of some of the church's greatest leaders and saints. Then ask the class to prepare and present dramatic sketches for the congregation that show the powerful love these people had for God.

___ An alternative to the suggestion above would be to ask a group of adults to prepare a dramatic reading of selected biblical passages. Each passage should be chosen for its ability to reveal the love of God that various biblical persons demonstrated in their words and actions.

___ Choose a hymn or chorus that praises God and proclaims the worshipers' love for God. Then ask one or more liturgical dancers to add motion to the hymn's words, so that the congregation may see their love and praise given visible expression.

Visuals

___ If you are going to hold a love-in, as suggested under "Responses to the Word" above, then pass out strings of 1960s-style love-beads to the worshipers. The worshipers could keep the beads as a reminder of the commandment that is "first of all."

___ Put the word out ahead of time, and invite people to bring flowers to the worship service to honor God and to proclaim their love. These could be a single bloom, or a huge bouquet. They could come from the worshipers' flower beds, or from the local florist. They could be cut flowers or potted flowers. Any type or any color is appropriate. The only guidelines are that worshipers should choose what they believe God would enjoy. At the beginning of the service, let the worshipers bring these flowers forward to place them at God's feet. Some forethought is needed to prepare a place to receive all the worshipers' tokens of love. After the service is concluded, the worshipers could take the flowers they brought to a neighbor, so that the neigbors would know they are loved, too.

___ If the "love of neighbor" is to be emphasized in this gospel lesson, then have a still photographer go around the community photographing scenes of people loving their neighbors. These photos can be taken to a photo store and blown up into life-size prints. Hang these prints around the sanctuary to visualize what Jesus means with the second greatest commandment. After the service the prints could be hung in other parts of the church building to keep Jesus' command in the minds and hearts of the congregation.

Anthems and Special Music

The Great Commandment — R. Johnson — SATB w/organ — AF
The Great Commandment — D. Moore — SATB w/keyboard — MF
The Word of God is Source and Seed — D. Hurd — Unison w/keyboard — from *With One Voice* — AF
You Are Not Far From the Kingdom of God — C. McCormick — SATB w/keyboard — SH

Organ and Other Keyboard Music

Joyful, Joyful, We Adore Thee (Hymn to Joy) — Procession of Joy — H. Hopson — CF
O Master, Let Me Walk With Thee (Maryton) — found in *Softly and Tenderly*, vol. 2 — D. Wood — SMP

NOVEMBER 6-12
PROPER 27
PENTECOST 25

Revised
 Common: Mark 12:38-44
Episcopal: Mark 12:38-44
Lutheran: Mark 12:38-44

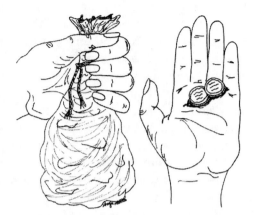

Note: Loving God and following Christ involves much more than just outward appearances. It involves one's heart — all of it.

"I tell you the truth, this poor widow has put more into the treasury than all the others."
– Mark 12:43

Angie Latta

Printed Resources

___ Greeting

Ld1: Beware of the scribes!
Ld2: Beware of those who want to impress you with their piety.
Ld1: Unless what you do in here is lived out there...
Ld2: You only heap up more condemnation upon your heads!
(Let the congregation respond by singing "A Charge to Keep I Have," "Come, Thou Fount of Every Blessing," or "Lord, I Want to Be a Christian.")

___ Prayer

O God, you send stars hurtling into space
    and fix the planets in their orbits.
 You set the volcanoes to boiling,
    and shake the land with earthquakes.
 You pile up the mountains
    and scoop out the oceans.
 You write the history of nations,
    and decide the fate of armies.
 You lift up presidents and heads of state,
    and set the times when they are brought down.
You are God, and there is no other like you.
    All power rests in your hands.
 The greetings of self-important mortals are nothing,
    because you call us "sons" and "daughters."
 Human banquets and places of honor have no meaning,

305

because you open to us the banquet in your eternal kingdom.
One word whispered in your ear is more precious
than all the long prayers recited to impress others.
We snub the world's minuscule powers and influence,
so that we may serve your overwhelming greatness.
Jesus has led us to give everything we have to you,
because everything we have is from you.
Our weakness is our greatest strength,
because it teaches us to depend upon your power.
We are nothing and you are everything,
yet your unconquerable grace anoints us with your love.
You draw us to your side with Jesus' great sacrifice,
and you give us unbelievable hope with his resurrection.
O God, our God, use your great power
to bring our deeds into harmony with our prayers. Amen.

___ Commissioning and Blessing

To give all you have in serving God
is to give as God has given to you.
Jesus saw the widow add her two copper coins to the treasury,
and what you add to the kingdom will be seen by its ruler.
Such giving is its own blessing and needs no other reward.
But do not be surprised when you receive more than you gave.
(The congregation can respond by singing "Blessed Be the Name," or some other appropriate chorus.)

___ Commissioning and Blessing

Ldr: The widow Jesus saw gave two copper coins.
When you give that much, it will be enough.
Cng: **Lord, teach us to trust you like the widow.**
Teach us to depend upon your love
to get us through each day.
Ldr: May the God whose name is love,
give you the widow's heart.
Cng: **Amen, Lord. Let it be so.**

Hymns and Choruses

(The asterisk [*] indicates hymns or choruses that are addressed to God and can be used as prayers.)

___ *"A Charge to Keep I Have"
___ *"Come Down, O Love Divine"
___ "Cuando El Pobre" ("When the Poor Ones")

___ "Humble Thyself in the Sight of the Lord"
___ *"I Want a Principle Within"
___ *"In My Life, Lord, Be Glorified"
___ "Jehovah-Jireh"
___ *"Lord Jesus, Think on Me"
___ *"Lord of All Good"
___ *"Lord, Teach Us How to Pray Aright"
___ *"Lord, Whose Love Through Humble Service"
___ "Seek Ye First"
___ *"Take Me In"
___ *"Take My Life, that I May Be"
___ *"We Are an Offering"
___ *"We Give Thee but Thine Own"
___ "What Does the Lord Require"
___ *"With All My Heart"

Reading the Scripture

___ Divide the reading between two people. Have the first read verses 38-40, and the second read verses 41-44.

___ Another way to divide the reading between two people is to have one read the narration, and the other read the words of Jesus.

___ Recruit a good storyteller from the congregation to recount this gospel lesson.

Responses to the Word

___ This is another of the many gospel lessons that would be good to use to challenge the congregation's financial support of the church's ministry. Filling out pledge cards, or estimate-of-giving cards, would be a proper response to this lesson.

___ If your congregation is one that provides financial statements to its members, then this would be a good Sunday to pass them out to the worshipers. But first, have them write their monthly income on a blank piece of paper (inserted in the worship bulletin?). Reassure them that they do not have to show this to anyone. Then give the worshipers their statements. Have them subtract the total of their last month's giving from their monthly income. Then tell them to add up all the other little donations, not recorded on their statements, that they have made to the congregation within the last month. This list could include Sunday school offerings, a donation to a youth fund-raiser, a special gift to missions, and so on. When the worshipers have had time to add up this list, tell them to subtract this from their income figure too. By this point the worshipers should have subtracted their regular offerings (recorded on their statements) and all their special offerings from their last month's income. Finally, have them draw a circle around whatever remains of their income after all these gifts to God. Then have the worshipers consider what position they would be in if they would also give this remaining amount of their income to God, too. When they have had a moment to reflect upon giving their whole paycheck to God, tell the worshipers that this is what the widow had done. Now they can understand why Jesus called attention to her giving. She had given everything, and trusted God to take care of her needs. Are we capable of such trust?

____ If this gospel lesson is read to a congregation of affluent people, then the preacher should lift up how Jesus contrasts a faithful life that avoids power, influence and wealth with the affluence enjoyed by many in the congregation. Such words will not be easy to hear. And what response would be proper? A prayer of confession would only allow another easy out for people who need to hear Christ's warning and need to let his words pierce the depths of their being. So, use silence as the proper response. Let the worshipers sit quietly reflecting upon the lesson they should learn from Jesus about how they should live today. Let them consider their own power, influence and wealth. Let them have time to decide quietly how they can be faithful. After three to five minutes of silence, let the worshipers join in a hymn of commitment.

Drama and Movement

____ Ask a group of adults to prepare one or two short skits that present a contemporary version of people pretending to be more pious than they truly are.

____ A group of Christian clowns could add some humor to the service by providing a clown's version of the gospel lesson. Three or four clowns could portray the scribes in their long robes and even longer prayers, as well as contrast the poor widow's offering with that of the rich.

Visuals

____ Here's a chance for a seamstress to have fun. This person can sew a banner depicting a scribe in a very long robe. The robe can be so long that it flows off the banner and onto the floor. Other figures can be shown bowing (as they do in Asia) in greeting to the scribe. Add the words, "Beware of the scribes," to the banner to drive the point of the lesson home.

____ Have someone from the congregation sketch the two copper coins for the cover of the worship bulletins. A bible dictionary would be a good source to check what they would have looked like in Jesus' day.

____ Give a children's Sunday school class black pens. Ask them to draw Jesus watching the poor widow and the rich people giving their offerings to the temple treasury. Use one or all of these drawings for worship bulletin covers by reproducing them on a copier.

Anthems and Special Music

God's Loving Call — W. Wold — Unison w/keyboard — CG

Organ and Other Keyboard Music

Lord Jesus, Think On Me (Southwell) — found in *Nine Easy Chorale Preludes for Lent* — J. Engel — MSM

Take My Life, That I May Be (Patmos) — Van Hulse — found in *The Parish Organist*, part 3 — CPH

NOVEMBER 13-19
PROPER 28
PENTECOST 26

Revised
  Common: Mark 13:1-8
Episcopal: Mark 13:14-23
Lutheran: Mark 13:1-8

Note: In the midst of all the terrible things that will happen in this world, Jesus' disciples are reminded not to be led astray, away from their Savior who opens the gates to the Kingdom.

"PEACE TALKS BREAK DOWN"

TROOPS MASSING ON BORDER

NEW MISSILE MORE ACCURATE, MORE DEADLY

INSURGENTS STOPPED NEAR CAPITAL

"WOUNDED OVERWHELM HOSPITALS"

TWO CARRIER GROUP ... E SHORE!

BOMBS EXPLODE IN CITY CENTER

"This is but the beginning of the birthpangs."

Printed Resources

___ Greeting

Ld1: Brothers and sisters, have you heard the prophecies?
      Many who come in the name of Christ
      are saying the end is near!
Cng: **"Beware that no one leads you astray."**
Ld2: But I have heard that we are going to be pulled into war!
      And there are already so many wars between the nations!
Cng: **"Do not be alarmed; this must take place,
      but the end is still to come."**
Ld1: But what about the earthquakes?
      There seem to be more than usual!
Ld2: And there are people dying of hunger!
      Famines are one of the signs of the end!
Cng: **This is but the beginning of the birthpangs.**

___ Prayer

**God of power and might,
    help us not to put our trust in human works.
The disciples were impressed with the temple's massive stones,
    but only one small fragment of its wall
    survived the Roman assault.
    Today people stand there and mourn their loss.**

310

Time and time again, people have built impregnable fortresses,
    assembled unconquerable armies and navies,
    and invented one ultimate weapon after another,
    only to see themselves go down in defeat.
There is nothing impregnable, unconquerable or ultimate,
    except for your love, your strength and your coming kingdom.
Keep us, O God, from going astray.
    Save us from being alarmed at all that must happen.
    Remind us that the terrors all around us
    are just the beginning of the birth pangs.
  Let the signs of your coming kingdom
    call us to greater dependence upon your faithfulness,
    today, tomorrow and all the days yet remaining. Amen.

___ Prayer

Almighty and merciful God,
    in a world where everything Christian is under attack,
    keep us true to our Savior, Jesus Christ.
Many are calling us to follow new ways,
    to accept their versions of the truth,
    and to adopt their more "enlightened" understandings.
Many try to alarm us by making long lists of troubles.
    "The world is falling apart," they cry out in panic,
    and they expect us to follow them in wrongheaded actions.
But you, O God, have not changed, and our Savior has not changed.
    Christians have always lived dangerous lives
    in a world overflowing with false prophets.
So keep us true to the one and only Savior, Jesus Christ.
    Keep us on the one and only path that leads to your kingdom.
    Keep us Christian, in a world full of so many other paths. Amen.

___ Commissioning and Blessing

Beware that no one leads you astray.
    There are many false prophets.
Do not be alarmed
    when you are faced with great troubles.
These are but the beginnings of the birthpangs
    that will establish Christ's kingdom on earth.
You have a Savior who has died
    so that you may live with God eternally. **Amen.**

Hymns and Choruses

(The asterisk [*] indicates hymns or choruses that are addressed to God and can be used as prayers.)

___ "Battle Hymn of the Republic"
___ "Be Bold, Be Strong"
___ *"By Gracious Powers"
___ "How Firm a Foundation"
___ "I Know Whom I Have Believed"
___ "In the Name of the Lord"
___ *"Jesus, Still Lead On"
___ *"Lord, Take My Hand and Lead Me"
___ *"O Lord of Light, Who Made the Stars"
___ "Soon and Very Soon"
___ *"Stand By Me"
___ *"When Peace, Like a River"

Reading the Scripture

___ Recruit three people to read the gospel lesson. One should read the narration, one the words of the disciples, and one the words of Jesus.

___ Have someone read verses 1-2. Then have the congregation sing the first two stanzas of "The Battle Hymn of the Republic." Then have verses 3-8 read, and after this the congregation concludes by singing the last three stanzas of the same hymn.

Responses to the Word

___ After the sermon, have the worshipers join in one of the prayers printed above.

___ Since the purpose of most apocalyptic writing is to strengthen the faithful during times of difficulty, invite the worshipers to sing some of the great hymns of faith as a response to the Word. Such hymns could include: "Am I a Soldier of the Cross"; "Stand By Me"; "By Gracious Powers"; "I Want Jesus to Walk with Me"; "Leave It There"; "How Firm a Foundation"; "A Mighty Fortress Is Our God"; or "Be Still, My Soul."

Drama and Movement

___ The vivid and dramatic content of Mark's thirteenth chapter deserves to be heard in its entirety. Assemble a group of dancers, a strong reader, and one or more musicians to provide a powerful reading of this apocalyptic chapter for the worshipers. The musicians may have a basic work in mind to shape their musical efforts, but they should remain free to improvise as necessary to give full expression to Mark's words. As the musicians add feeling and emotion to the words, the dancers have the job of helping the worshipers see the text's words and emotions. With a little imagination and some sweat, such a drama team could provide the congregation with a powerful and unforgettable experience of Mark's thirteenth chapter.

___ Write out descriptions of how people are being led astray in today's world. Give these descriptions to various people in the congregation. Have these people stand up and read these descriptions from their pews. These can be used either to introduce the sermon or to provide illustrations for the sermon.

Visuals

___ Gather your congregation's textile artists. Challenge them to make four banners depicting: (1) the Jerusalem temple broken into a heap of stones; (2) a war; (3) an earthquake; and (4) a famine.

___ Ask the church's youth group to construct a cardboard replica of the temple for a visual aid. They can research how it looked in bible dictionaries, and flatten large cardboard boxes for painting a replica. The cardboard will need to be supported by a wood frame, and the whole thing can be placed along one of the side walls in the sanctuary. If they would like, a replica of what remains of the temple (the Wailing Wall in Jerusalem) can be constructed for the opposing wall of the sanctuary.

Anthems and Special Music

(Mark 13:1-13)
Great God, Your Love Has Called Us — N. Cocker — SATB w/keyboard — from *With One Voice* — AF
Lord, Let My Heart Be Good Soil — H. Hanson — Unison hymn w/keyboard — found in *With One Voice* — AF
We Come to the Hungry Feast — R. Makeever — Unison w/keyboard, guitar — from *With One Voice* — AF

(Mark 13:14-23)
See above

Organ and Other Keyboard Music

Battle Hymn of the Republic (Battle Hymn) — found in *11 Compositions for Organ*, set 3 — C. Ore — CPH
Jesus, Still Lead On (Seelenbrautigam) — found in *Five Hymn Improvisations for Weddings and General Use* — P. Manz — MSM

PENTECOST 27

Lutheran: Mark 13:24-31*

*Material relating to this text can be found on the First Sunday of Advent.

CHRIST THE KING
PROPER 29

Revised
  Common: John 18:33-37
Episcopal: John 18:33-37 or
            Mark 11:1-11*
Lutheran: John 18:33-37

"My kingdom is not of this world."

Angie Latta

Note: Christ establishes his kingdom with or without our permission. And yet, Christ will not rule in our hearts unless we first give permission.

---

* See Passion/Palm Sunday for material on this text.

Printed Resources

___ Greeting

Ldr: Pilate had Jesus brought before him
      to ask if Jesus were the king of the Jews.
Cng: **Jesus, we have come before you**
      to affirm your authority over our lives.
Ldr: Jesus proclaimed that his kingship
      was not from this world.
Cng: **Jesus, bring your kingdom into our world,**
      and let it come soon.

___ Prayer

Our Father,
    each time we receive your holy communion,
    a new surge of Jesus' royal blood courses through our souls.
Jesus' kingdom may not be from this world,
    but we certainly feel the influence
    of his heavenly authority every minute of our lives.
Let the blood of Jesus' crucifixion be our truth,
    and let this truth govern us,
    until our earthly natures are transformed
    to harmonize with the heavenly kingdom that Jesus brings.
Amen.

____ Affirmation of Faith

We acknowledge that God creates all life,
    and that our lives continue
    only by the mercy of God,
    and that God sends Jesus to save us
    from being fatally separated
    from our Creator,
    the source and being of our lives.
We maintain that Jesus is the Christ,
    and that our lives are best lived
    under Jesus' rule, as the one
    who has power over life and death.
We are persuaded that Jesus' crucifixion, resurrection,
    and ascension to full glory and complete authority,
    are calls to all people to be united with God
    by living under the banner of Christ.
We testify that God's Spirit dwells in believers,
    and fills us with strength, courage, hope,
    peace, wisdom, faith and pure love,
    so that we can live boldly like Christ
    in eternal unity with our Creator.

____ Commissioning and Blessing

Go and serve your king in this world,
    so that you may be prepared
    for the kingdom that is coming.
And may all that you do be undergirded
    with the strength, authority and truth of Jesus Christ,
    in the name of Almighty God,
    Father, Son and Holy Spirit.
Amen.

Hymns and Choruses

(The asterisk [*] indicates hymns and choruses that are addressed to God and can be used as prayers.)

____ "All Hail the Power of Jesus' Name"
____ *"All Praise to Thee, for Thou, O King Divine"
____ "Alleluia, Alleluia"
____ "Alleluia! Sing to Jesus"
____ *"Eternal Ruler of the Ceaseless Round"
____ "Glorious the Day When Christ Was Born"
____ "Hail to the Lord's Anointed"

___ "Hallelujah! What a Savior"
___ "He Is Exalted"
___ "Jesus Shall Reign"
___ "Jesus! the Name High over All"
___ *"Lion of Judah"
___ "Majesty, Worship His Majesty"
___ "Morning Glory, Starlit Sky"
___ "Rejoice, the Lord Is King"
___ "The Lord Reigneth"
___ "There's Something About That Name"
___ *"Thy Kingdom Come, O God!"
___ *"We Bow Down"
___ "We Will Glorify"
___ "We've a Story to Tell to the Nations"
___ "Ye Servants of God"
___ *"You Are My God"

Reading the Scripture

___ Recruit three readers to read the scripture as follows:

Narrator: Then Pilate entered the headquarters again, summoned Jesus, and asked him,
Pilate: Are you the King of the Jews?
Narrator: Jesus answered,
Jesus: Do you ask this on your own, or did others tell you about me?
Pilate: I am not a Jew, am I? Your own nation and the chief priests have handed you over to me. What have you done?
Jesus: My kingdom is not from this world. If my kingdom were from this world, my followers would be fighting to keep me from being handed over to the Jews. But as it is, my kingdom is not from here.
Pilate: So you are a king?
Jesus: You say that I am a king. For this I was born, and for this I came into the world, to testify to the truth. Everyone who belongs to the truth listens to my voice.

___ Introduce the gospel lesson with this information about the context.

Our gospel lesson this morning comes from a longer narrative in John's gospel where Pilate interrogates Jesus concerning the charges that the religious leaders have brought against him. Jesus has already been before the religious leaders who had sentenced Jesus to death, even before he had been arrested. Because they have no authority under Roman government to execute anyone, the religious leaders have brought Jesus to Pilate. During this first part of Pilate's interrogation of Jesus, the questions turn into a philosophical discussion of the nature of kingship and truth. Listen now, as Pilate interrogates our Savior.

Responses to the Word

___ Have the worshipers affirm their faith in Christ's kingship by joining together in the affirmation of faith printed above.

___ The worship service could end with the congregation going out into the street and joining in a parade that proclaims and celebrates the sovereignty of Christ. See the third suggestion under "Visuals" below.

___ Invite the worshipers to come forward to the altar rail to submit their lives to the kingship of Jesus Christ.

Drama and Movement

___ In his book, *John*,[2] Fred Craddock provides an excellent outline of the dramatic scenes where Pilate pathetically shuttles back and forth between the Jewish authorities outside and Jesus inside. In 18:29—19:16 we see Jesus strong and well in control of his own destiny. We also see Pilate, the governor, as weak and bowing to the whims of his noisy subjects, the Jewish leaders. These leaders sound the cries of the world against God's chosen one. At the same time their hypocrisy is exposed as they refuse to ceremonially defile themselves by entering the Gentile Praetorium, but they hatch plots of murder in their hearts. Turn this over to a group of adults to produce a play portraying this explosive drama. The scenes are as follows:

vv. 29-32 Pilate inquires about the Jewish leaders' accusations against Jesus.

vv. 33-38a Pilate questions Jesus about his kingship.

vv. 38b-40 Finding no case against Jesus, Pilate asks the Jewish leaders if they want Jesus released. They ask for Barabbas.

vv. 1-3 Pilate has Jesus tortured and mocked.

vv. 4-7 Pilate repeats that he has no case against Jesus, and shows them that he has tortured Jesus. They cry out for death.

vv. 8-11 Pilate takes Jesus back inside and desperately tries to find a way out of his predicament.

vv. 12-16 Pilate goes outside and takes his official seat for judging cases. He pushes the Jewish leaders into acknowledging the Roman emperor as their king, before he sentences Jesus to death.

Visuals

___ Have volunteers construct a crown to slide down onto the main cross in the sanctuary.

___ This text is normally used on a special day in the Christian year, and yet the day is often sadly neglected in the church's celebrations. Why not let a large work of art declare the uniqueness of Christ the King Sunday? Work well ahead of time, and go to one of the congregation's best artists. Ask this person to create a work of art that can be displayed in the sanctuary on this day every year. (It might be displayed in another part of the church building the rest of the year.) In whatever medium the person works, have him or her portray Christ on the throne. This could be an oil painting, a tapestry, a huge banner, a carved or molded statue, a mosaic of colored tiles or stained glass, or any other medium. Give the artist the freedom to rely on his or her own inspiration to guide the content of the work.

___ Every year people provide big money to create flower-covered floats for the Tournament of Roses Parade and other such events. If people are willing to put this sort of money and work into celebrating a football game, then should the people of God not be willing to provide the money and work necessary to celebrate the rule of Christ? Many churches have large displays of poinsettias or lilies. Why not create a large flower-covered display of Christ on the throne by asking church members to underwrite the cost with memorial gifts. Unemployed persons could be paid to harvest wildflowers (if you live in the south), or to grow flowers just for use in this celebration. If the finished display is portable, it could be the center of a parade through the community's streets. The congregation could join in this parade, and other congregations, too, and all the people could sing songs proclaiming and celebrating the sovereignty of Christ. Candy, wrapped in papers printed with testimonials to the goodness of Jesus Christ, could be tossed to people watching the parade. Such an event would transform the nature of Christ the King Sunday.

Anthems and Special Music

(John 18:33-37)
See Passion/Palm Sunday

(Mark 11:1-11)
See Passion/Palm Sunday
Hosanna to the Son of David — J. W. Wesley — SATB w/keyboard, bongos — HF
Lift Up Your Heads, O Gates — R. Dirksen — Unison w/keyboard — from *With One Voice* — AF
Lord, Hosanna in the Highest — S. Glarum — SAB w/optional keyboard — GS
     (Also available in SATB)
The King Rides Forth — C. Means — SATB w/organ, baritone solo — HWG

Organ and Other Keyboard Music

Eternal Ruler of the Ceaseless Round (Song 1) — found in *36 Short Preludes and Postludes on Well-Known Hymn Tunes*, set II — H. Willan — CFP
Jesus Shall Reign (Duke Street) — found in *Festival Hymn Preludes* — R. Haan — SMP
Ye Servants of God (Hanover) — found in *International Collection of Nineteenth-Century Hymn Tune Preludes* — B. Owen — MAF

---

1. John H. Hayes, gen. ed., *Knox Preaching Guides, Mark*, by Ralph Martin (Atlanta: John Knox Press, 1981), p. 39.

2. John H. Hayes, ed. *Knox Preaching Guides: John*, by Fred B. Craddock (Atlanta: John Knox Press, 1982), pp. 132-133.

Appendix I

For Additional Choral/Organ Music see Appendix I in *Worship Workbook For The Gospels*, *Cycle A*

Additional Choral Music For The Advent Season

A Shoot Shall Come Forth — R. Horn — SAB w/keyboard — MSM
Comfort Ye My People — C. Young — SATB w/organ and treble instrument — HP
Creator of the Stars — D. Cherwien — SATB unaccompanied — RME
Magnificat — J. Biery — SATB w/organ — MSM
'Neath Vine and Fig Tree — H. Hopson — Unison/2-part w/keyboard — MSM
Rejoice Greatly, O Daughter of Zion — K. Kosche — SATB w/keyboard — CPH
Song of Mary: Magnificat — R. Schülz-Widmar — SATB w/organ — GIA

Additional Organ Music For The Advent Season

An Advent Triptych — J. Ferguson — MSM
Festal Voluntaries for Advent — various composers — NOV
Nine Seasonal Voluntaries for Advent/Christmas — H. K. Jones — CPH

Additional Choral Music For The Christmas Season

A Child is Born — L. Nester — SATB w/organ — ECS
A Cradle Song — D. Hurd — SATB w/organ — AF
African Noel — A. Thomas — SATB unaccompanied w/percussion — LG
He Came Here for Me — R. Nelson — SATB w/harp or keyboard — BH
Masters in This Hall — W. Brown — SAB w/organ — CPH
Sing We Merrily — S. B. Owens — SATB w/handbells — SEL
The Nativity — C. Callahan — Unison w/organ — RME
Child of Mary — G. Lawson — SATB w/organ — RME
Sussex Carol — D. Willcocks — SATB w/organ — OUP

Additional Organ Music For The Christmas Season

A Christmas Prelude on "In dulci jubilo" — C. Callahan — RME
Christmas Comes Again — W. Held — MSM
Five More Christmas Carols in a Baroque Style — J. H. Schaffner — CPH
Four Carol Meditations — G. Martin — BEC
Nine Seasonal Voluntaries for Advent/Christmas — H. K. Jones — CPH
Three Preludes on Christmas Hymns — J. D. Peterson — AF
Toccatina on "Go Tell It on the Mountain" — G. Bales — RME
'Twas in the Moon of Wintertime — M. Lochstampfor — AF

Additional Choral Music For The Epiphany Season

Arise, Shine! — J. Martinson — SATB w/organ — AF
Brightest and Best of the Stars of the Morning — M. Larkin — SATB unaccompanied — MSM
Come, Ye Lovers of the Feast — J. M. Thompson — SATB w/organ — AF
Now Shine, Bright Glow of Majesty — J. Becker — SATB w/organ — MSM
O Chief of Cities, Bethlehem — R. Schultz — SATB unaccompanied — MSM
O Love, How Deep — A. Fedak — SATB w/organ, cong., opt. brass and timpani — SEL
Star in the East — D. A. White — SATB w/organ and opt. percussion — SEL
We Three Kings — R. Davidson — SATB w/organ — BH

Additional Organ Music For The Epiphany Season

An Epiphany Suite — C. Callahan — MSM
Festal Voluntaries for Christmas and Epiphany — various composers — NOV
Three for Epiphany — P. Manz — MSM
Two Hymn Improvisations for Epiphany — M. Burkhardt — MSM

Additional Choral Music For The Lenten Season

A Lenten Love Song — H. Kemp — Unison w/keyboard — CG
A Lenten Walk — H. Hopson — 2-part w/organ, opt. handbell, timpani — AF
A Litany — C. Fountain — SATB unaccompanied — PAV
Come, Ye Sinners — D. A. White — 2-part w/keyboard and treble instrument — AF
Drop, Drop, Slow Tears — S. B. Owens — SAB w/organ and opt. handbells — MSM
Give Me Jesus — L. L. Fleming — SATB unaccompanied — AF
God Give Us Grace These Forty Days — J. M. Thompson — Unison w/keyboard — CPH
Guide Me, Savior, Through Your Passion — H. Gerike — Unison w/organ and opt. canon — GIA
Jesu, Word of God Incarnate — C. Saint-Saens/W. Livingston — SATB w/keyboard — TP (Coronet)
Lord, for Thy Tender Mercies' Sake — J. Hilton/K. L. Scott — 2-part w/organ — MF
O Dearest Friend — K. Kosche — SATB w/organ, opt. cong. and treble instrument — MSM
Responsory for Lententide — M. Reger — SATB w/organ — AF (Chantry)
Solus ad Victimam — K. Leighton — SATB w/organ — OUP
Ubi Caritas — J. Langlais — SATB w/organ — HTF
Wash Me Thoroughly From My Wickedness — G. F. Handel/A. Lovelace — 2-part w/ keyboard — HIN
What Wondrous Love — D. H. Williams — 2-part w/organ — AMSI
When I Survey the Wondrous Cross — H. Mollicone — SATB unaccompanied — ECS
Wilt Not Thou Turn Again, O God? — P. Dietterich — SAB w/organ — SMP
Without Love — A. R. Petker — 2-part w/keyboard — PAV

Additional Organ Music For The Lenten Season

A Lenten/Easter Suite — A. Fedak — SEL
Festal Voluntaries for Lent, Passiontide and Palm Sunday — various composers — NOV
Four Hymn Improvisations for Holy Week — M. Burkhardt — MSM
Six Lenten Chorales for Organ — P. Kickstat — MSM

Additional Choral Music For The Easter Season

Alleluia — W. A. Mozart/M. Burkhardt — Unison w/keyboard, 2 treble instruments — MSM

Alleluia! Christ Is Risen! — W. Mathias — SATB w/organ

Canticle of Praise — C. Callahan — SATB w/organ — RME

Christ Is With Me — G. Coleman — 2-part w/keyboard and opt. SATB choir, treble instrument — CPH

Christ Our Passover — J. Rickard — SATB w/organ, cong., opt. brass, timpani — PA

Gloria, Alleluia — G. F. Handel/P. Liebergen — ALF

Good Christian Friends Rejoice and Sing — H. Hopson — 2-part w/organ — CPH

He is Risen — C. Cope — Unison w/organ, opt. descant — OUP

Let Us Love One Another — A. Sherman — Unison or 2-part w/keyboard — SMP

Now Glad of Heart — S. B. Owens — SATB w/organ, brass and timpani — PA

On This Day the Lord Has Acted — F. Burgomaster — SATB w/organ — PLY

The Song of the Tree of Life — R. Vaughan Williams — Unison or 2-part w/keyboard — OUP

This is the Day that the Lord Has Acted — G. P. Telemann — SAB w/organ and strings — HAN

Wake, My Soul with Joy and Gladness — J. Horman — Unison/2-part w/keyboard — CG

Additional Organ Music For The Easter Season

A Lenten/Easter Suite — A. Fedak — SEL

Postlude on "Easter Hymn" — E Kerr — RME

Postlude on "O filii et filiae" — E. Kerr — RME

Three for Easter — J. Biery — MSM

Additional Choral Music For The Pentecost/General Season

Come, Down, O Love Divine — D. Busarow — SAB w/organ — CPH
Come, Holy Ghost, in Love — E. Bullock — SAB w/organ — OUP
Come, Holy Ghost, Our Souls Inspire — J. G. Reutter/J. Floreen — Unison w/keyboard —
    AF
Gracious Spirit, Holy Ghost — J. Erickson — Unison w/organ and opt. descant — AF
Filled with the Spirit's Power — D. Busarow — SATB w/organ and opt. treble instrument
    — CPH
Hail Thee, Spirit, Lord Eternal — R. Wetzler — 2-part w/organ — AF
Hymn to the Holy Spirit — R. Currie — SATB w/organ — GIA
Lord of All Being — H. Willan — SATB w/organ — CFP
O Be Joyful in the Lord — HRH Albert/W. Peterson — SATB w/organ — HTF
O Come, Creator Spirit Blest — F. J. Haydn/K. L. Scott — SATB w/keyboard — MSM
Spirit Divine, Attend Our Prayers — S. Wright — SATB w/organ and opt. brass — GAL
Veni Jesu — L. Cherubini/D. Weck — SAT w/keyboard — HP

Additional Organ Music For The Pentecost/General Season

A Fancy on Westminster Abbey — R. Baker — RME
Come, Let Us Join Our Cheerful Songs — R. Boursey — AF
Eight Hymn Preludes — E. H. Meyer — CPH
Fantasia on "O God, Our Help in Ages Past" — A. Fedak — SEL
Four Hymn Preludes — P. Gehring — CPH
Gift of Finest Wheat — C. Callahan — CPH
Organ Variations on Six Chorales — J. Berthier — GIA
Music for Organ — C. Hampton — WB
Prelude on "Kingsfold" — D. Lasky — RME
Sent Forth: Short Postludes for the Day — R. Powell — AF
Seven Hymn Reflections — M. Sedio — AMSI
Ten Hymntune Preludes for Manuals Only — A. Mann — GIA
Thine the Praise, vol. 1, 2, 3 — R. Powell — CPH
Twentieth Century Hymn Tune Settings — J. Biery — MSM

Appendix II

Publishers

Abbreviation	Company
AF	Augsburg-Fortress
ALF	Alfred Music
AMC	American Music Center
AMSI	AMSI Publishers
AE	Arista Editions
AG	Agape
AP	Abingdon Press
AUR	Aureole
BAR	Barenreiter
BBL	Broude Brothers Limited
BEC	Beckenhorst
BEL	Belwin-Mills
BH	Boosey and Hawkes
BM	Boston Music
BOU	Bourne Music
BP	Broadman Press
BRA	B. Ramsey
BRE	Breitkopf and Hartel
BRO	Brodt Music
CFE	Composers Facsimile Edition
CF	Carl Fischer
CFP	C.F. Peters
CG	Choristers Guild
CH	Chester Music
CM	Chappel Music
CMP	Chantry Music Press (Augsburg Fortress)
COB	Coburn Press
CP	Curtis Press
CPH	Concordia Publishing House
CPP	CPP Belwin
DUR	Durand
EB	Eboracum
EAL	Edward Ashdown Limited
EBM	Edward B. Marks
ECK	E.C. Kirby
ECS	E.C. Schirmer
EV	Elkan-Vogel
FBM	Fred Bock Music
FOR	Forster Music
GAL	Galaxy

Abbreviation	Company
GIA	GIA
GM	General Music
GS	G. Schirmer
GVT	Gordon V. Thompson
HAN	Hanssler
HF	Harold Flammer
HIN	Hinshaw
HP	Hope
HS	High Street
HTF	H.T. Fitzsimons
HWG	H.W. Gray
INT	International
IAI	Ionian Arts Inc.
JFB	J. Fischer Brothers
KAL	Kalmus
KH	Kirkland House
LG	Lawson-Gould
LIL	Lilenas
LMP	Ludwig Music Publishing
LOR	Lorenz
MAF	McAfee Music
MB	Mayhew-Brodt
MCA	MCA Music
MER	Mercury Music
MF	Mark Foster
MK	McKee (Associated)
MMP	Masters Music Publication
MSM	Morning Star Music
NAK	Neil A. Kjos
NOV	Novello
OD	Oliver Ditson
OUP	Oxford University Press
PA	Paraclete Press
PAV	Pavanne
PLY	Plymouth
PP	Providence Press
RD	Roger Dean
RDR	R.D. Row
RIC	Ricordi
RME	Randall M. Egan
RSCM	Royal School of Church Music
SAL	Salabart
SB	Stainer and Bell
SC	Schott
SH	Shawnee Press

Abbreviation	Company
SHM	Schmitt, Hall, and McCreary
SMP	Sacred Music Press
SOU	Southern
SP	Somerset Press
SPC	Selah Publishing
STB	Stuart Beaudoin
STP	Studio Publications
SUB	Summy Birchard
TC	Terra Continuo
TP	Theodore Presser
TRI	Triune Music
TUS	Tuskegee
UE	Universal Editions
WAL	Walton Music
WAT	Waterloo
WB	Warner Brothers
WIM	Western International Music
WL	World Library
WM	Word Music

Appendix III

Time of Service_____

Day in Church Year_____Date_____

Pastor's Planning Worksheet

Scriptures (* preaching text)

    Old Testament_____

    Psalm_____

    Epistle_____

    Gospel_____

    Creative Reading?_____

    _____

    _____

Liturgical Color_____

Communion?_____

Baptism?_____

Special Emphasis/Day_____

_____

_____

_____

Sermon Focus_____

_____

_____

Need of congregation to be addressed:

    Need to learn_____

    _____

    Attitude to be instilled or developed_____

    _____

    Behavior to be changed_____

    _____

Sermon Title_____

Response to the Word_____

_____

Children's Talk_____

_____

Special Notes _____

_____

Time of Service_____

Day in Church Year_____ Date_____

Worship Team Planning Worksheet

Hymns

Number_____ Title_____

Number_____ Title_____

Number_____ Title_____

Number_____ Title_____

Service Music

Prelude Title_____ Composer_____

Musicians_____

Introit Title_____ Composer_____

Musicians_____

Act of Praise_____ Composer_____

Musicians_____

Offertory Title_____ Composer_____

Musicians_____

Choral Response after Lord's Prayer_____

Composer_____ Musicians_____

Choral Response after Benediction_____

Composer_____ Musicians_____

Postlude Title _____ Composer_____

Musicians_____

Other Special Music

Title_____ Composer_____

Musicians_____

Title_____ Composer_____

Musicians_____

Visuals_____

_____

Time of Service_____

Day in Church Year_____ Date_____

Worship Team Responsibility List

Responsibility	Name	Phone Number
Preacher	_____	_____
Assisting Preacher	_____	_____
Liturgist	_____	_____
Head Usher	_____	_____
Elevator Usher	_____	_____
Usher	_____	_____
Usher	_____	_____
Usher	_____	_____
Acolyte	_____	_____
Acolyte	_____	_____
Choir Director	_____	_____
Organist	_____	_____
Pianist	_____	_____
Soloist	_____	_____
Soloist	_____	_____
Ensemble Leader	_____	_____
Drama Director	_____	_____
Liturgical Dance Director	_____	_____
Mime Director	_____	_____
Clowning Director	_____	_____
Puppet Director	_____	_____
Liturgical Artist	_____	_____
Altar Guild Chairperson	_____	_____
Floral Artist	_____	_____
Bulletin Cover Designer	_____	_____
Communion Steward	_____	_____
Communion Steward	_____	_____
Communion Steward	_____	_____
Communion Steward	_____	_____
_____	_____	_____
_____	_____	_____

Index

Gospel Lections

All the lessons from the gospels included in the Revised Common, Episcopal and Lutheran lectionaries are listed below. Preachers not using these lectionaries can use this index to find where their chosen lessons are treated. The numbers on the right indicate pages in this book. The Roman numerals "I" and "III" indicate the first and third volumes of this series, and "NA" indicates that the lesson is not treated in any of the three volumes.

13:31-33, 44-49a	Proper 12, Pentecost 10 A	I
13:31-33, 44-52	Proper 12, Pentecost 10 A	I
13:44-52	Proper 12, Pentecost 10 A	I
14:13-21	Proper 13, Pentecost 11 A	I
14:22-33	Proper 14, Pentecost 12 A	I
15:(10-20) 21-28	Proper 15, Pentecost 13 A	I
15:21-28	Proper 15, Pentecost 13 A	I
16:9-15, 19-20	Ascension A	NA
16:13-20	Proper 16, Pentecost 14 A	I
16:21-26	Proper 17, Pentecost 15 A	I
16:21-27	Proper 17, Pentecost 15 A	I
16:21-28	Proper 17, Pentecost 15 A	I
17:1-9	Transfiguration A	I
18:15-20	Proper 18, Pentecost 16 A	I
18:21-35	Proper 19, Pentecost 17 A	I
20:1-16	Proper 20, Pentecost 18 A	I
20:17-28	Lent 4 A	I
21:1-11	Advent 1 A,	I
	Passion/Palm A	I
21:23-32	Proper 21, Pentecost 19 A	I
21:28-32	Proper 21, Pentecost 19 A	I
21:33-43	Proper 22, Pentecost 20 A	I
21:33-46	Proper 22, Pentecost 20 A	I
22:1-10 (11-14)	Proper 23, Pentecost 21 A	I
22:1-14	Proper 23, Pentecost 21 A	I
22:15-21	Proper 24, Pentecost 22 A	I
22:15-22	Proper 24, Pentecost 22 A	I
22:34-40 (41-46)	Proper 25, Pentecost 23 A	I
22:34-46	Proper 25, Pentecost 23 A	I
23:1-12	Proper 26, Pentecost 24 A, 26 A	I
24:1-14	Pentecost 27 A	I
24:36-44	Advent 1 A	I
24:37-44	Advent 1 A	I
25:1-13	Proper 27, Pentecost 24 A, 25 A	I
25:14-15, 19-29	Proper 28, Pentecost 26 A	I
25:14-30	Proper 28, Pentecost 25 A, 26A	I
25:31-46	Christ the King A,	I
	Christmas 2 C,	III
	Christmas 2 B	I
26:1—27:66	Passion/Palm A	I
26:14—27:66	Passion/Palm A	I
(26:36-75) 27:1-54 (55-66)	Passion/Palm A	I
27:11-54	Passion/Palm A	I
28:1-10	Easter Day A	I
28:16-20	Trinity A	I

MARK

1:1-8	Advent 2 B	14
1:4-11	Bapt of Lord B	51
1:7-11	Bapt of Lord B	51
1:9-13	Lent 1 B	101
1:9-15	Lent 1 B	101
1:12-15	Lent 1 B	101

335